Ground Wars

Ground Wars

PERSONALIZED COMMUNICATION IN POLITICAL CAMPAIGNS

Rasmus Kleis Nielsen

PRINCETON UNIVERSITY PRESS

PRINCETON AND OXFORD

Copyright © 2012 by Princeton University Press
Published by Princeton University Press, 41 William Street, Princeton, New Jersey 08540
In the United Kingdom: Princeton University Press, 6 Oxford Street, Woodstock,
Oxfordshire OX20 1TW

press.princeton.edu

Library of Congress Cataloging-in-Publication Data

Nielsen, Rasmus Kleis, 1980-
  Ground wars : personalized communication in political campaigns / Rasmus Kleis
Nielsen.
      p. cm.
  Includes bibliographical references and index.
  ISBN 978-0-691-15304-9 (cloth : alk. paper)—ISBN 978-0-691-15305-6 (pbk. :
alk. paper)   1. Political campaigns—United States—History—21st century.
2. Communication in politics—United States—History—21st century.   I. Title.

  JK2281.N54 2012
  324.7'30973   dc23

                                                              2011032746

British Library Cataloging-in-Publication Data is available

This book has been composed in Sabon

Printed on acid-free paper. ∞

Printed in the United States of America

10 9 8 7 6 5 4 3 2 1

Contents

Never doubt that a small group of thoughtful, committed citizens can change the world; indeed, it's the only thing that ever has.
—President Jed Bartlet in Aaron Sorkin's *The West Wing* (originally attributed to Margaret Mead)

"There is so little one can do." [Pause.] "One does it all." [Pause.] "All one can."
—Winnie in Samuel Beckett's *Happy Days*

Acknowledgments

While working on this book, I have enjoyed the intellectual and academic opportunities that Columbia University and the many other great universities in and around New York City offer. I have learned much from my teachers, colleagues, and friends in the PhD program in Communications; from the CODES seminar and Contentious Politics workshop organized through the Department of Sociology at Columbia; from seminars in the Mellon Graduate Fellows Program hosted by ISERP; from the Politics and Protest workshop at the Graduate Center, CUNY; and from frequent visits to and conversations with people from the New School for Social Research and NYU. Through the good offices of Yochai Benkler, I also had the opportunity to work for six weeks at the Berkman Center for Internet and Society at Harvard University in the summer of 2009. The final push for this book came while I was working on other projects at the Reuters Institute for the Study of Journalism at the University of Oxford in the United Kingdom, and while waiting to take up a new position at Roskilde University (RUC) in Denmark.

Many friends and colleagues have taken the time to read and comment on parts of my work. I like to think of academic work as a form of intellectual craftsmanship embedded in a community of inquiry, and I am grateful to the people who at various points have helped me realize that idea. I would like to thank in particular—though in no particular order—Amy Stuart, Benjamin Peters, Chris W. Anderson, Daniel Kreiss, David Karpf, Frank Moretti, Elena Krumova, James M. Jasper, Jonah Bossewitch, Josh Whitford, Lucas Graves, Monique Girard, Quinn Mulroy, Robbie McClintock, Ruthie Palmer, Solon Barocas, Tom Ogorzalek, W. Russell Neuman, and the late Charles Tilly. All of them have helped me along the way.

If I ever advise someone on their road toward a PhD, I hope I can offer what Michael Schudson offered me while I was at Columbia—constant encouragement to follow my own intuitions, tempered with attentive criticism and close readings of all I sent him, and an appropriate dose of skepticism and uncommonly common sense when I got carried away (which I do). He stands as a model of intellectual integrity and the right kind of ambition for me, and it has been a privilege to work with him. In their own ways, both David Stark and Todd Gitlin have pushed me to improve my work. David never ceases to be able to reframe my own understanding of what I am doing, and he leads by example when it comes to pushing academic work beyond the confines of what any individual researcher can accomplish by maintaining a wonderful intellectual community around him. Todd never let me forget the big questions that lurk—and should lurk—behind our otherwise specialized academic endeavors.

What little I knew about ethnographic fieldwork when I started this project I learned from Herbert J. Gans, a master craftsman still passing on the craft, and he has kindly commented on several chapters along the way. Rodney Benson and Rogers M. Smith read through the manuscript, and both of them taught me much about my own work, things that have helped move this piece of work to becoming a book. David Karpf, Daniel Kreiss, and Herbert J. Gans all went far beyond the call of duty and read the entire revised book manuscript in the fall of 2010. They have given me more constructive criticism than I could possible hope to process. Two anonymous reviewers provided both encouragement and further possibilities to pursue. My editor at Princeton University Press, Eric Schwartz, has been exemplary in nudging me along toward completion; it has been a pleasure to work with him as well as with Beth Clevenger and Janie Chan, who both helped with production. Senior people at VAN not only gave me their time, but also permission to reprint screenshots of their company's work. I thank all of the above for their time and effort, and acknowledge that it is my responsibility alone that I have not responded effectively to all of their thoughtful comments. I will build on all they have taught me in the future. You never stop learning, nor should you.

My family has been unflagging in their support of my work as an academic and my decision to pursue my vocation a world and some six thousand kilometers away. Though we have spent years far from each others' everyday lives, I have never felt that we were truly separated. What we share I appreciate more and more. Martha Pichardo—always my first reader, my first critic, and so much more—has lived with this project for years. It would be embarrassing for both of us if I tried to put into writing how much I owe her, so I won't. I will try to show it instead.

I feel privileged to have been in a position to do the research for this book, and I am deeply grateful for all the help I have received along the way. But this project is not simply the outcome of my own intellectual endeavors and the environment in which I found myself. It is also the result of an extensive engagement with the realities of electoral politics. I have learned more from the people involved in campaigns than I can ever hope to teach them, and I thank them all for letting me into their world. Insofar as what follows can repay some of my debt, it is because I have had an opportunity to see campaigns from many different perspectives and have had more time to think about what I saw than any staffer, volunteer, or part-timer. If I can convey these different views effectively enough, even seasoned campaigners may be surprised to learn about how what they do looks to others.

Ground Wars

Welcome to the Campaigns

At 7:55 P.M. we stop calling, and the campaign office is suddenly quiet. Nobody seems to know what will happen next. People just sit in front of their phones. After a few minutes, somebody says quietly, "It's eight o'clock." The polls are closing now. There is nothing more we can do.

People begin to get up; some start talking; a few grab snacks from the table in the volunteer room. Kesari, one of the field organizers, goes around hugging people. She has tears in her eyes as she says, again and again, "I can't believe it's over!" She is hoarse from exhaustion and from making hundreds of phone calls. Someone turns up the volume on the TV, but all the news is about the presidential election. Nobody seems to care. We want to know what will happen here, in New Jersey. We want to know if Linda Stender will be the next House Representative from the 7th district.

By now there are mostly staffers left in the office, along with a handful of volunteers who have stuck around until the end. The field director comes out from the back room and asks all the field organizers to go with him. They will be getting the returns from around the district and comparing them to their vote goals. Everybody else is told to go to the Crowne Plaza Hotel in Clark, where the "election night celebration" will be. (The staffers consider it hubris to call something a victory party.)

I drive with Philip, one of the volunteers. He says, "I can't remember the last time I made so many calls." We have both been on the phones for a couple of hours straight. He came back to the office from his last canvass around 6:00 P.M., having knocked on doors for two hours after getting off work. Upon his return, he was put straight onto the phones. I have walked two shifts with different partners myself and have also made calls this evening. We are but a drop in an ocean. Hundreds of people have knocked on doors and made phone calls for Stender and the Democratic Party in this district, not only today, but every day for the last couple of months. Some of these people are campaign staffers, many volunteers, several hundreds have worked as paid part-timers, and more have been mobilized by allies in the labor movement and elsewhere.

Philip and I get to the hotel and make our way to the room booked for the campaign. About fifty people have already arrived, including five journalists and two camera crews. More people are filing in. The reporters circulate among the guests, but no one seems to want to talk to them. Everybody is watching the two TV sets, one tuned in to CNN for national politics, the other to News12, a local cable news channel covering this race and another competitive contest in southern New Jersey. I scan the crowd and recognize most of the people. The finance staff is here, a couple of local elected officials and party regulars, some guys from the union locals who have supported Stender all the way, at least a dozen volunteers, and two or three people who have worked on the paid canvass. The finance director says quietly to me, "She's upstairs with her family, waiting for the returns." A few precincts have already started to report. The news is not too good. Leonard Lance, the Republican candidate, is up by ten points or more in most areas. The atmosphere is growing tense, but we are still waiting to hear from some of the Democratic base areas—there is still hope for Stender.

Around ten, the field organizers start filling in at the back of the room, carrying drinks. They look like they are attending a funeral. They clearly know something we do not. I get myself a drink and find Jack, the volunteer coordinator. He is crushed. "We lost the undecided eight to one. I can't fucking believe it. We are the worst campaign in America." I protest that it's not over yet, but he says, "No, we have an internal poll that we didn't tell anyone about, and I've seen the returns—it *is* over. We spent three million dollars and blew it. We suck."

Our conversation at the back of the room is beginning to draw attention from those around us. Many people are still waiting to see the final results on TV. Someone says, "As long as Woodbridge hasn't reported, there's still hope." Jack shakes his head and whispers to me, "We'll lose by ten." The minutes tick by. Seventy percent of the precincts have reported now and Stender is nine points down. Jack is right. It's over.

At about ten-thirty, News12 cuts to broadcast Lance's acceptance speech. A few people hiss and boo, but halfheartedly. A few minutes later Stender enters the room with her family in tow. She gets a standing ovation, lasting several minutes. People are chanting, "Linda! Linda! Linda!" stamping their feet, and applauding. She delivers a brief concession speech, thanking us for our support, congratulating Lance on his victory, and saying she had hoped things would have ended differently.

In short, she says what she is supposed to say; it's nothing special— except for the self-control it takes when years of hard work, constant compromises, and personal sacrifices have come to nothing. Stender's eyes are moist as she speaks. I feel a lump in my throat. Several people in the audience are crying. And then it's over. Stender leaves and people start to get up. Philip says, "I gotta go work tomorrow. I think I'll call it a night." Jack says, "It's not even eleven!" Jack has nothing to do tomorrow. His job here is done.

I notice on the CNN news ticker that Connecticut's 4th district, the other area where I have done my research on political campaigns, has been called for the Democrat Jim Himes. It feels somewhat inappropriate, given the mood here, but I step out to make a few calls to congratulate some of the staffers and volunteers who have worked for Himes. The corridor is quiet; a janitor is picking up some empty glasses. For him, I guess, this is just another night at the Crowne Plaza Hotel. Most of the people I get through to in the Connecticut district are simply euphoric. One staffer is more contemplative. He says, "When they called it for us, I had this sick feeling inside. I was sure it was a mistake—you know, 'Dewey Defeats Truman.' I was so sure we would lose this." He is the only one who asks how the "Stender people" are doing. I don't know quite what to tell him.

I get off the phone, write a few notes about my conversations, and return to the "election night celebration." That, too, is over. Most people have left. The lights are up. There are empty chairs everywhere, crumbled snacks on the carpet, and a little bit of confetti in a corner. (Someone must have thought there would be something to actually celebrate.) It all looks so sad to me. The staffers have retreated to the hotel bar. I go to join them, and we all get more drinks. People start talking about the future, about what's next. At the stroke of midnight the room grows quiet as the CNN cameras zoom in on a family of four who have stepped out in front of a quarter of a million people in Grant Park, Chicago. The bartender cranks up the volume, and we hear Barack Obama speak: "If there is anyone out there who still doubts that America is a place where all things are possible, who still wonders if the dream of our founders is alive in our time, who still questions the power of our democracy, tonight is your answer." Kesari's eyes are glued to the screen. She says quietly, "I'm so happy." The field director says, "Yeah, that's great, but it's not my victory. I still lost tonight."

* * *

This book is not about Linda Stender or Jim Himes, or about winning or losing, but about the hundreds of thousands of phone calls and door knocks that campaigns and the people who work on them make in pursuit of victory. It is about how those calls and knocks work as a form of political communication, what the campaigns that generate them are like, and what it means for those involved. Thus it is also, ultimately, about American democracy.

CHAPTER 1

Personalized Political Communication
in American Campaigns

EPISODE 1.1

Charlene is in her late thirties, African American, and looking for a job. Her home is in Bridgeport, Connecticut, a decaying, de-industrialized city with an unemployment rate over 10 percent and about 20 percent of the population living below the poverty line. Right now she is making ten dollars an hour canvassing for the Connecticut Democrats' coordinated campaign—and gets a gas card every week too. "It helps pay the bills," she says. She finished her Microsoft Office User Specialist class at Workforce, Inc., this afternoon, and since then we have been out walking door-to-door, talking to voters.

Charlene knocks on the door, holding her clipboard with the Jim Himes for Congress flyers and a map of the area in one hand and a PalmPilot with our script, walk sheet, and talking points in her other hand. I stand a couple of yards behind her, clutching my own clipboard and PDA (personal digital assistant), watching the house for any signs of life. We are about to leave when an elderly white woman opens the door. We know from our list that she is probably Anna Rizzo, a seventy-seven-year-old registered Democrat who lives here. She is our target because she is an infrequent voter. Ms. Rizzo leaves the door chain on, and asks, "What do you want?" Charlene says, "We're here to tell you about Jim Himes, the Democratic congregational candidate." I flinch as she says "congregational." She has done it before, just as she again ignored the script we have been instructed to use. Ms. Rizzo closes the door without a word. We write her down as "Not Home." She will be contacted again soon because she has been identified as a part of one of the target universes—sometimes called "lazy Democrats"—and because the campaign has her phone number and address.

"This is a bad list," Charlene says to me as we walk toward our next target, a couple of houses down the street. "I can't believe they've sent us out here. What a waste of time. Well, well—that's their problem."

EPISODE 1.2

It is late afternoon in Fanwood, New Jersey, Linda Stender's hometown, a town she has served as mayor and state assemblywoman for years and now hopes to represent in Congress. Her campaign office is in a worn-down demolition-slated building just across from the train station. Today we are four people working the phones, calling voters to tell them about Stender and ask them a few questions about where they stand on the upcoming election. Everyone on the phones is a volunteer. All are well over sixty (except me). We sit in a room separate from where the staff works.

Paula gets what she calls "a live one," her first since she arrived twenty minutes ago. So far she has just been leaving messages. She reads the first lines of her script to the voter, asking who he plans to vote for in the fall. It turns out he is leaning toward Stender's opponent, state senator Leonard Lance. Paula immediately gets into an argument with him. "I can't believe you want to vote for a Republican after what Bush has done to our country! Dragged us into a criminal war for oil, undermined the Constitution, handed over billions in tax cuts to the wealthiest!" They talk for a few minutes. From what we can hear, it is a spirited discussion.

After she puts down the phone, Paula says to the rest of us, "I can't believe there are people out there who aren't Democrats." We all chuckle. Clearly, Stender's campaign staffers and her outside consultants have an inkling that there are some voters in the district who aren't Democrats. Stender ran as a progressive in 2006 and lost narrowly to the incumbent Republican, Mike Ferguson. This cycle she is running as a moderate for what is now an open seat, without using her party affiliation or the name of the Democratic presidential nominee in her literature and advertisements. But many of the volunteers still see her—and present her to voters—as the woman they support, "the old Linda."

EPISODE 1.3
Election Day is only a week away, and the field organizers are struggling to whip the GOTV (Get Out the Vote) program into shape. People are on the phones constantly, calling paid part-time canvassers and potential volunteers, trying to get them to confirm their availability over the weekend. There are thousands of shifts to be filled, walk packets to be assembled, call sheets to be printed. This is a major logistical operation, with many moving parts, pursued under intense time pressure.

One of the field organizers complains that his volunteers are "flaky" and won't commit. The field director is stressed out: "We need more bodies!" He makes a call and then shouts to one of his deputies—who is technically employed by the state party and not the candidate—"We've got twenty more labor guys coming in. I need you to cut more turf. I'll send you the lists." Jack, the volunteer coordinator, is calmer, almost serene. He leans back and comments on the commotion around us: "We'll have to close some locations; it'll never work with all those phone banks. Multiple locations: great in theory, bad in practice. But they won't listen. We don't have time for this."

Around 100 million Americans were contacted at the door or over the phone by various political organizations during the 2008 elections.

Millions of volunteers and tens of thousands of paid part-time workers did the contacting. Thousands of full-time staffers organized their efforts. At the surface it looked like nothing new under the sun. Even if the number of contacts made varies over time (and it has increased dramatically from 2000 onward), canvassing voters, by foot or by phone, is a staple of American politics. In some ways the conversations among people in 2008 probably were not all that different from those of 1988 or 1968: "Who do you plan to vote for?" "Here is why you should support my guy." "Now, remember to go and vote." That is the basic blueprint as campaigns try to identify where people stand, sway the undecided, and bring out their supporters. Volunteers who cut their teeth on Michael Dukakis's or even Hubert Humphrey's campaign for the presidency can still use their experience at the door many years later when confronted with an uninterested, unfriendly, or otherwise unapproachable voter who does not care much for "that one," the man who later became President Obama. At the face of things, on the front stage, canvassing seems largely unchanged.

But behind the scenes hundreds of specialists toiled at their computers to make it all possible, to maximize the instrumental impact, and to try to keep it all under control. Away from the doors and off the phones, staffers, volunteers, and part-timers used new information and communication technologies ranging from by now mundane things like cell phones and email, to emerging tools like social networking sites, and to specialized technologies like tailor-made campaign Web pages and dedicated software solutions for targeting and management. In Washington, D.C., and in innumerable offices and coffee shops around the country, consultants crunched numbers to make sure their client campaigns made the most of it all. The work done to sort index cards with voter information and to physically cut and paste the walk sheets for a canvass in 1968 or 1988 had little to do with what it took to update detailed Web-accessible voter files, synchronize personal digital assistants, and print turf maps in 2008. In political campaigns new technologies have not replaced older forms of communication as much as they have revived them.

The backstage changes are not only technological, they are also institutional. When Barack Obama topped the ticket in 2008, many of the organizations that had provided much of the manpower to knock on doors for Dukakis and Humphrey—most importantly labor unions and local Democratic Party organizations—were no longer what they used to be. Candidates and their staffers today have to piece together their own campaign operations from a wider, less structured, and more unruly universe of allies, volunteers, and paid part-timers. The supposedly old-fashioned practice of contacting voters directly on behalf of a candidate or party is deeply intertwined with the most recent advances in online-integrated software and database management; it is also deeply influenced by contemporary changes in how the major parties and their closest allies organize and are organized. Like campaign practices in general, these various forms of voter contact are characterized by both change and continuity.

This book deals with how American political campaigns pursue what I call "personalized political communication"—premeditated practices that use *people* as media for political communication. The main forms of this method of communication are door-to-door canvassing and phone banking, central parts of what political operatives call the "ground war." I analyze this subject not to assess its impact on electoral behavior, but to identify the implications that ground war practices have for how we understand processes of political communication, for how we understand campaigns, and for how we understand what it means to take part in them—an important form of political participation, a part of what it means to have a government that is created at least partially "by the people." How campaigns are waged matters, not only for electoral outcomes but also for what democratic politics *is*.

Personalized political communication on the large scale we have seen in recent elections requires resources that are well beyond those commanded by campaign organizations built around individual candidates. I show how this type of communication is pursued instead by wider "campaign assemblages" that include not only staffers and consultants but also allied interest groups and civic associations, numerous individual volunteers and paid part-timers, and a party-provided technical infrastructure for targeting voters. Close scrutiny of how such campaign assemblages engage in personalized political communication leads me to challenge the dominant view of political communication in contemporary America—that it is a tightly scripted, controlled, and professionalized set of practices that primarily represses turnout and turns people off politics in its cut-throat pursuit of victory. I highlight how even as they bankroll negative advertisements, feed the horserace coverage, and resort to direct mail attacks, campaigns also work hard to get out (especially partisan) voters and get people involved in (instrumental) forms of political participation. Analysis of how campaign assemblages wage ground wars leads me to dispute the widespread idea that American politics is increasingly the province of a small coterie of professionals as well as the romantic notion that canvassing and the like represents some purer form of "grassroots politics." I demonstrate how even well-funded competitive campaigns for federal office continue to rely on a wide range of nonprofessional elements, how the campaign organizations themselves are at most unevenly professionalized, and also how even the most seemingly innocent volunteer canvass is tied in with specialized targeting technologies and staff expertise.

Finally, attention to campaigns' and staffers' instrumental need for people to engage in the labor-intensive work of personalized political communication, of contacting voters one at a time, at the door or over the phone, leads me to suggest that when elections are competitive and ambition is thus still made to counteract ambition, today's political operatives and political organizations have a renewed self-interest in getting people to participate in the political process as volunteers and voters. Ground war campaigns are highly instrumental in their orientation; they pick and choose who they talk to and try to turn out, discriminate consciously and unconsciously in who they mobilize as volunteers, and have not even a semblance of internal democracy. But they actively encourage participation and generate higher turnout, and that is a good thing for a democracy plagued by widespread indifference and a sense of disconnect between people and politics.

Ground war campaigns and practices of personalized political communication offer a privileged point for observing American democracy in action. Working for a candidate or a party at election time is a paradigmatic form of political participation, something millions of people do every year. Most of them, whether they are volunteers or part-timers, will be asked to knock on doors or make calls and talk to voters. Canvassing and phone banking are intensely social, organized, and outward-oriented activities; they cannot easily be done in isolation from the privacy of one's living room like making an online donation to a candidate or writing out a check to be mailed to a campaign committee. Personal contacts confront participants with parts of the electorate, bring them together with others who are involved, and introduce them to the organizational and technological intricacies of contemporary campaigns. They offer an opportunity to try to influence (however slightly) electoral outcomes; meet people with a passion for, or a professional commitment to, politics; and, as one volunteer put it, "take a real-life lesson in practical politics." To understand practices of personalized political communication is therefore to understand a crucial component in civic and political life.

My analysis of recent ground wars is based primarily on ten months of ethnographic fieldwork on the Democratic side in two competitive congressional districts during the 2008 elections: Connecticut's 4th district and New Jersey's 7th district. The episodes I recount throughout this book, and all quotations without any other reference, come from the hundreds of hours I spent as a participant-observer in these two districts. Other than the names of candidates, all other names are pseudonyms, and a few scenes and locations are obscured further to protect the anonymity of the people involved, but all events are described as I witnessed them. Close examination of this unique firsthand evidence provides new insights into political communication and into how political organizations operate today. It sheds light on the practices of political participation that these organizations constitute and make possible. The data I have is not always representative and rarely complete, but it provides for a close-up portrait of American electoral politics as it is practiced on the ground.

POLITICAL PRACTICE ON THE GROUND

Personalized political communication represents only one arm in the arsenal employed by contemporary campaigns. The ground war is fought under the cover of an "air war" waged by thirty-second television spots and spin. Canvassing and phone banking have something in common with these other forms of political communication that campaigns engage in, including "paid media" (advertisements), "earned media" (public relations), direct mail, and digital marketing—most notably their instrumental intent and their organizational origin. But they also have logics of their own. I focus on these distinct logics here because they are important, and because they have received little attention. A rich literature deals with the impact and implications of television advertisements, news coverage, and other forms of mass-mediated political communication, but few people outside the campaign world itself know much about how ground wars are fought. This book is thus not focused on the twists and turns of the two campaigns I followed. It does not purport to address their outcomes. It is not about why Jim Himes won in Connecticut or why Linda Stender lost in New Jersey. Instead, I deal with how it became possible for their two campaigns, initially made up of just the candidate and a handful of staffers, to pursue personalized political communication on a large scale and ultimately reach about 20 percent of the electorate in each district in person, by knocking on tens of thousands of doors and making hundreds of thousands of phone calls.

If one considers the rough average of three contacts per hour that campaign staffers expect from both those canvassing door-to-door and those on the phones, it becomes clear that personalized political communication on such a scale is an enormous logistical challenge. Contacting approximately 100 million people across the nation, as the numerous campaign assemblages that faced off at various levels during the 2008 elections did, takes about 33 million hours of work—and on top of that comes the effort that goes into gathering the people to do it, coordinating their work, and choosing which voters to talk to. Whereas the mass-media- and direct-mail-dominated politics of the last decades of the twentieth century sometimes resembled what Robert M. Entman has called a "democracy without citizens," run by a small number of consultants and funded by big-dollar donors, the resurgent interest in personalized political communication means that parties and campaigns today need people—lots of people—to wage ground wars.[1]

The average congressional district has a population of about 700,000 and between 300,000 and 400,000 registered voters. With high turnout expected in a presidential election year, a competitive race at hand, ample financial resources, and a strategic decision from the outset to try to call and canvass every potentially Democratic voter at least once, the staffers working on the two campaigns I followed aimed at contacting more than 100,000 people at home. Assisted by hundreds of volunteers and part-timers, as well as additional people mobilized by their allies in the labor movement and elsewhere, these campaigns got through to an estimated 20 percent of the electorate at least once, generating about 100,000 door knocks and around a 150,000 phone calls between Labor Day and the end of October, and at least another 100,000 knocks and calls over the "GOTV weekend," the get-out-the-vote effort during the last four days leading up to the election.[2] In the two campaigns I studied, paid part-time workers did most of the canvassing, volunteers did most of the phone banking, and allied organizations ranging from labor unions to progressive activist groups provided some help for each of these activities, along with additional "bodies" for the final push to get out the vote. (Campaign staffers made thousands of contacts themselves but spent most of their time organizing the overall effort.)

Every single one of the countless knocks and calls made served one or more of the same three instrumental purposes: to persuade swing voters (those who have no fixed political allegiances and whose votes can thus determine election results), to motivate base voters to turn out, and to gather more information about the electorate for further contacts. Every call or knock was predicated upon the participation of players well beyond the core of full-time staffers in the campaign organization itself. Every one of these contacts entailed potentially fraught encounters with voters, came with numerous organizing challenges, and had to be effectively targeted to be worth the effort.

To demonstrate what such ambitious ground war campaigns mean for political communication and for how we understand contemporary forms of political organization and political participation in America, the rest of this book deals not only with the act of contacting voters but also with the organizing and targeting that make these countless conversations possible. Together, processes of contacting, organizing, and targeting define how personalized political communication works. The episodes scattered throughout the text include some of the elements that must be considered in this type of communication—the different communities of staffers, volunteers, and part-timers involved; the various technologies they use; the data their work is based on; the different moti-vations and conceptions of politics at play; and the whole heterogeneous edifice that is constructed around candidates in competitive districts to conduct field operations, to wage ground wars, to pursue personalized political communication.

Political practice on the ground does not single-handedly decide elec-tions or define levels of political participation. Political scientists have long demonstrated the importance of broad economic trends, demo-graphic developments, and party identification for electoral outcomes.[3] Sociologists have established the importance of socioeconomic status and social ties for civic engagement.[4] But campaigns matter—at the margin for who wins and who loses, and in terms of political participation because they constitute one of the pathways by which people can get involved in politics.[5] The central role played by formal and informal intermediar-ies in encouraging, shaping, and sustaining civic engagement has led to detailed studies of, for example, antiabortion activism, environmentalist groups, and movements for urban renewal, but, curiously, not of political parties and campaigns.[6]

Close attention to the work that goes into fighting ground wars brings to light an everyday life in campaigns that is far from the glamour that some associate with politics. Personalized political communication is rarely covered by journalists, who are more interested in who said what to whom and who is ahead. It plays no part in television drama series like *The West Wing* (1999–2006; much loved by many campaign staffers). It receives little breathless commentary on cable channels or political blogs. Field operations belong to the electoral backstage, where people who are not candidates, policy specialists, or high-profile consultants work hard in relative obscurity to bring about these countless contacts. To make vis-ible the daily practices that make personalized political communication possible on a large scale, this book focuses on what I actually saw people say and do on the ground in the campaigns, and not on how canvassing and phone banking are depicted in the press or by prominent political operatives marketing themselves and their work. It is only on the basis of such firsthand evidence that a clear analysis of the logics at play, and the implications they have, becomes possible.

PERSONALIZED POLITICAL COMMUNICATION

As mentioned above, I use the category "personalized political communi-cation" to refer to practices of political communication that use people as media. In the United States, campaign staffers refer to these type of com-munication interchangeably as the "ground war," the "ground game," or as "field operations," whereas volunteers often call them "grassroots" activities, part-timers talk about them as "work," and voters may simply think of them as a nuisance. The most common forms are door-to-door canvassing and phone banking, the practices in which most people who staff, volunteer in, or work part-time for American campaigns are engaged. Typically more than half of a campaign's full-time staff is assigned to the ground war effort (and more than that in large campaign organizations). All volunteers are asked to help with it. Paid part-timers are hired to work on it.

While most of what I analyze here as personalized political communication is synonymous with what the staffers call "field," the analytical category introduced serves to highlight the distinct character of these practices as forms of political communication. It also reminds us that comparable kinds of personalized political communication operate in different ways in different settings, whether animated by an archetypical political machine à la 1930s Chicago, new forms of privatized political patronage as in parts of contemporary New York City, or a rapid churn of college students working for profit-oriented companies offering plug-and-play canvassing operations to parties and interest groups that are willing to pay the price.[7] These different entities all communicate with large numbers of target voters one-on-one, but they also represent different kinds of political organizing and constitute different forms of political participation.

Personalized political communication is *personalized* insofar as people serve as media for a message that originates elsewhere. It is thus distinct from mass-mediated and computer-mediated communications, the usual focuses of political communications research, just as it is distinct from direct mail and "robocalls" (instances of what have been called "medio" communication).[8] In the case of earned and paid media, technological objects serve as channels between senders and receivers, while in the case of canvassing, human subjects are the intermediaries between political organizations and voters. This type of communication is *political* in the most ecumenical sense of the word. The people engaged in it perceive it to be political; the organizations involved are generally perceived to be political; and most of what is disseminated has direct bearing on electoral outcomes, the authoritative distribution of values, and the constitution of society. It is *communication* in the basic sense of a process for sharing symbols in time and space (symbols that go well beyond the semantic content of the words involved, including enthusiasm, attitude, and, in particular at the door, the embodied symbolism of class, gender, and race).[9]

For those who are disinclined to think of people as media, with all the instrumental overtones this concept has, think "messenger" and what that means. The communications scholar Klaus Bruhn Jensen provides a threefold definition of media as the *materials* that function as a delivery system between a sender and a receiver, the *modalities* afforded (text, sound, visuals, etc.), and the *institution* (or organization or other entity) that makes mediation possible.[10] When people function as media, we simply have subjects playing (at least part of) the material role we are accustomed to thinking of objects as playing. Communication through people is not necessarily face-to-face or unscripted. It can be conducted over the phone. It can be more or less affable or uncomfortable in form, more or less personal or impersonal in its content. What differentiates it from mass communication and medio communication is the element of live interaction, either in the flesh or mediated, live interaction that routinely takes callers and canvassers off message, interactions that most of those involved frequently find rather stressful. Personalized political communication involves interpersonal communication between the caller or canvasser and the voter contacted. But this does not make it a "direct" form of communication, since the entire interaction is orchestrated and brought about by a larger campaign assemblage working on behalf of a candidate who is not there at the door or on the line. (Speeches at rallies and candidate-voter interactions like those Richard Fenno has studied are arguably the closest we can come to political communication without mediation.[11])

The category of personalized political communication highlights a whole range of practices that most research on political communication has largely ignored. The emphasis has been on advertisements and news coverage. Both communications researchers and political scientists have concentrated on communication through technological media and their institutionalization in particular, and not on processes of communication more generally. Attention has been directed toward traditional mass media such as television, radio, and newspapers as well as today's increasingly digital networked technologies.[12] In this manner the study of political communication resembles the wider discipline of communications, with its inherited focus on mass media output and institutions. The most important exceptions to the focus on technological media have been a series of studies of the role of "social communication" in politics—analysis of how people talk about politics among themselves, unprompted by political organizations.[13] These studies of various forms of "water cooler" and primary group conversations have supplemented the field of political communication just as the study of interpersonal communication has supplemented mass communications research. But the practical division of labor between the study of technologically mediated communication, on the one hand, and unprompted social or interpersonal communication, on the other, leaves out the entire terrain that the category of personalized political communication highlights: the premeditated and often large-scale use of people as media, animated by larger assemblages. We see this not only in political campaigns but also in different ways in social movements, civic associations, religious proselytizing, and in direct marketing efforts, all trying to reach audiences through personalized communication. In all of these instances, people serve as media for messages that originate elsewhere and engage in practices that need to be understood in terms of both their impact on the target audience and their implications for the people and organizations involved.

Despite the fact that the American National Election Studies survey series clearly documents that tens of millions of people have been contacted in person or by phone every cycle in the post–World War II period and the fact that hundreds of millions of dollars have been spent on generating all of these contacts in recent elections, the ground war has generally remained, in the words of two political scientists, "in the shadows" in conversations about electioneering and campaign communications.[14] Figure 1.1 shows the percentage of people who have reported that they were contacted in person by the major parties in each presidential election year since 1956. (On top of this come additional contacts made by interest groups and others.) The postwar figure is typically around 25 percent, with occasional dips to 20 percent in the 1950s and 1990s and an extraordinary climb to over 40 percent since 2000. These millions of contacts have provoked relatively little interest among political scientists. Some have analyzed campaign organizations and the interplay between various allied groups at the state and local level, and some touch on field in more wide-ranging treatments of campaigns and elections.[15] But only a few have focused directly on the use of people as media for political communication.[16]

The most important recent research focused on the impact of ground war efforts is arguably the series of randomized natural experiments initiated in the late 1990s by Donald P. Green and Alan S. Gerber and their various collaborators.[17] The growing literature inspired by their work seeks to identify the immediate and direct effect of voter contacts on people's electoral behavior through rigorous research designs complete with control groups. It generally shows that personalized political communication is more effective than advertisements, direct mail, emails, and robocalls in getting people out to vote, and it can also influence who they vote for. The impact seems to differ to a considerable degree based on the kind of contact made (knocks are generally more effective than calls, live interactions vastly more so than any alternative). Free-flowing conversations, for example, seem to be more effective than more tightly scripted ones, and contacts from people who are somewhat familiar to the voter seem more effective than contacts from total strangers.

Overall, the experimental literature has consistently demonstrated that personalized political communication has considerable and measurable

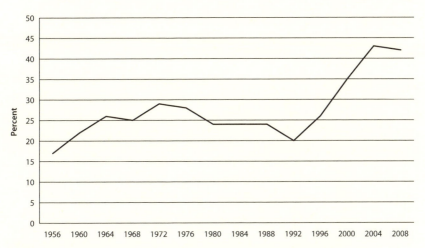

Figure 1.1. **Contacted in person by either major party 1956–2008.**
Question: "Did anyone from one of the political parties call you up or come around and talk to you about the campaign this year?"
Source: American National Election Studies, 1956–2008 (presidential election years only).

immediate short-term effects on people's voting behavior. These findings are entirely in line with what previous generations of social scientists have found.[18] They have been not only noticed by political operatives but also anticipated, replicated, and expanded by internal studies conducted by the AFL-CIO, the Republican National Committee, and others. Such research affirms that field efforts aimed at swing voters sometimes sway them and that get-out-the-vote programs using people as media actually do get out the vote. And yet, although all of these studies recognize, at least in passing, what a challenge it is to orchestrate large-scale ground war campaigns, few study how they are conducted. To put it bluntly, we know that personalized political communication happens and that it works, but we do not know *how* it works and what that means. That is the question I pursue in this book.

GROUND WARS AS PERSONALIZED POLITICAL COMMUNICATION

In a sense it is surprising that campaigns still bother with canvassing and phone banking. Living in what some think of as a "communicative cornucopia" and faced with increasingly ubiquitous computing, multimedia convergence, nonstop cable news and blogging, and the proliferation of mobile devices that are supposed to make it all available to us "anytime, anywhere," it seems almost impossibly quaint that someone would knock on your door to talk to you about an upcoming election. The idea of a thorough "mediatization" of politics, the dominance of "media logics," is central to today's discussions of political communication in the postindustrial world.[19] Though the evidence suggests a recent increase in the number of people who are contacted in person by political parties and others, analysts have long predicted a decline in personalized, live interaction as a tool for campaigns and the gradual disappearance of old-fashioned practices like canvassing as they are replaced by mass- and computer-mediated communication.[20]

The basic conclusion in research on mediated politics is that while traditional political institutions (government, parties, interest groups, etc.) remain central to most political processes, they are increasingly dependent upon and shaped by the media organizations that possess the means to communicate with people, partially because the development of "parties without partisans" and the shift in interest groups and civic associations from "membership to management" has left them without the organizational capacity and raw manpower to contact people in a more personalized fashion.[21] Even if analysts disagree about how to name the phenomenon and how developed it is, there is broad agreement on what has been called its "mutagenic" implications, the idea that while political institutions remain distinct, they are shaped by mediatization because they internalize the logics of the mass media to be able to communicate through them.[22] Gianpietro Mazzoleni and Winfried Schulz, who coined the term *mediatization*, argue that "the mass media . . . have assumed the character of 'necessity' in the political domain."[23] Manuel Castells has taken this idea to its logical extreme in his most recent work, claiming that "the media have become *the* social space where power is decided."[24]

It is important to notice in these two quotes the slide from "the mass media" to the more general "the media," because it alerts us to an underlying premise that should make us wary of Castells's use of the definitive singular. It is clear that communication (and thus media, defined as delivery systems) is a necessary part of politics—as it is of any social practice. Politicians and their associates need to communicate with people to reach their goals. It is less clear that particular historical formations, such as the conglomeration of mass media–based news and entertainment organizations we refer to in casual conversation as "the media," are necessary. Indeed, if one takes a step back from exceptional events like American presidential elections, it is sometimes striking how little news coverage politics attracts, how few political advertisements are present in the vast sea of marketing, and how ingenious political organizations are when it comes to finding ways of communicating that are not dependent on (autonomous) journalists or (expensive) advertising.[25] The two congressional campaigns I followed, two of the most competitive House races in the entire country, were each subject to just a few dozen articles in the main regional and local papers throughout all of 2008 and very little television coverage. The traditional mass media, and with them a central part of the mediatization thesis, do not look like all they are purported to be when you can cram the total accumulated coverage of the candidates in an important federal election onto a few newspaper pages. This dearth of journalistic attention and the harsh competition for eyeballs for advertisements is part of the reason why practices of personalized political communication remain stubbornly alive despite all predictions of their imminent demise.

There simply is no evidence that supports the idea of a consistent decline of face-to-face communication in politics in the United States. There have been some variations, as figure 1.1 documents, and the mass media have grown throughout the twentieth century—and grown increasingly powerful and important, no doubt—but they have not crowded out everything else nor put an end to the development of other practices of communication. Campaigns need to spread the word, and they cannot rely on "the media" alone to do it, no matter how much they massage reporters or how many thirty-second television spots they buy. There is simply too much content out there, too little attention being paid. Hence, campaigns develop what political operatives call a "layered" approach. They rely not only on advertisements and news coverage but also on direct mail, digital marketing, and field operations. As Barack Obama's campaign manager, David Plouffe, put it, the goal is "to be on our target voters' network TV, cable, satellite, and on-demand; on their radios; all over the internet; in their mailboxes; on their landlines and their cell phones . . . [and] at their doorsteps. . . . Balanced communications across *all mediums* is critical in any messaging effort today."[26] From a campaign staff point of view, people are just one medium among many. Research in political communication needs to deal with all of these different layers and to recognize that while some forms of political communication have faded away over time (we do not see many torchlight processions these days), they rarely follow one another in a neat succession of distinct epochs, as some would have it.[27] Different practices of political communication seem to coexist and to be mixed and matched by campaigns on the basis of their own perceived interests, the ideas and know-how they have, the resources at their disposal, and the communications environment around them.

Thus, in the 1970s and 1980s, when the three national television networks reached more than 50 million Americans every evening and regional newspaper monopolies reached most households in "their" media markets, it might have made sense to base one's strategy primarily on paid and earned media. But that is no longer the communications environment in which campaigns operate.[28] The more or less monolithic mass media began to crumble in the 1990s, faced with the rise of cable TV and later the Internet. Consultants and senior campaign staffers are acutely aware of this. When asked to explain the rationale behind investments in seemingly old-fashioned practices of personalized political communication, political operatives point not only to research documenting its impact or to the development of new tools like the predictive modeling algorithms and online-integrated database technology that facilitate field operations today. They also talk about several current trends discussed in the academic study of communications. They point to problems of *oversaturation*, sometimes bringing up the idea that individual Americans are subject to several thousand advertising messages every day, and argue that this situation blunts the impact of television advertisements and direct mail.[29] They point to an increasing *audience fragmentation*, where the spread of cable television, falling newspaper circulation, and the increasing proliferation of specialized publications online and off-line combined with vast disparities in people's interest in political information make it ever more difficult to reach a broad audience through any one given media.[30] Finally, they point to the oft-documented *limited effects* of mass communication and direct mail when it comes to actually influencing people's immediate political behavior, in terms of both voting preferences and turnout.[31]

The combination of these developments makes it particularly difficult for campaigns to communicate effectively with key targets like swing voters and infrequently voting partisans—many of whom pay little attention to news and who frequently are not interested in (or even decidedly disenchanted with) electoral politics. Given the litany of complaints, any kind of communication that, like personalized political communication, allows for *unique contacts* that stand out from the media torrent, reaches a clearly defined universe of *individual targets*, and has *measurable effects* starts to look attractive to campaigns involved in close races. Back in 1992, after the midterm elections, political scientist Paul S. Herrnson surveyed hundreds of congressional campaigns and found that staffers rated door-to-door campaigning well below paid and earned media in terms of impact and importance.[32] When he repeated the study after the 2002 midterm elections, he found that operatives now saw ground war practices as among the most effective means of communication, more so than television advertisements, email, or the Internet.[33]

In the early years of the twenty-first century, the strategies and priorities of the major parties have gradually come to reflect this change of mind among political operatives. In the 1990s parties and campaigns allegedly turned away willing volunteers because they did not know what to use them for.[34] Today they are clamoring for help because labor-intensive field operations again have become a key concern in competitive races, a central part of their strategy. This resurgent interest in the use of people as media is important because it has led to the increased number of contacts we have seen in the first decade of the twenty-first century and has had a clear impact on electoral results—especially by increasing voter turnout.[35] But personalized political communication is also important because of the implications its large-scale pursuit has for political organizations themselves and for those involved—it constitutes one of the main forms of political participation available today. Field operations affect electoral outcomes, this we know. What is less often discussed is that they also have their own "mutagenic" implications for the forms that campaigns take. Changing strategic priorities with a greater emphasis on phone calls and door knocks are driving today's political campaigns toward a slightly more open and inclusive form than what we have known during the last decades of the twentieth century.

THE PURSUIT OF PERSONALIZED POLITICAL COMMUNICATION

Ground wars are *projects*, distinct and temporary tasks defined by clear criteria for success—that is, victory—and an equally clear deadline: Election Day. They depend on many factors, including the overall political and economic climate, the demographics of the district at hand, the nature of the competition, and the resources available. Most of these variables are not under the control of those involved in a given campaign. In the United States, decennial redistricting carried out in oft-distant state capitols; the cold, dead hands of the Founding Fathers who defined the electoral system; and the processes that lead to the nomination of whoever a candidate happens to be running against have a large say in how a given ground war will be waged. In a district that for one reason or another is not competitive, personalized political communication may not even be worth the trouble (and as we shall see, it involves a lot of trouble)—and only 10–20 percent of all congressional elections are effectively competitive, with only a dozen or so states in play at the presidential level. But in close elections, every little bit counts. A common saying among political operatives is that a good field program can make a difference of between 1 and 5 percent.[36] There is certainly more art than science to such estimates, but, as mentioned above, research at least documents that field can make *a* difference. A few percent may not sound like a lot, but remember that six of the sixteen postwar presidential elections were decided by less than a 5 percent margin. So were four Senate races and thirty-three races for the House of Representatives in 2008 alone. In such cases, as in competitive elections at all levels, a good ground game can be decisive, and the work of putting together a set of elements to pursue it begins when consultants and staffers think their candidate may be within striking distance of victory.

I call such a set, arranged around a common ground war project in a particular district, a *campaign assemblage*. I use the concept to refer to a heterogeneous collection of elements engaged in concerted action. The notion of an "assemblage" is appropriated from recent work in social theory, organizational sociology, and science and technology studies.[37] A campaign assemblage is not a thing "out there" in the sense that a human being is, but rather a name for a combination of technologically augmented organizations, groups, and individuals whose combined capacities for action are brought to bear on a shared project. In a few corners of the United States, where the finely meshed networks associated with the parties and political machines of yore still exist or have found new forms, one can perhaps think of personalized political communication as something pursued by a single organization or as a set of firmly institutionalized practices. In parts of Boston, Chicago, or Philadelphia, an identifiable set of trans-organizational routines may recur from election to election, cycle after cycle, as the same people gather at the behest of the powers that be and spread the word to the voters. But, as I show in chapter 2, this is not the standard scenario today.

EPISODE 1.4

"What about the unions and the party? Won't they do much of the work for you?" I ask. The senior staffer looks at me for a moment, then says, "I wish. First of all, the unions aren't what they used to be. Second, we don't always get along so well—think NAFTA and all that. Third, what party? That, too, is sort of crumbling, at least on the ground, and where it's not, there are usually various complications." "Like what?" "Ah, you know, people have their own agendas."

The major parties in America, and their most important respective allies, have changed, and even the most powerful cannot provide a complete ground war machinery.[38] The ground war is only partially institutionalized and is fundamentally dependent on the active, dynamic, and contingent creation of temporary and ad-hoc campaign assemblages. Campaign organizations, the unevenly professionalized temporary vehicles set up around candidates, are not in a position to do all the work themselves either. Take the two districts where I did my research. According to the Federal Election Committee, Jim Himes: Democrat for Congress spent a total of $3.9 million in 2008, Linda Stender for Congress $2.6 million. (In both districts national, state, and local party committees and many other allies spent substantial sums on top of that.) In Connecticut's 4th district the Democratic candidate's expenditures alone came to $13 per vote cast on Election Day; in New Jersey's 7th, $9 per vote. (By way of comparison, Barack Obama's campaign raised and spent close to $750 million on the presidential race, or a little less than $6 per vote cast across the country.) In addition to buying some television advertisements and a lot of direct mail, these millions of dollars were used to build campaign organizations that grew from basically being the candidate and a fund-raising operation in the winter and early spring of the election year, to a nucleus of senior staffers (campaign manager, finance director, communications director, field director, and a few more to assist them) by the late spring, and finally into a fully articulated operation with about twenty full-time staffers by June.

More than half of a campaign's staff work on the ground war effort. They all share an instrumental view of what they are doing. They are, in the words of one, "in it to win it." Apart from the field director and inter-mediary staffers such as the deputy field director, the canvassing director, and the volunteer coordinator (if there is one), most of the staffers working on the ground war are recent college graduates or students taking a semester off from school. This, then, is what a well-funded congressional campaign organization in a competitive district has available for the ground war: a handful of people with a few cycles' worth of experience and a dozen new recruits. There is simply no way that these people alone, most of whom will be working on the campaign for less than six months, can meet the goal of contacting 20 percent of the electorate in a district— about a hundred thousand people—in person.

So to accomplish this goal, wider campaign assemblages are brought together. When I refer simply to "campaigns," these assemblages are what I refer to. The notion of assemblages is useful here not only because it can encompass the whole set of actors involved in field operations (and not only the staffers in the campaign organization), but also because its invocation of the verb "assemble" highlights the work that goes into holding these temporary teams together. Campaigns look like monolithic entities only when seen from afar. Up close it becomes clear that they are composites of temporary campaign organizations, durable allied organizations, and hundreds or even thousands of individual volunteers and part-timers enrolled for the duration of the project. The ground war in a single congressional district involves not only the candidate's campaign organization, the staffers who populate it, and the consultants they contract with. It also involves, with variations from place to place, the campaign organizations of other candidates (running for everything from president to the board of education); the state party; one or more of the party campaign committees from the state capital or Washington, D.C.; local party organizations and political entrepreneurs; allied interest groups such as unions, activist groups, and sympathetic civic associations (whether religious-, ethnic-, or issue-based); plus communities of volunteers and part-timers. The various allies involved blur normal distinctions between different advocacy or interest group coalitions and have machine regulars and reformers, manufacturing unions and environmentalists, affordable housing advocates and lobbyists for developers temporarily working together side by side, sharing the same ground war project—often because they hope for something in return if the candidate wins.

The volunteers and part-timers involved are recruited as individuals (but from very different and only partially overlapping demographic groups). Hundreds of volunteers come in and help out on a congressional campaign for everywhere between a few hours once to dozens of hours a week for months. They come with different expectations—some want to write speeches or work on policy, others just to "help." All will be asked to canvass and phone bank. (See figure 1.2 for a list of the volunteer opportunities advertised by the New Jersey campaign.) Depending on district demographics, they tend to be white, college-educated, older, and often affluent. They are typically motivated by political partisanship, a sense of citizenship, and sometimes a love of the game. They want to win, but they also see campaigns as a communal activity and a form of civic engagement.

Staffers have ambivalent relations with volunteers. On the one hand, volunteers are widely recognized as the most effective ambassadors for the candidate and the party. "Volunteers are the best, no doubt about it," says one staffer. On the other hand, they are unpredictable, sometimes unwilling to focus on canvassing and phone banking, and occasionally so ideologically invested in the project that they are reluctant to accept tactical advice. Volunteers are often seen by staffers as "high maintenance." "There are so many egos you need to massage," says one volunteer coordinator, adding, "In that sense, part-timers are easier."

Most campaigns have many more volunteers than staffers involved, but rarely enough to reach their contact goals. While political operatives and national political organizations have increased their emphasis on, and budget allocations for, field operations from the early 2000s onward and generated more and more contacts, the number of volunteers mobilized by campaigns and by local party organizations has not increased as much as the number of contacts has. Volunteer recruitment is considered progressively more important, but local networks are often weak and the work of getting people involved remains, in the words of one staffer, "haphazard" and only one among many priorities. Mobilizing people and keeping them involved has not been a major concern for parties and campaigns in the latter half of the twentieth century, and the

Volunteer Opportunities

For more information about these and any other volunteer opportunities with the Stender campaign, please call or e-mail at ███-███-███ or ███████@lindastenderforcongress.com

Morning Phonebanking

Date: Daily, Monday through Friday
Time: 10:00 AM – 12:00 Noon
Location: Campaign HQ, 256 South Avenue, Fanwood, NJ

Click Here for Directions

Evening Phonebanking

Date: Daily, Monday through Friday
Time: 5:00 PM – 8:00 PM
Location: Campaign HQ, 256 South Avenue, Fanwood, NJ

Click Here for Directions

Weekday Canvassing

Date: Daily, Monday through Friday
Time: 5:00 PM – 8:00 PM
Meetup Location: Campaign HQ, 256 South Avenue, Fanwood, NJ

Click Here for Directions

Weekend Canvassing

Date: Saturdays
Time: 10:00 AM – 12:00 Noon or 1:00 PM – 3:00 PM
Meetup Location: Campaign HQ, 256 South Avenue, Fanwood, NJ

Click Here for Directions

Figure 1.2. **Volunteer opportunities in New Jersey.**
These were the options listed on the campaign organization's website. (The initials in the email address have been removed to protect the staffer's anonymity.)

number of people who volunteer has declined. As recently as the 1960s and early 1970s, the American National Election Studies routinely found that 5–6 percent of all respondents reported having worked for a candidate or campaign during election time. But the number fell throughout the 1980s and 1990s and reached a nadir of 2 percent in 1996. Even with a renewed focus on volunteer recruitment by campaigns, participation

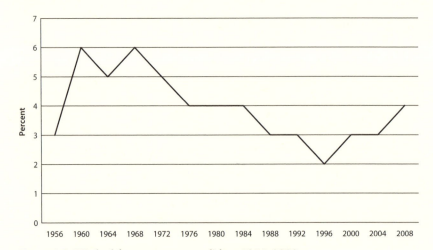

Figure 1.3. **Worked for a party or candidate 1956–2008.**
Question: "Did you do any {other} work for one of the parties or candidates?"
(Beyond attending a meeting, wearing a button, or donating money.)
Source: American National Election Studies, 1956–2008 (presidential election years only).

has been inching upward only slowly since then, reaching 4 percent in 2008 (see figure 1.3). As one senior staffer said to me, "We never get enough volunteers; we always want more."

EPISODE 1.5
Election Day is less than two weeks away, and John, the field director, is stressed out. "It's usually about now that I start having trouble sleeping and get heart palpitations." Over a slice of pizza with salami and a can of Dr. Pepper, he spends his five-minute break explaining that the campaign needs to fill eighteen hundred volunteer shifts and find about two hundred people for eight hundred paid canvassing shifts before the GOTV weekend kicks off.

He is pretty strung out and hard to have a sustained conversation with, but I ask him how things are coming along. He is tapping his feet incessantly as he says, "Well, you know we've got about sixty paid canvassers already, and all the guys are out recruiting. I think we have maybe a hundred signed up. All the organizers will have to work every day recruiting." "What about volunteers?" I ask. "You'll have to ask Jack about that. I think he said he has about a hundred and sixty scheduled, so you can imagine. He has a lot of work to do."

Despite their pronounced preference for relying on volunteers and on allies (most of whom can rarely mobilize large numbers of members for personalized political communication), the two campaigns I followed eventually ended up employing about two hundred people working part-time as paid canvassers or phone bankers for ten dollars an hour or so—people like Charlene in episode 1.1. Their use of paid casual labor is hardly unique. Unions and other interest groups also sometimes find they have to pay people to do work when they have too few member activists to do the job.[39] Even the Barack Obama campaign, with its estimated 3 million volunteers, also resorted to paid phone banks in 2008.[40] Staffers have ambivalent relations to part-timers too; on the one hand, they are aware that part-time workers are not always the best ambassadors for the cause—poorly trained and motivated as they often are—but on the other hand, part-timers are seen as more dependable than volunteers. And as one campaign manager put it, "It is more important that we do field than that we have volunteers do it." Paid part-timers are used to close the gap between the ambitious contact goals that staffers set for themselves and what they expect they can accomplish with the help of allies and volunteers.

Those who are hired for this work are predominantly either young students who do it on the side of their studies to earn a little cash or people (some of them older) who need the money to tide them over because they find themselves without permanent employment. In the districts I researched, there were many more blacks and Latinos among part-timers than among the volunteers. Some part-timers care about politics, and all would like "their" candidate to win, but most say they are mainly involved for the weekly paycheck. For them, campaigning is a casual job. And it is sold to them primarily as such, not as a political or civic enterprise (see the recruitment flyers from New Jersey reproduced in figure 1.4).[41] Staffers may be rather particular about whom they hire for these jobs to begin with, but this quickly comes to an end as the imbalance between supply and demand becomes clear. One field organizer, in the span of two months, went from describing who he was looking for to do part-time paid canvassing as "Someone local, who knows the community and who cares about politics" to the rather less demanding idea that "We need people who aren't crazy and don't look crazy." (In 2000 Jon Corzine's campaign for Senate memorably ended up busing in men hired en masse at homeless shelters in Pennsylvania for its GOTV weekend in neighboring New Jersey.) "You should see some of the people who come in," the field organizer added. I did see them, and they were ordinary Americans, most of them either uninterested in politics and simply taking the job to earn a little on the side or people who had found themselves in a tough spot where any job was better than no job.

EPISODE 1.6

Luis is still short of his recruitment goals for the paid canvass, and when I ask him about them, he shrugs and says, "I've stopped thinking of it as two hundred people; now I'm just trying to fill all eight hundred shifts. I just need

Campaign Jobs

Easy work ! Great Pay !

$75/Shift

Saturday Nov 1st   9 AM – 3 PM
                               3 PM – 9 PM
Sunday Nov 2nd   11 AM – 5 PM
Monday Nov 3rd   3 PM – 9 PM
Tuesday 4th (ELECTION DAY) 3 PM- 8PM

Call 908-490-1380
to schedule a shift.
_____@njdems.org

Paid for by the New Jersey Democratic
State committee. Not authorized by any candidate or
candidate's committee. Printed in house.

Campaign Jobs

$10/Hour

4:00 – 9:00 PM Mon-Thurs
10:00 – 3:00 PM Sat
1:00 – 6:00 PM Sun

Call 908-490-1380
to schedule a shift.
_____@njdems.org

Paid for by the New Jersey Democratic
State committee. Not authorized by any candidate
candidate's committee. Printed in house.

Figure 1.4. Two flyers used for part-time recruitment in New Jersey.
One was used in September and October ($10/hour), the other for GOTV weekend ($75/shift). (The initials in the email address have been removed to protect the staffer's anonymity.)

more bodies." He shakes his head and continues: "I'd have loved to have, you know, teams of kids canvassing their home turf wearing their local high school sweatshirt. But we're short, so that's not going to happen." On the wall behind him is a black-and-white photocopied flyer that he picks up and hands to me. "Have you seen this?"

It is an irregularly cut half page of letter-size paper with a stylized drawing of a donkey—a common mascot symbol for the Democratic Party—trumpeting "Campaign Jobs" in a large font. The subtitle reads "Easy work! Great Pay!" A month and a half earlier, the campaign tried to recruit part-timers to go canvassing for the Democratic Party. Two weeks ago the flyers were encouraging people to work to "Get Obama elected" (in a solidly pro-Democratic state). Now it has come to this. Luis says, "That's my favorite slogan so far. Fuck Obama, fuck the party. Easy job, great pay, that's what it's all about." He shakes his head and turns to his computer.

Staffers like Luis, a canvassing director, spend a lot of their time tied to their desk in front of their computers. Political ground wars, like the rather more dramatic forms of warfare they take their name from, are deeply dependent on back-end logistics and increasingly tied in with new information and communication technologies—a whole range of mundane, emerging, and specialized tools used for communicating with constituents, mobilizing volunteers, organizing work, and targeting voters.[42] The most important back-end tools involved in personalized political communication are a combination of databases and online-integrated interfaces used for planning canvassing and phone banking, gathering response data from voters, and targeting them for further contacts.

EPISODE 1.7
Luis says, "All those databases, microtargeting, and all that stuff, it really has changed campaigns a lot. It used to be all about TV; now it's more like a junk mail company, you know? We're trying to reach out to people in person." I ask him to give examples of what has changed, and he says, "Where do you want me to begin? I mean, just back in 2006 we didn't have a turf-cutter, so I had to pull a list of voters from each precinct, then export it to Excel, then import it to Microsoft Streets and Names, call up all the pushpins on a map, mark the map with a line around the area—which then wouldn't really be the precinct, but what the hell—then remove the pins and print it. That would be my master copy." He laughs and says, "It took me a weekend and a half to cut the turf for all the canvassers!"

I say that sounds convenient but hardly like a revolution, and he grows more serious and responds, "Look, this has led to a much better field. Now that the party maintains those databases, we can use all these new kinds of targeting, meaning that we can, when we need to, reach much larger universes of voters for persuasion and for GOTV [get-out-the-vote]. Sometimes we joke—you know, 'What did we do before the Internet?'—but seriously, we wouldn't have had such a large ground game this year if the consultants hadn't been able to identify so many targets for us."

Despite some hopeful prognostications to the contrary, the rise of the Internet and the development of new, networked "social media" has not brought about a massive increase in popular participation in politics or radically empowered citizen activists to take on entrenched interests.

A few exceptional outliers aside (like Howard Dean in the Democratic presidential primary in 2004 and Ron Paul in the Republican presidential primary in 2008), most political organizations use available information and communication technologies to supplement, extend, and augment existing practices, not to transform them. The most important new tools adopted by field campaigns in the 2000s are predictive modeling algorithms leveraging vast amounts of data kept by the political parties in online-accessible databases and continuously updated by the response data generated by campaigns themselves. The "new political targeting" has emerged as an increasingly dominant targeting scheme in Democratic field efforts.[43] It allows campaigns to target individual voters for persuasion and activation with greater accuracy and expands the universe of potentially "valuable" targets beyond what could be identified in the past.

The notion of campaign assemblages is used here to unpack the black box of field operations; to conceptualize its relational character; and to grasp how interdependent, loosely coupled elements develop the capacity to pursue personalized political communication together, all the time retaining their distinct character as they eschew formal organization and fail to solidify into anything one would recognize as a single entity or institution. All the different actors touched on above—the campaign organizations and the staffers working in them, various allied groups and organizations, the communities of volunteers and part-timers—and the technologies they rely on play a role in the story told in the rest of this book. All are involved in the pursuit of electoral victory; all can tell us something about political communication, political organizations, and political participation. Each campaign assemblage contains both old elements and routines and new components and challenges, each involves both temporary and durable organizations, and the evidence suggests that they differ from party to party and from district to district.[44] The ground war machinery assembled around Democratic *candidates* in a particular district does not have the solidity and stable characteristics of the Democratic *Party* in the same place. (Even the latter is, of course, a complicated contraption.) In fact, many people who are working hard to get a particular candidate elected balk at the idea that they are involved in a capital-D Democratic campaign, preferring more general notions such as "liberal" or "progressive" and making it clear that, to quote one activist, "we are not doing it for *their* sake."

This suggests how—in contrast to advertisement time or direct mail blasts—the use of people as media (however recruited) comes at a price for campaign organizations that goes beyond simply writing a check. People can be unruly, and the same activist energies that can help put a Barack Obama or a Ronald Reagan in the White House can also propel a George McGovern or a Barry Goldwater to the top of the ticket. While all the people involved in a campaign assemblage recognize the electoral project and want to win, different elements have different motivations, different views of what is and ought to be going on, and they are rarely accountable to the campaign and its manager the way subordinates in the campaign organization itself are. This situation is a cause for great concern and constant consternation for staffers striving to control what is going on, and it is just one example of how personalized political communication has implications well beyond its instrumental impact.

STUDYING PERSONALIZED POLITICAL COMMUNICATION

Most of the work that goes in to ground war projects takes place in a back region that we know little about. Campaigns' internal documents are rarely made available to researchers, and in any case they capture only part of what is going on. The millions of contacts made are ephemeral and leave no qualitative record that speaks to their dynamics. Thus, to get at the inner workings and intricate details of the ground war, the bulk of my analysis is based on my own original ethnographic fieldwork. The appendix at the end of this book discusses the research approach in detail, but here are the basics: From February until November 2008 I engaged in participant-observation in two congressional districts (Connecticut's 4th and New Jersey's 7th), focusing in each case on the campaign assemblage that evolved around the Democratic candidate for the House of Representatives (Jim Himes and Linda Stender, respectively). I chose these two districts because they looked likely to be competitive races with considerable stakes and thus good examples of how well-funded, high-priority, federal-level campaigns pursue personalized political communication. For ten months I attended local party meetings, visited various political organizations and associations (from powerful unions to marginal activist groups), and, especially during the last three months, worked practically around the clock alongside staffers, volunteers, and part-timers on the ground. The result was firsthand experience with the look, feel, and everyday practice of electoral politics, retained in the more than one thousand pages of field notes I wrote.

In the one sense that matters most to those involved, the two campaigns could not be more different—Jim Himes won, Linda Stender lost. But this aside, their internal operations were similar enough that throughout this book I stress mostly the commonalities between them as examples of how campaign assemblages built around Democratic candidates pursue personalized political communication in competitive elections today. To supplement the data from my fieldwork, I have conducted fifty-nine off-site interviews with people involved, both directly in the districts and through various other parts of the assemblages based in Washington, D.C., the respective state capitals, and elsewhere (campaign committees, data and software providers, and consultant companies). Finally, I have gone through what was—until Barack Obama started winning states in the Democratic presidential primary—a limited amount of news coverage of ground war operations in various campaigns.

Interviews and secondary sources have played an important supplementary role in developing my argument, but they would have been insufficient on their own. When you talk with people about what they do, they are likely to, consciously or unconsciously, provide a very selective version. Although I did learn a lot through such conversations, a lot of the material from my interviews basically suggests that everything done is effective, that everybody is good at what they are doing, and that everyone works together smoothly. (As it happens, it turns out that this is only one part of the story.) Secondary sources are also useful additions but again have a similar performative dimension that one must take into account. News coverage is oriented toward the spectacular and often limited to the story the professionals want to tell about their effort—how well it works, how much it matters, how finely targeted it is. Many political operatives I spoke with marveled at, for example, how effectively Republican operatives had shaped the news coverage of the Bush-Cheney field operations during the 2004 presidential elections. Others were equally impressed with how well journalistic writings about the Obama effort in 2008 were spun by the campaign.

What you see on the ground is rather different and rarely put on display. Outsiders are not particularly welcome behind the scenes. In my experience, even when volunteers and part-timers turned out to be open-hearted, many of the staffers and consultants were professional paranoids (even when promised anonymity). Much information on contact numbers, volunteer recruitment, and sources of funding was kept from me; many meetings off-limits; and many documents never made available, even after the campaigns were over. Often it was only when instrumental interests overrode concerns about secrecy that information was shared with me—so passwords that had been guarded jealously one week would be handed over the next if that meant I could train a few volunteers to make phone calls or enter data about voters.

The fact that I took upon myself such tasks flows from the idea that ethnographic fieldwork is based on social exchange.[45] In addition to making it more difficult to maintain the conventional scientific standing as an outside observer, this means that what you get depends on what you give. In ground war operations the fieldworker enters an assemblage built around a shared goal—that of winning the election—and must find one or more roles that can secure continued access without compromising the validity of the study or standing in the way of that purpose. There is no room for tourists on campaigns. I engaged in participant-observation, typically assuming the position of what some staffers call a "super-volunteer," someone whom they can depend on to show up when promised and who will "do the work" without too much goofing off. I tried to follow a classic ethnographic dictum and did what I could to avoid situations where my opinions would be solicited. I also turned down repeated job offers, thinking that going fully "native" as a field organizer would severely truncate the view I could get of the wider assemblage. Basically I offered the campaigns some of my time in exchange for some access and considerable freedom of movement, and the informal deal remained more or less intact until the elections were over. The data I have no doubt remain incomplete in some details, but do, I believe, capture a larger picture nonetheless.

In this chapter I have situated the study of personalized political communication in relation to existing work on political communication, political organizations, and political participation and have provided a basic outline of my argument about the development of ground war practices, campaign forms, and how they are related to civic engagement and democracy. Chapter 2 further elaborates the setting by tracing the recent history of—and controversies around—personalized political communication in the Democratic Party in particular. These parts provide the starting point. The central question, pursued in greater detail in the remaining chapters, remains how personalized political communication is pursued by American campaigns, how it is produced by assemblages arranged around ground war projects and faced with a fast-approaching deadline on Election Day—and what that means for American democracy. I had no idea that the Obama campaign would put such emphasis on field operations and personalized political communication when I began developing this project in the fall of 2007. But precisely because many of the practices pursued by the Obama campaign, dependent as they were on the extraordinary amounts of money and numbers of volunteers that the candidate attracted, were so exceptional, I am glad they are not at the centerpiece of this book. I chose competitive congressional districts because they seemed more likely to serve as what sociologist Robert K. Merton has called "strategic research sites," sites that exhibit an object of analysis in an accessible form that enables systematic scrutiny of previously untouched problems and potentially opens up new terrains for inquiry.[46] The two cases I analyze here are cases *for* the study of personalized political communication as well as cases *of* how it is pursued by American campaigns. It is precisely because they are unexceptional but still competitive, well-funded, and important contests—and not always unique presidential elections or the more common uncontested, moderately endowed, and always already decided races—that they provide interesting research sites. Close scrutiny here of two cases from the same party and in comparable districts has helped me identify logics I suggest are widespread throughout competitive and well-funded Democratic campaigns. I hope further research will test and no doubt revise the ideas developed here and determine how relevant they are for Republican campaigns and others too.

OUTLINE OF THE BOOK

In chapter 2 I outline the development of the ground war in the early twenty-first century, with particular focus on the Democratic Party and its allies. I trace the resurgent interest in personalized political communication among top political operatives over the last ten years, the increased investments in field made by both campaigns and national party organizations, but also the continual slow decline in many areas of the local organizations that have historically mobilized much of the manpower needed. The "labor guys" mentioned in episode 1.3 are not as numerous as they used to be, nor are party regulars. It is in part because of the absence of a firmly institutionalized "permanent campaign" infrastructure for field operations that wider campaign assemblages are built today.

In chapter 3 I turn from the recent history of the ground war to a detailed analysis of a few of the millions of contacts made in 2008 to address the question of how personalized political communication between campaigns and voters plays out at the individual level. The interactive character of encounters between callers/canvassers and voters helps explain why personalized political communication consistently seems to go "off message" and why most of those involved find the work so stressful. Sometimes, as with Ms. Rizzo in episode 1.1, entreaties appear to come across as invasive and uncomfortable, while conversations like Paula's with the unnamed Republican in episode 1.2 are perhaps more conventionally satisfying (though nerve-rackingly undisciplined from a staff point of view).

In chapter 4 I analyze how the diverse elements enrolled in campaign assemblages organize their pursuit of the shared ground war project, and then I return to the relations staffers have with sympathetic interest groups and with volunteers and part-timers. Here I unfold the distinctions outlined above, between the campaign organizations populated by the staffers, the wider networks of allies around them, and the communities of volunteers and part-timers enrolled to serve as media for personalized political communication. On closer inspection, the ground war turns out to be neither the kind of "grassroots politics" that some romantics think it is, nor as thoroughly professionalized as many have suggested American campaigns are today. There I go back to the tensions illustrated by part-timer Charlene's criticism of the areas the staffers had sent us to in episode 1.1, to the reasons Paula and the rest of the volunteers worked in a room of their own in Fanwood in episode 1.2, and to the uneasy relations between staff and volunteers hinted at in episode 1.3.

In chapter 5 I deal with how campaigns target their limited resources and decide which voters to contact. I analyze several aspects of a recently emerged and increasingly dominant new targeting scheme that integrates predictive modeling done by outside consultants, everyday work done by people in the campaigns, and the online-integrated and easily accessible national voter file maintained by the Democratic National Committee and the state parties. This new scheme dramatically improves staffers' ability to focus efforts on persuadable voters and infrequently voting partisans and significantly expands the universe of potentially valuable targets. But, as I show, despite the availability of these methods, even some parts of the Democratic Party itself choose to opt out and pursue their own alternative targeting schemes to retain some autonomy from the national and state parties. In chapter 5 we go to Washington, D.C., and to Somerset, Massachusetts, to understand why Charlene and I found ourselves at Ms. Rizzo's doorstep in episode 1.1, who were on the list Paula and the other volunteers called through in episode 1.2, and how the campaigns got the contact information in the first place.

Chapter 6, the penultimate part of this book (before an appendix on research methods with a more detailed discussion of some of the methodological issues touched on briefly above), presents my conclusions by relating the detailed analysis of how American campaigns pursue personalized political communication to the wider questions raised in this chapter—questions about how we understand political communication more generally, about political organizations, and about the practices and possibilities of political participation that electoral contests offer.

* * *

In this book I make a case for reinterpreting our overall understanding—and judgment—of political communication in the light of how field operations work. Even if negative advertisements and cynical news coverage spread by print, broadcast, and the Internet are "out of order" and depress voter turnout and engagement (as political communication literature sometimes permeated with something akin to distaste for its object suggests), ground wars are waged at the same time with equal vehemence by unevenly professionalized, heterogeneous, and temporary campaign assemblages that leverage people as media for political communication in the face of considerable costs and many practical challenges to do the *exact opposite* among a given candidate's own imagined constituency: to turn them out, get them involved, and make them care, however momentarily, about politics. Ground wars are full of sound and fury; adversarial, unequal, and plagued by internal conflicts, they are far from poster children for a picture-perfect democratic process. But they are inching the actually existing American democracy toward a slightly more inclusive form. And that, I believe, is a good thing.

CHAPTER 2

The Ground War Enters the Twenty-first Century

EPISODE 2.1

"I don't think you'll see much field in that district; I think you'll see mostly mail and television." This prediction was made by an experienced campaign manager and high-level political aide who had worked for much of the 1980s and 1990s in one of the two states where I did my research. Given my interest in the ground war, it was hardly what I hoped to hear in the background interview I conducted in early April in her elegant Manhattan pied-à-terre, but such is life.

EPISODE 2.2

"This cycle, the D-trip [the Democratic Congressional Campaign Committee (DCCC)], the state party, and the campaign are pumping hundreds of thousands of dollars into what will probably be the largest field effort this district has ever seen." That was the view of one senior staffer working in the district in question, confidently expressed in an on-site conversation in early August and later corroborated by both the executive director of the state party and the DCCC regional field director.

EPISODE 2.3

"I swear to God, we must have had the worst fucking field operation in the whole goddamn country." So went the colorful postelection verdict of one of the staffers who fought in that particular ground war, delivered with equal parts anger and regret over coffee in a postelection interview in a West Village café.

The last ten years have seen a resurgent interest in the ground war among political operatives. The three episodes above illustrate both their change of mind and the difficulties they are having in actually executing field operations in practice. Personalized political communication has been integral to American campaigns since active electioneering became socially acceptable in the early nineteenth century. The rambunctious "politics of parties" that replaced a more deferential "politics of assent" manifested itself in a wide array of new campaign practices that were unheard of in the first years of the Republic.[1] In the late eighteenth century, public office was rarely contested but usually handed to a locally respected property-owning white man by his peers. In later years, however, when candidates no longer "stood" for election but "ran" for office, campaigns took a more active turn and began to engage in everything from torchlight processions and mass meetings with surrogate speakers to various last-minute efforts by party activists to round up and drag voters out, all in aggressive pursuit of victory on Election Day.[2]

Present-day practices of door-to-door canvassing and phone banking are heirs to such attempts to systematically leverage people as media for political communication. Knocking on doors is one of the many rituals and routines of American politics, a thing that campaigns "just do." But the long historical pedigree of calling on voters at home does not explain the investments that parties and campaigns make in the ground war today. Nor does it explain the dramatic increase in the number of people contacted in recent years or, for that matter, the new technologically assisted forms political contact takes as auto-dialing, various Internet tools, and online-integrated databases are leveraged for electoral purposes. Instead, the waxing and waning of personalized political communication seems to depend on how instrumentally effective those who run campaigns think it is and on whether the resources to pursue it are available—people to contact voters, organizers to coordinate the work, data to target it, and money to fund it. In the nineteenth century ground wars were waged by the parties, and in the twentieth century they were increasingly conducted by their member-based interest group allies, whether in the labor movement or on the religious right. Today they involve a wider set of actors working together.

In this chapter I analyze the development of the ground war in the early twenty-first century, with particular focus on the Democratic Party and its allies. I show how top political operatives began to value personalized political communication once again, and I follow the increased investments made by campaigns and national parties in field operations. Yet I also illustrate how the local party organizations and member-based allied organizations who have traditionally animated Democratic efforts in many areas continued their slow decline. Politicians, parties, interest groups, and media organizations may find themselves locked in a "permanent campaign" in other respects,[3] but the history outlined here shows how partial and incomplete the firmly institutionalized underpinnings for waging ground wars are. Party organizations in general try to be "in service" to candidates, as political scientists have long argued;[4] however, while they can help campaigns find staffers, connect with consultants, and sustain some elements of a technological infrastructure for targeting voters, they can rarely supply the manpower needed for large-scale, labor-intensive ground war efforts.[5] It is in the absence of the "standing armies" of yesteryear's mass parties and political machines—or even the ability to mobilize volunteers and conscripts in substantial numbers through interest group allies—that candidates and campaign staffers have to build wider assemblages in order to be able to fight effectively in competitive elections.

THE GROUND WAR IN THE LATE TWENTIETH CENTURY

The problem that Democratic campaigns faced as top operatives regained an interest in personalized political communication in the late 1990s and early 2000s was that the party organizations and interest group allies in the labor movement and elsewhere that previously had provided most of what was needed to wage an effective ground war no longer could do so. Starting with what historian Michael McGerr has called "the decline of popular politics" in the late nineteenth century and the rise in the early twentieth century of an increasingly mass-media-based and mail-based "politics of information," party organizations have gradually ceased to be deeply embedded in people's everyday lives and lost the ability to leverage large numbers of party regulars for campaign purposes.[6] (And they never had much of a presence in the first place in many of the midwestern and western states.) Though political machines and vibrant local parties survive in some places, civil service reforms that undercut networks of patronage, widespread disenchantment with the political process, changing campaign practices downplaying the importance of popular involvement, and the rise of new political players such as advertisement-funded commercial media organizations and a variety of increasingly important interests groups have all challenged the position that parties occupied in American politics for much of the nineteenth and twentieth centuries.[7]

Political parties remain central to how the country is governed, how large parts of the electorate orient themselves, and how campaigns are organized. But they are no longer the main means by which office seekers communicate with voters. They have lost this role not simply because of stylistic changes in how campaigns are waged but also because the parties themselves have changed. The postwar years saw the rise of a new kind of volunteer activism driven by an intrinsic and often ideologically motivated interest in public policy that many of the more materially motivated party regulars found perplexing and even pernicious.[8] But the overall trend of the postwar years has been what has been characterized as the "breakdown" of local party organizations and the networks they have sustained.[9] This is not a universal phenomenon, as talented local organizers have kept individual committees alive or groups of activists have been energized by particularly charismatic candidates. (Arguably, for a new generation of Democrats, Howard Dean and Barack Obama have been what Adlai Stevenson was for the "amateur democrats" James Q. Wilson studied, and MoveOn is just one of several Internet-assisted activist groups laying claim to a progressive reform heritage.[10]) But in an interview, one experienced Democratic operative described the situation today in this way: "About ten percent of the more than two hundred thousand precincts in the United States have active organizations at the local level. Many others have fallen apart as people die, drop out, move, et cetera. There is definitely a resurgence now, but we have a long way to go." In place of the politics of parties, the late twentieth century saw an increasingly candidate-centered form of politics, the rise of political consultants based outside the parties, and ever more active electoral engagement by a wide range of interest groups.[11] And as the networks and organizations that historically mobilized and motivated party activists—whether regulars or reformers—withered away, labor-intensive personalized practices were in many cases supplanted by capital-intensive media and mail campaigns.

For years the labor movement—arguably the single most important organized ally of the Democratic Party—was a partial exception to this trend. Its political efforts continued to involve massive field programs and get-out-the-vote efforts.[12] But as membership, union density, and organizing capacity declined in the face of demographic shifts, economic changes, wavering leadership priorities, and from the 1980s onward increased anti-union activity from big business and from Republican administrations in Washington, D.C., weakened unions also turned from member-based efforts to professionally managed mass media and mail for much of their electoral work.[13] This shift was in line with a more general transformation of American civic life that accelerated in the 1960s and 1970s, summed up by Theda Skocpol as a shift from "membership to management" and characterized in particular by the abandonment of trans-local membership-based organizing in favor of centralized staff-controlled, direct-mail-based operations.[14] Thus, even though many of the newer interest groups that grew in importance from the 1960s onward—environmentalist organizations, women's rights groups, and the LGBT movement in particular—often supported Democratic candidates in significant ways, their help rarely took the form of boots on the ground.

At the end of the twentieth century, Democratic field efforts were basically dependent on a weakened labor movement and whatever other elements of support individual campaigns could assemble from an uneven population of more or less functional local party organizations, various networks of progressive activists, and other sympathetic civil society groups (most notably African American churches and some ethnic-based associations). The main vehicle for these efforts was something called "the coordinated campaign," pioneered by Democratic National Committee (DNC) chairman Ron Brown and his political director, Paul Tully, who from the 1980s onward worked to encourage some orchestration of the various candidate campaign, party organization, and sympathetic interest group activity in a given area. This typically took the form of ground wars waged by paid part-timers and people recruited en bloc from allied membership-based organizations on behalf of all Democrats running in a particular district. While these efforts—typically pursued through temporary organizational vehicles registered under some generic name, like "Victory '08" (to take a contemporary example from my New Jersey case study)—have occasionally been well funded and generously staffed, they could rarely rely on party regulars and volunteers alone. Things have come a long way since the middle of the nineteenth century, when historians estimate something like 7 percent of the adult male population were actively involved in party campaigning on a regular basis, and turnout reached almost 80 percent.[15] As mentioned in chapter 1, the American National Election Studies survey series shows that the percentage of people reporting they have worked for a political candidate or campaign has declined from 5–6 percent in the 1960s to 3–4 percent in the 1970s and 1980s and to a nadir of 2 percent in 1996.

As a consequence of the lack of interest and investment in the ground war and the changing character of the organizations that have historically waged it, the number of Americans contacted in person by parties and their allies remained at a low level throughout the second half of the twentieth century. As many observers started to worry about declining turnout during these years—the low point for presidential elections was less than 50 percent of the voting age population in 1996—political scientists argued that this was at least partially attributable to the absence of large-scale ground war efforts by parties and their allies.[16] But given the intellectual, institutional, and organizational changes of the past decades, this seemed unlikely to change. One oft-cited article asked in apparent despair in 2000 whether "the long-term decay of civic and political organizations has reached such a point that our society no longer has the infrastructure to conduct face-to-face canvassing on a large scale."[17] At this point, Pippa Norris's prediction that we would see a continual "decline in face-to-face communications," that personalized political communication would continue to wither away, seemed plausible, not only because political operatives did not seem to care much about it but also because they did not seem to have the resources to pursue it.[18]

But then, in the early years of the twenty-first century, things began to change—and the rest of this chapter outlines, election cycle by election cycle, how interests and investments in ground war efforts changed from 2000 to 2008 and beyond. My analysis draws on secondary sources culled from transcripts of various conferences for political operatives, articles from trade magazines like *Campaigns and Elections* (today called *Politics*), and material from the news media, combined with my own

interviews with several senior current and former staffers and consultants as well as existing scholarship in political science. On this basis I
trace how top political operatives rethought the value of the ground war
over these ten years. I also examine how the priorities of the national
Democratic Party organization changed as some tried to build a stronger infrastructure for ground war efforts, and I illustrate how different
developments often were at the local level as state, county, and municipal
party organizations in many cases continued to wither away, depriving
campaigns of one traditional source of manpower.

I look at the thinking of prominent operatives because much research
suggests they play a key role in both devising campaign strategies and
designing party and campaign organizations.[19] However, the actual developments in how the latter then allocate resources are influenced by many
other factors, too, so I look at both D.C.-based national-level organizations like the Democratic National Committee and the Democratic Congressional Campaign Committee, which scholars argue provide important
infrastructural support for campaigns, and at examples of local organizations on the basis of a series of studies carried out in Mahoning County,
Ohio, tracing the evolution of the local party organizations there over
more than a decade.[20] The area around Youngstown is not perfectly representative for developments across the country, or even in the two districts
where I did my own research, but the work done there by John C. Green
and his various collaborators represents the only example of sustained
scrutiny of local party organizations and their campaign activities that
cover the period I deal with here. And if the local organizations in a Democratic base area in a state that has been a battleground for every presidential election since 1992 have continued to deteriorate throughout the
decade, even as top operatives and party leaders increasingly underlined
the importance of field campaigns and organizing—as the evidence from
Ohio suggests they did—then odds are that local developments are not
determined by professional or national priorities elsewhere either. What
little has been written about state- and local-level party organizations in
Connecticut and New Jersey suggests that the parties also continued to
decline in importance in these historically well-organized states.[21] Therefore, I pay separate attention to each of the three strands of the story of
how the ground war entered the twenty-first century.

2000: LOSING THE BATTLE, WINNING THE GROUND WAR

Meeting in Cambridge, Massachusetts, just weeks after the close and contentious 2000 presidential election had been decided by a controversial
Supreme Court vote, the Democratic and Republican operatives who

gathered for the ritual "Campaign for President" postelection conference that the Institute for Politics at Harvard University has hosted since 1972 agreed on only one thing: the Democrats and their allies won the ground war even as they lost the battle for the White House. In the 288-page transcript of a conference that found time to discuss both the candidates' spouses and Vice President Al Gore's kissing technique, the hundreds of thousands of volunteers, part-timers, and staffers who worked on the ground receive little attention—only a brief exchange at the end of the conference where Republican top strategist Karl Rove points out that "one of the Gore campaign's greatest unsung successes [was] Election Day."[22] He went on to praise the work of Gore's campaign manager: "Early on, literally in 1999 when we knew that she was going to be associated with the campaign, we started studying what Donna [Brazile] would do about getting out the vote. So we began early, building a huge get-out-the-vote apparatus. And we did. We built the largest, biggest, baddest, best-funded get-out-the-vote operation on the Republican side. . . . Our mistake was that we assumed that this would be big enough to overcome [the Democratic] efforts. It wasn't."[23] This 2-page aside is the first substantial mention of the ground war in many iterations of this conference, a key forum for discussions of how campaigns are and should be won. The 1992 and 1996 versions, for example, had nothing on the subject, even as money, media, and individual events are discussed in great detail.

At the subsequent "Electing the President" conference at the University of Pennsylvania—another recurring high-profile event—Rove was again alone in touching upon the subject. He summed up his feelings about the situation on the ground as "labor envy."[24] And rightly so, for the apparatus that took Gore over the top in the popular vote (if not the Electoral College) in 2000 was not exactly capital-D Democratic, but assembled well beyond the party itself. One observer estimated that the Gore campaign fielded about ninety thousand volunteers on Election Day.[25] The AFL-CIO alone mobilized an additional one hundred thousand volunteers for GOTV work in 2000—about ten times as many as in 1996—and on top of that came the efforts of individual unions themselves.[26] In spite of serious and sustained disagreements with the Democratic leadership and the Clinton White House over trade policy—NAFTA in particular— the labor federation budgeted $46 million for political activities in 1999–2000, and individual unions spent tens of millions on top of that. As opposed to the 1996 campaign, with its high-visibility (and ultimately ineffective) $30 million television campaign, the AFL-CIO's effort in 2000 was focused on mobilizing members to engage in the finely targeted "labor-to-labor, labor-to-neighbor, neighbor-to-neighbor" program that the labor federation's national political director, Steve Rosenthal, had pushed for since the late 1990s.[27] A trial run of the more personalized approach during the 1998 midterm elections had produced encouraging results, in terms of both turnout and persuasion. According to survey data, the share of the electorate made up of union households increased from 14 percent in 1994 (the previous midterm election) to 23 percent in 1998, despite dwindling membership. Research commissioned by the AFL-CIO found that 81 percent of the workers who had had a conversation with a volunteer in the workplace or at the door supported union-endorsed candidates, as opposed to 61 percent of those who had not been contacted personally.[28]

After the election the importance of these findings seems to have been particularly clear to Republican operatives. George W. Bush led Al Gore by several percentage points in the final polls in 2000 but lost the popular vote by more than half a million votes. Rove, among others, attributed this to the Democrats' labor-fueled advantage on the ground, and he immediately sought ways to counter this factor in coming elections.[29] The Bush-Cheney campaign had actually mobilized more volunteers than Gore-Lieberman and their allies—450,000 by one estimate—so the problem was not simply one of getting boots on the ground.[30] Republican operatives needed to improve how they organized and targeted their efforts. The tools and techniques they adopted were similar to those the unions had already pioneered in their attempt to merge traditional organizing strategies with techniques developed in direct marketing: the mobilization of partisans to reach out personally to voters (at the door, on common ground like the shop floor or in church, or over the phone), targeted on the basis of detailed and increasingly individualized data, organized predominantly by full-time staffers, and supplemented with paid part-timers and productivity-enhancing technologies like predictive dialing when too few bodies were available.[31]

While the Gore campaign and its labor allies won the ground war in 2000, little was done to prepare for the next one; aside from within the labor movement, up-to-date means for organizing and targeting personalized political communication were not institutionalized in or around the Democratic Party. Whereas the Republicans moved to close the "ground gap" that Rove had lamented, the early years of the twenty-first century must stand as a transitional period rather than a transformative one for the Democrats. When Terry McAuliffe took over as chair of the DNC in 2001, he declared that his goals were to reinvigorate the withering activist base, invest in technological infrastructure, and raise money to close the financial gap between the two parties. Arguably, he achieved only the latter.

Even as the DNC struggled to update the computer systems in the national headquarters (more on this in chapter 5) and McAuliffe set fund-raising records, developments elsewhere threatened to unravel the basic blueprint for field operations that the Democrats and their labor allies had followed for decades. While for much of the twentieth century elections had been characterized by largely unregulated donations and often wanton spending by wealthy individuals, corporations, and labor unions, the Federal Election Campaign Act (FECA) that took effect after the 1972 elections introduced a semblance of control, regulation, and oversight. FECA ensured a degree of disclosure, some limits on contributions to candidates and parties, and regulated cooperation between candidates and third parties such as interest groups, corporations, and party organizations.[32] The act was quickly challenged as unconstitutional by a wide variety of interest groups intent on maximizing their political impact, and while the Supreme Court upheld all of FECA's contribution provisions in the landmark case *Buckley v. Valeo* in 1976, it invalidated limits on independent expenditures as long as these were not coordinated with candidate campaigns or did not expressly advocate the election or defeat of an individual candidate. Thus, coordination and what in legal parlance is called "candidate advocacy" continued to be regulated and had to be funded with "hard money" (contributions raised within the FEC framework). "Issue advocacy," on the other hand, was deemed political expression and thus an exercise of First Amendment rights and exempt from most of this regulation. In addition, party organizations were still free to fund activities that did not advocate for the election of any particular candidate but sought to register people and bring out the vote for the whole party ticket—activities such as field programs. This was the opening that the Democratic Party's seasonal and temporary "coordinated campaigns" were designed to exploit. To finance them, party organizations raised vast amounts of so-called soft money, unlimited contributions by corporations, unions, or wealthy individual donors unregulated by FECA. According to the Federal Election Commission (FEC), the DNC and the two "Hill Committees," the DCCC and its Senate counterpart, the DSCC (Democratic Senatorial Campaign Committee), channeled a grand total of almost $250 million in essentially unregulated soft dollars in 2000, much of it from labor unions and much of it spent on field.[33] This was the approach that had produced the "unsung success" on the ground in 2000 and brought Gore to within an inch of the presidency. The problem for the Democrats was that it was about to be challenged by the Bipartisan Campaign Reform Act, passed in Congress in 2002 and effective after that year's midterm elections—a reform I return to below.

While senior staffers and top consultants from both parties agreed that the Democrats might have lost the battle but won the ground war in 2000, and Republican political operatives operated in Washington, D.C., to try to win the next round, things often looked very different at the local level. Consider a few key words used to describe the coordinated Democratic effort on the ground in Mahoning County, Ohio: "in disarray," "weak," "poor."[34] Although as recently as in 1992 Bill Clinton could count on the remnants of a traditional political machine, the county party was in shambles by 2000; a reform slate had ousted the regulars but turned out to be unable to maintain the organization without the enthusiasm of fighting the good fight or the patronage that had animated the machine. The regional field director working for Gore's campaign in the area faced internal squabbles between different Democratic organizations and fractions and the fact that he had less money and only half the staff that had been available to Clinton's field staff in 1996. In fact, the 2000 coordinated campaign in Mahoning County seemed to have less of everything compared to the last presidential election: there were fewer volunteers, worse facilities (with no store-front office and too few phone lines), and poor data available for targeted efforts. The 1992 effort had relied on the machine's network of precinct captains to target voters and areas known to the local operatives and activists, and the 1996 campaign had access to data allowing them to target only precincts where Democrats had won 65 percent or more of the vote in past elections.[35] But the only data available in 2000 was outdated information from the 1998 gubernatorial election and a raw list of all registered voters in the county. This made effective targeting virtually impossible, defanging the whole operation. In the end, John C. Green and Rick Farmer concluded that players like the Ohio Legislative Black Caucus and various local unions had a stronger field program running in Mahoning County 2000 than the party organizations and the coordinated campaign that formally represented the Democratic Party on the ground in this base area of a battleground state.

2002: THE LAST HURRAH

Shortly before the 2000 elections, political science professors Alan S. Gerber and Donald P. Green from Yale University published an article in the *American Political Science Review* that was based on using randomized field experiments to test the relative effectiveness of door-to-door canvassing, phone calls, and direct mail when it comes to getting out the vote.[36] They showed that field campaigns are a demonstrably cost-effective way of increasing turnout. As made clear in chapter 1, their work, and the literature it has spawned, constitutes one premise for this book, since they demonstrate that ground wars *matter*. The reason to highlight it here is different, however—namely, that Gerber and Green's work quickly began to attract a kind of attention rarely afforded specialized social science research. Newspapers like the *New York Times*, the *Washington Post*, and *USA Today* all reported their findings (often by way of political professionals), and so did the trade magazine *Campaigns and Elections*.[37]

The Yale studies and the research that followed not only validated much of the work done by Rosenthal and the AFL-CIO, but were also in line with the ideas that animated a set of natural experiments orchestrated by Karl Rove and Ken Mehlman at the Republican National Committee (RNC).[38] The 2002 election saw the first trial runs of what the Republicans called "STOMP"—the Strategic Task Force to Organize and Mobilize People—and the so-called 72-hour program (the moniker comes from the experience in 2000 when Bush's seemingly solid lead in the polls evaporated over the last three days before the election). STOMP was an organizational vehicle that was supported by the Republican leadership and meant to push representatives in safe districts to channel resources (money, staff, volunteers) to competitive races across the country.[39] The 72-hour program was designed to build local volunteer bases willing to work with staffers from Republican campaigns and party organizations and combine them with data-based targeting to try to match individual canvassers with voters who had some affinity with them (shared church affiliation, living in the same neighborhood, etc.). The program was aimed at keeping people actively involved in conducting voter registration in the lead-up to elections and rolling them out in the final days to turn out the Republican vote.[40] The GOP continued to rely mainly on conservative activists for manpower, but from 2002 onward they were tied into a whole new assemblage. The first tests were in low-profile local races across the country in 2001 and in the trial-by-fire competitive Senate races in Georgia, Minnesota, and South Dakota in 2002.[41] The lessons learned went into honing the program for Bush's reelection campaign.

It is worth fastening on to three remarkable details about STOMP and the 72-hour program. The first is that it went largely unnoticed at the time, in line with the limited attention paid to field operations in general. Four years later, *Time* magazine could still refer to the 72-hour program as the Republicans' "secret weapon."[42] The second is how well it worked. Much in line with the general tenor of the Yale studies and Rosenthal's experience at the AFL-CIO, internal Republican research suggests that a large-scale investment in a well-organized and well-targeted ground war could swing several percentage points in close elections.[43] The third is that unlike the millions spent on advertisements, spin, and mail every election year, Rove's experiments left something behind. Thousands of volunteers had been mobilized to contact voters and might be willing to help again in the future, staffers had gained valuable experience in organizing and executing field operations, and data and technologies for targeting had been tried and tested. Most of these resources remained available to fight another day. The Republican leadership at the time aimed at building a lasting conservative majority partially based on political organizing and campaign innovation.[44] Having troops on the ground was part of the plan.

The Democratic and liberal-progressive efforts in 2002 did not have a similar level of ambition, but were instead what political scientists David B. Magleby and J. Quin Monson have called "the last hurrah."[45] Flush with the kind of soft money that campaign finance reform would soon ban (and channel elsewhere), various party organizations and their allies stuck to an unusually well financed version of business-as-usual during this cycle, essentially sticking to the traditional combination of a party-coordinated campaign and a determined effort by labor and any other membership-based allies present in each district.

Understanding the torpor on the Democratic side—relative to the innovations of the Republicans—requires a look at where the parties stood in 2002. The Republican Party had a clear leadership and an organizational center of gravity in the people working on President Bush's reelection effort, most notably Rove in the White House and Mehlman at the RNC.[46] The Democrats had no presumptive 2004 nominee or clear leader and did little to develop their ground war resources. Instead they relied again on the labor movement. The AFL-CIO alone spent $20 million in 2002, mainly on field, a good deal more than the $15 million spent by the party committees themselves.[47] The unions maintained a higher-than-average turnout among their members that cycle, too, and again delivered a majority of them to the Democratic ticket. Even as the number of organized workers continued to decline, Rosenthal's ongoing commitment to and investments in personalized political communication helped the labor movement increase the unionized part of the electorate. His strategy was thus a clear success for the AFL-CIO. But from the perspective of a broader progressive coalition in pursuit of an electoral majority, it also suffered from several limitations, based as it was on the organizational strength of a declining labor movement with at best a weak presence in many parts of the country and only tenuous connections to growing parts of the Democratic constituency (most notably Latinos, younger voters, college-educated women, and, especially outside the Northeast, African Americans). These were limitations that Rosenthal and others would try to confront, with varying degrees of success, over the coming years.

They did so under a radically different campaign finance regime. In March 2002 Senator John McCain and Senator Russ Feingold finally managed to push the previously mentioned Bipartisan Campaign Reform Act (BCRA)—also known as the McCain-Feingold Act—through Congress. The legislation took effect after the 2002 elections. The goals were twofold. On the one hand, the act was meant to ban "soft money" by restoring the contribution limits and regulations that had been part of the FECA but were later pushed back by the Supreme Court in *Buckley v. Valeo*. It did so through the new category of "federal election activity," a term used to describe practices beyond candidate and issue advocacy, such as voter registration, identification, and get-out-the-vote efforts— precisely the generic campaign activities that soft dollar–funded coordinated campaigns had so far engaged in on the Democratic side. From 2002 onward, not only candidate campaigns but also all kinds of party committees had to fund such activities with hard dollars raised and spent under FEC regulations. (The Levin Amendment makes some exceptions for state and local parties, dependent on state legislation.) On the other hand, it sought to bring restrictions and disclosure to corporate and labor spending. This was accomplished by basically banning the use of corporate or union money for any kind of electioneering, whether candidate advocacy, issue advocacy, or federal election activity, except through dedicated political action committees (PACs) using funds raised explicitly for political purposes. Thus, after 2002, parties could still make coordinated or independent expenditures and pursue field programs, but they had to raise hard dollars to do so. They could not serve simply as conduits for soft dollars from large donors. Many thought the Democrats, with their more pronounced reliance on soft money and labor-powered field operations, would be particularly hard hit by the reform.[48]

Of course, corporations, unions, and wealthy individuals wishing to get involved could still donate within the regulations outlined by the BCRA and enforced by the FEC or could engage in electioneering by raising funds through political action committees to do so, but they could no longer simply funnel money into joined efforts coordinated by party organizations. Instead, they began to operate via nonprofit groups often referred to by their Internal Revenue Code section numbers as 501(c)s and 527s.[49] The BCRA drove soft money out of most candidate and party efforts and limited the ability of unions, corporations, and wealthy individuals to get directly engaged in party politics, but it also set the scene for 527 groups as the new vehicle of choice for soft money trying to find a way to influence elections. Such groups would emerge as some of the most important players on the ground in 2004.

The 2002 elections in Ohio unfolded largely untouched by these changes in how top operatives viewed the ground war and how different national party organizations tried to engage in it. The Republican ticket—topped by incumbent governor Bob Taft—won every statewide election without the Democratic Party putting up much of a fight. In Mahoning County, the later governor Ted Strickland cruised to reelection in the 6th Congressional District, and state senator Tim Ryan won the 17th Congressional District, from which Representative James Trafi-cant had been expelled in June after being convicted of taking bribes, filing false tax returns, racketeering, and several other counts in an ugly reminder of the less savory side of machine politics.

2004: OUTSOURCING THE GROUND WAR

Whereas the 2000 postelection conferences in Cambridge and Philadelphia barely touched on the ground war, it was the talk of both towns in 2004—and for good reason. While political polarization and population growth account for parts of the increased turnout in that year's presidential election, one team of political scientists estimated that increased ground war efforts on both sides mobilized an additional *13 million voters* on Election Day, expanding the electorate by almost 10 percent.[50] By now, senior staffers and consultants in both parties and many interest groups had embraced the ground war (well before anyone seriously believed Barack Obama would be the 2008 nominee), and national organizations had begun to allocate resources accordingly. Strong feelings about the upcoming election no doubt motivated additional activists. Mary Beth Cahill, who managed John Kerry's campaign for the presidency, did not mince words when she spoke at the University of Pennsylvania's "Electing the President" conference: "The amount that both campaigns and both national committees spent on field and volunteers is an enormous sea change in political tactics and in terms of emphasis."[51] In 2004 the presidential campaign assemblages spent more money on personalized political communication than ever before; they also fielded more staffers, volunteers, and part-timers than had been seen for decades. Matthew Dowd, a top strategist for the Bush-Cheney reelection effort, reported at the same conference that the Republican presidential campaign alone had spent *five times more* on field in 2004 than in 2000. (In contrast to expenditures on media and mail, precise figures for field costs are hard to calculate, since most are salary and FEC filings do not require job descriptions.) The GOP thus continued to build on the investments made in the previous years and further developed their ground war capacities. The Democratic effort was extraordinary as well but again was pursued in large part outside the party. The cornerstone was the newly established 527 group America Coming Together (ACT)—headed by Steve Rosenthal—funded by the kinds of interest groups and wealthy individual donors who previously would have contributed soft dollars to the party's coordinated campaign efforts. Instead, Rosenthal's new entity spent about $80 million on mobilizing more than 4,000 full-time staffers, 45,000 paid part-time canvassers, and about 70,000 volunteers in seventeen battleground states.[52] By comparison, the DNC spent about $20 million to put 2,000 people on the ground for the final months of the campaign, most of them via a company called (apparently without irony) Grassroots Campaigns, Inc. MoveOn, by far the largest of the new online progressive groups, boasted a $5 million neighbor-to-neighbor program staffed by 500 organizers, largely run by the same company. The *Almanac of American Politics* estimates that about 250,000 people volunteered for Democratic candidates on Election Day and no less than 1.4 million on the Republican side (mobilized perhaps by a more charismatic presidential candidate, the polarizing tactics of the GOP and its allies, the substantial investments Republicans had made in organizing over the previous years, and the time and effort put into engaging with new activists).[53]

Broadly speaking, the elements enrolled in the Republican and Democratic ground war assemblages were the same—voters were contacted at the door or over the phone by paid part-timers or volunteers, mobilized and organized through diverse organizations by campaign staffers, and targeted on the basis of detailed and often individual-level quantitative data. But the elements were arranged in very different ways. The Republican efforts had been planned years in advance (with the party's nominee a given and his people in the White House and the RNC coordinating the efforts). The GOP ground war machinery mobilized many of the staffers and activists who had been involved in 2000 and 2002, was organized by party operatives who by now had considerable field experience, and drew on and further refined internally hosted and individualized data that the RNC had initially acquired to pursue direct mail campaigns and fund-raising but had now put to new uses as well. While many Democratic operatives I interviewed doubted whether the Republican field effort actually came close to being the almost too perfect machinery that *New York Times Magazine* writer Matt Bai (and others) described as the "multi-level marketing" of the president, no one denied that the Republicans did very well on the ground.[54] Whereas in 2000 Bush had underperformed relative to his polls a few days out, in 2004 the final count was much closer to what had been predicted. With STOMP and the 72-hour program, Rove seemed to have reached his goal of closing the "ground gap" he had lamented in 2000. In 2004 he had few reasons to envy the Democrats and their allies anything.

While the Republicans built on the combination of internally institutionalized resources and the external interests and activists they still attracted, the Democrats had, in *Washington Post* reporter Thomas Edsall's words, essentially "outsourced" their 2004 ground war to ACT.[55] To abide by the regulations instituted by the McCain-Feingold Act, this group had to operate apart from official Democratic Party organizations and from the Kerry campaign itself in particular. Its ability to raise and spend soft money was predicated upon remaining at least nominally within the domain of issue advocacy and mobilization efforts, not coordinated expenditures or candidate advocacy. The Kerry campaign and the various Democratic Party organizations obviously fell into the latter category. (ACT eventually accepted that it had ventured into this terrain too; in 2007 it was at the receiving end of the third-largest civil penalty in the history of the Federal Election Commission.[56])

So from the 1980s until the early years of the 2000s, Democratic coordinated campaigns had served to channel soft money from various large donors through different parts of the party apparatus and into field operations, typically for the whole ticket in a given area. In 2004 many of these dollars flowed through ACT and similar entities. The purpose and partial success was clear: Rosenthal and the AFL-CIO had demonstrated the power of personalized political communication in the labor programs he had headed for three cycles in a row. They had also encountered their limitations. Labor could effectively reach the roughly 25 percent of the population who were parts of households with one or more union members, and in 2004 the AFL-CIO spent another $45 million and mobilized more than two hundred thousand volunteers to do so. But by pooling data and resources through ACT and other umbrella organizations like America Votes, a coalition of liberal and progressive interest groups could reach well beyond that to other parts of the Democratic base—and they did, and turnout increased substantially. That was the success. The downside was that unlike the individual interest groups involved (and the party itself), ACT had no core constituency, fundamental interest, or underlying purpose to ensure its continued existence after the election. It never established itself as the permanent "shadow party" that some people initially saw it as.[57] Rosenthal and others had hoped that the organization would serve to reinvigorate the activist base and the organizational and technical infrastructure that he and others argued the Democratic Party had allowed to wither even as the Republican Party invested in its own.[58] In the end, little came of this. Like a medieval war machine, ACT was dismantled after the battle, its elements repurposed or left behind. Liberal billionaires George Soros and Peter Lewis, who had contributed about a quarter of the total budget, pulled out. The various unions, most notably the Service Employees International Union (SEIU), which had made similarly massive contributions, turned to other tasks as they and others left the AFL-CIO to build the new Change to Win federation. Less than a year after the election, the largest 527 group of the 2004 cycle was effectively no more.[59] Organizations like MoveOn maintained a permanent presence online but had yet to engage in local organizing, a level at which the network of local parties and various union locals—in many places largely atrophied—remained the main organized source of potential volunteers for Democratic campaigns.

The development on the ground in Mahoning County during this cycle again illustrates the ongoing mismatch between the increased high-level interest and national investments in personalized political communication and the continued coordination problems and slow deterioration of local organizations on the ground. In Ohio, as in battleground states across the country, ACT was the most important element in the Democratic ground war assemblage. A coordinator was hired for Mahoning and neighboring Trumbull County in late 2003 and basically started building a field operation from scratch. Local labor unions not only contributed through the money channeled to ACT and through volunteers channeled to the coordinated campaign. They also engaged in their own well-funded and well-staffed "Take Back Ohio" program, aimed at contacting every union member in the state in person. But the local Democratic Party in Mahoning, John C. Green and Daniel Coffey dryly note, "was not the asset to the 2004 presidential campaign that it had been in previous elections . . . it lacked volunteers and finances."[60] Unlike in 2000, it is important to observe that with ACT involved, money was not the central problem this cycle, but mobilizing people and organizing and targeting personalized voter contacts still were. The combined effort was deemed "uncoordinated" by Green and Coffey, who also quote staffers complaining about the lack of volunteers, the uneven quality of the paid canvassers, and poor data for targeting. One professional called the information available "worthless."

2006: FIFTY STATES OR NOT?

Many outside observers and inside operators concluded that the Democrats and their allies lost the ground war in 2004, blaming everything from poor organizing and coordination, to the absence of serious attempts to mobilize volunteer activists, to the dearth of quality data and up-to-date database technology for targeting.[61] In the aftermath of the election, the Republican machine seemed formidable—a lasting "Red America" built on razor-thin electoral majorities, donor largesse, and effectively institutionalized and highly disciplined political organizing.[62] For Democrats, if there was a silver lining on these dark and dismal clouds, it took the form of Howard Dean's extraordinary primary campaign and the persistently growing presence of Internet-assisted "netroots" activist groups like MoveOn.[63] Both demonstrated that Democrats and progressives, too, could leverage new technologies to raise money and connect with potential activists.

Most of the political operatives I have spoken with deemed the overall Dean effort in the 2004 presidential primary a fiasco, rhetorically asking how he, in the words of one person I interviewed, could "piss away" $50 million, the AFL-CIO endorsement, and considerable momentum going into Iowa and end up with only fifteen Vermont delegates to show for it. If one image of the Dean campaign that stuck with many outside observers was its strong volunteer support, one that made a great impression on campaign staffers and consultants was the inability of throngs of poorly organized out-of-state activists in orange hats to make much of a difference in the Iowa caucus. Despite this, some Dean alumni—most prominently his former campaign manager, Joe Trippi—made names for themselves and exported the campaign's fund-raising and mobilizing practices to other efforts.[64] Other Dean staffers would soon go on to populate the most important of the national party organizations—the DNC itself.

Dean's primary campaign—and his claim, echoing that of the late senator Paul Wellstone, to represent "the Democratic wing of the Democratic Party"—won him many friends among party activists but few among party leaders. When he announced his candidacy for the chairmanship of the national party, dominant figures among the congressional Democrats like Senate minority leader Harry Reid and House minority leader Nancy Pelosi openly sought to find an alternative to him but found too many, and the opposition to Dean never coalesced around one candidate. On February 1 the Association of State Democratic Chairs voted overwhelmingly for Dean (against the recommendation of their executive board). The day after, the AFL-CIO announced that it would remain neutral in the contest, freeing its affiliates to make their own endorsements—and many of them backed Dean, as did other central players, like the Service Employees International Union and the American Federation of Teachers. This basically sealed the deal, and on February 12, 2005, a new party chair was elected against the express will of leading elected officials and key parts of the party establishment and on the basis of state party, labor, and rank-and-file party activist backing—in other words, with the support of the central players in Democratic ground wars.

Dean ran for chair on his old campaign slogan, "You have the power." Like basically every other candidate for the job, he argued that the Democratic Party needed to pursue what he called a "50-state strategy" to rebuild its local organizations, technical infrastructure, and activist base.[65] This was partially red meat for the state party representatives, who cast roughly a quarter of the votes for national chair, but it was also a clear swipe at how McAuliffe and his predecessors had let the all-consuming focus on the next election's likely swing states become the modus operandi of the DNC itself—a supposedly national operation. When Dean took office in February 2005, he outlined his job in the usual terms, promising to take care of fund-raising and representative functions but also pledging to try to expand the party's organizational capacities, mobilize its base, and improve the targeting infrastructure to help Democrats "win elections at every level in every region of the country."[66] The main difference between Dean and his predecessors turned out to be that he actually did pretty much all of what he said he would do, rather than simply raise money (if anything, fund-raising was the one thing he turned out not to be so good at, despite his prodigious success with Internet-assisted online fund-raising during the 2004 primary). Taking on staff many of the people who had been part of his primary campaign, Dean worked to give the DNC (and through it state and local parties) what they needed to challenge the Republicans and reclaim the edge on the ground they had lost over the last cycles. Under his chairmanship, the party sought to develop new mobilization capacities (such as the new online platform "Party Builder," based on the experiences and tools of his primary campaign), organizational resources (putting two field organizers on the ground in every state at the national party's expense), and building a new database to replace the dysfunctional "Demzilla" system built during McAuliffe's tenure.

In retrospect, the 50-state strategy has been widely considered a success.[67] It is easy to forget how controversial it was at the time. Prominent former Clinton advisers like James Carville and Paul Begala challenged Dean's plans, the latter calling the program "hiring a bunch of staff people to wander around Utah and Mississippi and pick their nose."[68] Even at the modest thirty thousand dollars or so annually that young staffers come at, carrying out Dean's idea across the country eventually added up, and the closer the party came to the 2006 midterm elections, the higher the pressure was for him to do what DNC chairs have historically done: focus on fund-raising and channel resources to the congressional campaign committees. The DSCC and the DCCC, as usual, wanted to spend the dollars raised on television and mail in their attempts to capture a few swing districts. As an unpopular war in Iraq turned the national electoral climate in favor of the Democrats, Senator Charles Schumer and Representative Rahm Emanuel, chairs of the two Hill committees, increasingly tried to push Dean to put the 50-state program on hold and cough up the money so that they could make the most of the opportunity at hand. But Dean stood his ground. Relations between him and Emanuel famously deteriorated to the point where their aides feared the two temperamental men would come to blows. Their disagreement was basically about the balance between long-term party building and short-term campaign goals. Both of them saw the organizations they headed as meant to help Democratic candidates for public office. But they disagreed on what priorities should follow from that. Schumer and Emanuel—tasked with winning the midterm elections—wanted money here and now. Dean, accountable to all the state parties, insisted on investing in the broader and more long-term infrastructure. Ultimately the 50-state strategy survived the onslaught, and since the midterms ended in a landslide victory for the Democrats, we will never know how it would have been evaluated had it turned out to come at the expense of potentially decisive seats in Congress.

The dramatic struggles between various parts of the national Democratic Party meant little in Ohio. The House races in Mahoning County offered no excitement in 2006, with Representative Tim Ryan cruising to reelection in the 17th district, and state senator Charlie Wilson easily winning the 6th House district, which Ted Strickland had vacated to run for governor. But the gubernatorial election, Sherrod Brown's attempt to capture Mike DeWitt's Senate seat, and a host of other statewide races meant that state and local Democrats had plenty of reasons to wage ground war. In 2005 Chris Redfern had won the chairmanship of the Ohio Democratic Party, running on his imaginatively named "88-county strategy" aimed at expanding the party's infrastructure and organizational presence across the state.[69] Mahoning County had voted in its usual solid fashion for Democrats for president and for the House back in 2000, but in 2004 Republican DeWitt had captured 47 percent of the vote in the county, running 12 percentage points ahead of George W. Bush on top of the ticket.[70] The Democrats needed to do better in 2006 to win the statewide offices, and Redfern invested heavily in this effort, eventually increasing the number of full-time staffers at the state party from five to more than forty with the aim of pushing the Republicans in all areas. And yet a local veteran operative who had served as Northeast regional director of ACT two years before told reporters that the party and the local unions around Youngstown were not engaged in any on-the-ground organizing that year.[71]

2008: THE RUN-UP

With widespread popular demand for change in Washington, two wars seemingly going nowhere, the economy teetering on the brink of disaster, and no incumbent president or vice president running for the first time in fifty-six years, 2008 was bound to be a special election, and much has been written about it already. What I touch on here are only those factors that pertain directly to the question of how the ground war developed. All staffers and most volunteers in the two campaigns I studied followed the presidential primaries and the general election closely. Several were at one point or another directly involved in it, and many tried to draw their own lessons from what they saw and heard. But few highlighted the same source of inspiration as the top Democratic operatives speaking at the Harvard University and University of Pennsylvania conferences after the election. (In an implicit nod to the ground war's rise to prominence, Obama for America's field director, Jon Carson, was the first field staffer to figure as a speaker at one of the two events.)

Obama's campaign manager, David Plouffe, was frank when he spoke in Philadelphia: "We studied the Bush [2004] campaign pretty carefully. They did a great job."[72] And indeed, while the allies around it came from the traditional progressive coalition, the well-funded, disciplined, generously staffed, and volunteer-rich Obama for America campaign organization probably did have more in common with the Republican effort in 2004 than with the much more sprawling and polycentric assemblage that had surrounded Kerry's candidacy that year (not to mention the rambling Dean campaign). With widespread political disenchantment and the fear that many disgruntled voters would simply stay at home, there was never any doubt that field would be a major priority for the fall campaign or that the Democrats would handle it differently this time around. The ACT model of an externally funded and run field program and the idea of wholesale outsourcing canvassing to companies like Grassroots Campaigns, Inc., was widely seen as discredited by the 2004 experience.[73] Dean's work at the DNC and investments made at the state level by many other party organizations since then had helped strengthen the organizing and targeting infrastructure of the party. The general idea moving forward was to build a post-BCRA kind of coordinated campaign to integrate various campaign and party efforts and to establish an effective division of labor with allied interest groups. But the concrete planning would have to await the outcome of the Democratic presidential primary.

A closer look at the Hillary Clinton and Barack Obama campaigns that squared off in 2007–2008 suggests that they ran their field operations in somewhat different ways, and because the drawn-out primary meant that both built substantial campaign organizations across the country, it was clear that the winning campaign would eventually shape the general election effort in important ways. Starting out as the presumptive nominee, Clinton had won the "talent primary" early on and attracted many of the most prominent Democratic operatives in the country. Her national field director, Guy Cecil, could draw on experienced ground warriors like Karen Hicks and Michael Whouley as senior advisers. The plan plotted out by chief strategist Mark Penn, however, put the emphasis in the primary on the strength of the Clinton brand, paid and earned media, and help from the party establishment and allied interest groups. On the assumption that little could be done to expand the primary electorate beyond the hard core of regulars who always participated, field remained tangential, and from Iowa onward the Clinton campaign consistently had fewer staffers and offices on the ground than the Obama campaign.[74]

On the Obama side, campaign manager David Plouffe and chief strategist David Axelrod prioritized field from the start, assuming that they would have to expand the electorate to win the primary and that they could not rely on existing party organizations in doing so.[75] Throughout the spring of 2008 they spent money early and often on putting staffers on the ground in every state where they thought they could win convention delegates. Building a large operation that grew to employ more than five thousand field organizers by the time of the general election, they sought to combine the best elements of the Dean campaign's Internet-assisted volunteer mobilization with time-honed organizing practices adopted from community, labor, and faith-based organizing and a strong focus on message control. In his reflections on the campaign, Plouffe did highlight the value of the MyBarackObama website in helping the campaign mobilize people, but he also underlined that those who got involved were put to decidedly off-line use: "the truth is [that] most of the people who signed up online ended up phone banking and canvassing."[76] As was the case throughout the first decade of the twenty-first century, new technologies did not as much replace personalized political communication as they reinvigorated this (at first glance) apparently archaic campaign activity.

Interviews with former staffers and volunteers suggest that the campaign did not always and in all states live up to the idealistic slogan that the Iowa state director, Paul Tewes, had coined: "Respect. Empower. Include." Sometimes Obama offices would be run by old hands from previous Democratic campaigns and would work in the old ways. One insider called the New Hampshire primary campaign a "business-as-usual disaster." But the Obama staffers often tried to offer a different approach designed to change the character of campaign activism. Starting in March 2007 the campaign organized a series of events called "Camp Obama," eventually training more than ten thousand people in basic organizing and campaign techniques. In time, everyone who volunteered to help would be asked to do the usual things—knock on doors, make phone calls, enter data. But often their first task after training would be to recruit more people to join them, a task usually reserved for staffers. Estimates of how many people volunteered for Obama varies. One figure given by the campaign itself is a total of about 3 million people over the course of the primary and the general election.[77] Although extraordinary by the standards of recent elections (twice the figure given for Bush in 2004 and a massive six times the figure for the Democrats that year), and frequent media claims to the contrary, this was not the largest political mobilization in American history. As recently as 1964 the Barry Goldwater campaign mobilized a similar number of volunteers, and the U.S. population has grown by about 50 percent since then. Campaign work is not as common today as it was in the 1960s.[78]

But the "machinery of hope" that was built around Obama's extraordinary charismatic appeal to both volunteers and donors was substantially larger than and different from the campaign built around Kerry, the DNC, and ACT four years before.[79] Going into the general election, its various legal incarnations, "Obama for America," the "Campaign for Change," and the state-level equivalents, channeled much of what in the past would have flown through a party-led coordinated campaign or outside efforts through a campaign-dominated assemblage active primarily in twenty potential swing states and almost exclusively oriented toward winning the presidential election. Though many journalists portrayed the Obama campaign as having "reversed" traditional top-down forms of campaign organizing, it is more precise to say that it managed to combine a clear hierarchy with a broad-based network of volunteers. (This is how field director Jon Carson described it.[80]) The campaign went to great lengths to control not only volunteers' hard work but also allies' various efforts. In the summer of 2008, when some civil liberties groups and a large number of activists took issue with Obama's Senate vote on an amendment of the Foreign Intelligence Surveillance Act (FISA) and voiced their discontent on the MyBarackObama website, new media director Joe Rospars made clear that the campaign was running Obama, and not "the consensus of the people on the email list," for president.[81]

Internally the campaign organization was focused on message control, clear lines of command, and the use of quantitative metrics to continually ensure that everyone involved met their targets and kept up with the game plan.[82] In its relations to volunteers, donors, and outside allies, the campaign strongly emphasized that it wanted everything possible to flow through its own channels rather than through other entities, and the top operatives did their utmost to fold the DNC infrastructure and organizing capacity built under Dean's tenure into the main campaign organization itself. This was no mean feat. As Axelrod put it, "The greatest challenge has been [that] there is this enormous outpouring of good will and interest in this campaign and people wanting to volunteer, wanting to do things, and there is an enormous organizational challenge in trying to figure out how to marshal all that goodwill. And you don't want people to go away and say, gee, they weren't interested in my help, you want to get those people engaged."[83] And they were engaged, mostly through the campaign organization itself, but also by the wider assemblage of allies in the labor movement and beyond: the AFL-CIO reported fielding a quarter of a million volunteers in the final four days of the election, the Change to Win unions led by the SEIU mobilized tens of thousands more, as did netroots groups like MoveOn and other interest groups, activist networks, and civic associations.

The situation in Ohio in 2008 illustrated both the strengths of the Obama campaign's approach and the limitations it might have for less generously endowed campaigns. The local chapter of the Campaign for Change integrated all Obama-related ground war efforts from the national- and state-level party organizations and worked alongside well-funded interest group efforts by labor and others to run a comprehensive and centrally controlled field effort. But the local party organizations and candidates were left in the "periphery" of the assemblage, writes Melaine Blumberg and her co-authors.[84] According to local sources, the county party and its chair were on bad terms with the state party and never integrated into the Obama effort. Data was not shared between the larger national and state campaign assemblages and the local organizations, targeting and training remained separate, and down-ticket races were mostly ignored in the scripts and literature used by the Campaign for Change. It was reported that "numerous party faithful who had been instrumental in many [previous] presidential elections felt ignored."[85] Obama did eventually carry Mahoning County by a large margin but actually fell short of Kerry's results from 2004. His ground war illustrates here as more widely that with enough money, volunteers, and interest group support, it may not matter much that local party organizations are left by the wayside. But most candidates, of course, will never command the resources Obama had in 2008 and will struggle to build comparable campaign organizations.

AFTER 2008: THE IMPERMANENT CAMPAIGN

Most campaigns have to marshal many different elements in pursuit of victory, since no one institution or organization has what it takes to win. Though different party organizations try to service candidates the best they can, there is no "permanent campaign" on the ground, only partially institutionalized forms of organizing expertise, targeting technologies, and resources that can be combined in a wider assemblage of campaign organizations, allies, volunteers, and part-timers cobbled together for each individual election. America Coming Together in 2004 represents the most determined attempt to date to build a comprehensive field operation outside the formal candidate campaign and party organizations, and it fell short of realizing its founders' and funders' goals. Barack Obama's 2008 campaign organization is the most ambitious recent attempt to build a comprehensive field operation around a single candidate. And even this extremely well funded and generously staffed campaign, buoyed by an extraordinary outpouring of volunteer support, relied heavily on interest group allies from labor and elsewhere.

The less successful efforts of Obama's 2008 rival, John McCain, illustrate not only how differently field operates for candidates with fewer resources at their disposal but also how weakly institutionalized ground war resources remain. In the aftermath of the 2004 election, some observers marveled at the strength of the machinery Karl Rove had assembled and predicted a future "one party country."[86] But though this apparatus was certainly powerful, it also turned out to be fragile. Four years later, McCain seemed to be largely on his own, having to fight anew for wholehearted support from many of the interest groups and activist networks that had supported Bush, and struggling to bring up to speed the backend apparatus maintained by the RNC.[87] Volunteers are not at the beck and call of political operatives, alliances must be constantly affirmed, and party organizations have to be continually maintained.

This has been clear in the years after 2008 as well. After his inauguration Obama announced that the remnants of his campaign organization—including its 13-million-strong email list—would continue as a "special project" within the DNC (indirectly replacing the 50-state strategy, which was being quietly wound down).[88] Renamed Organizing for America (OFA), the new entity was most immediately tasked with issue advocacy on behalf of Obama's legislative agenda (some even suggested it would take up community organizing), but it was also created with at least one eye firmly on the 2010 congressional midterms and especially the 2012 presidential election. OFA was meant to circumvent some of the restrictions that the transition from the campaign trail to the Oval Office imposed on Obama and to keep the core of his 2008 supporters engaged, all without alienating too many parts of an existing party structure wary of parallel structures.[89] Manned by veterans from the 2008 campaign organization, OFA got tens of thousands of people to contact their representatives during the 2009 budget battle and the protracted 2009–2010 confrontation over health care reform.[90] It also tried, with less success, to mobilize volunteers on behalf of the Democratic candidates in the 2009 special election for the Senate in Massachusetts and for governor in New Jersey and Virginia. These candidates ultimately had to rely largely on their own assembled supporters for field operations.

OFA's first major electoral test came with the 2010 congressional midterms. Over the summer it was involved in attempts to clear the field for several Democratic incumbents who were in danger of drawing strong primary challenges, including, very controversially, the recently converted longtime Republican Arlen Specter in Pennsylvania (this drew considerable criticism from progressives). With the political climate against incumbents in general and the Democratic Party more particularly, and with the Supreme Court's 2010 *Citizens United v. the Federal Election Committee* decision, which overturned key campaign finance provisions and opened the floodgates for vast increases in independent expenditures (mostly coming from pro-Republican business interests), hard-pressed party leaders and operatives hoped that OFA and the fabled Obama field operation could help stem the losses in the general election. Through this vehicle the DNC made a substantial effort, funding $20 million worth of advertisements and direct mail and $30 million worth of GOTV assistance, fielding three hundred organizers on the ground in key races around the country, and generating 10 million personalized voter contacts.[91] Executive director Jennifer O'Malley called it "the largest ground game the DNC has ever participated in" in a midterm election.[92] The DNC provided significant support in many cases, but the scale and scope of this support should be kept in perspective—Democratic candidates for Congress raised and spent $878 million themselves and built their own campaign assemblages, and on the ground they often relied heavily on help from the usual suspects in the labor movement.[93] The AFL-CIO reported that its Working Families Vote program alone, with its emphasis on personalized political communication, mobilized two hundred thousand volunteers, made 48 million phone calls, and knocked on 8.5 million doors.[94]

In a sense, 2010's Organizing for America was akin to the Republicans' 72-hour program in 2006—talked up in press briefings as a potential game changer in the face of inauspicious polls, undoubtedly important (though not as impressive as some had forecast, partially because of an ebb in activist support), but ultimately not enough to turn the tide. It did offer congressional Democrats some much-needed help (whether it was enough to outweigh the damage done to incumbents by the president's oft-repeated refrain of "Congress is broken" is another issue), and it allowed staffers loyal to Obama to reach out again to his 2008 supporters and to road-test organizing techniques and technological innovations with an eye toward 2012 (much as Rove and his people had done between 2000 and 2004). But this was not a "permanent field campaign," despite claims to the contrary.[95] When the president formally announced his reelection bid on April 4, 2011, OFA was folded into the Obama for America 2012 organization. It was time to start reassembling the troops around the candidate. It was time to build a new campaign assemblage.

* * *

The early years of the twenty-first century witnessed a renewed interest in personalized political communication among top political operatives. Ground war practices like door-to-door canvassing and phone banking that as recently as the late 1990s had been consigned to the historical dustbin as quaint and irrelevant relics of a bygone era are today seen as essential tools in any competitive race and are increasingly combined with new technologies used for mobilizing volunteers, organizing part-timers, and targeting voters. The lack of concern for field displayed by the experienced operative quoted in episode 2.1 at the outset of this chapter has been replaced by the emphasis illustrated by episode 2.2. The resurgence of field is fueled by the hundreds of millions of dollars spent on ground wars over the last ten years to generate increasingly impressive numbers of contacts, despite an only moderate increase in the overall number of campaign volunteers. From the national level of central party committees and presidential campaigns, and much of the way down the ladder of party organizations and candidate campaigns, personalized political communication is no longer an afterthought, but instead an important priority.

Ongoing organizational disputes over how to allocate finite resources— most vividly illustrated by the clash between Dean at the DNC and Emanuel at the DCCC in 2006—underline that field is far from the only concern. Both campaigns and party organizations continue to spend most of their money on the televised "air war" and on direct mail. Ongoing differences about how funds should be distributed by party organizations represent reasonable disagreements over what the most effective mix of advertisements, mail, and field is in a particular area. They also represent different takes on the relative importance of the short-term goal of winning *this* election, in *this* district, *this* year versus the long-term goal of strengthening a party's infrastructure and organizational presence on the ground. Being a party "in service" is no easy task, especially when there are so many different party organizations involved in serving (with accompanying turf wars), so many candidates to serve (with conflicting interests), and so many different ways to serve (with different means, at different times). Divergent priorities by individual campaigns reflect senior staffers' and consultants' view of how to make the most of the precise resources at their disposal in the particular situation they find themselves in.

The last ten years have seen determined efforts to expand and institutionalize the parties' resources for waging ground wars, with much progress made in terms of technical expertise and data in particular. But the manpower involved, the bodies on the ground, is still mobilized for each occasion. Both volunteers and allies remain clearly beyond campaign control. While attempts have been made to strengthen party organizations, especially at the national level, local organizations and networks of activist support are still weak in most places. And as one staffer, working for a member-based allied interest group, puts it, "They have to come to us for help. We like it like that. The party is already powerful enough as it is."

Attempts are being made to revive organizing in many areas to get people reengaged in civic life in a more ongoing fashion, ranging from labor unions gearing up for large organizing drives, over new netroots groups like MoveOn establishing local "councils" to supplement their online efforts, and to party initiatives like Organizing for America. But we have yet to see systematic evidence of a large-scale resurgence of sustained organized political activism at the local level. While some individual campaigns have attracted unusual numbers of volunteers in recent cycles and the number of contacts made have increased dramatically, survey data from the American National Election Studies suggests that the overall number of people who report having worked for parties or candidates has increased only slightly from their historic lows in the 1990s and reached only a modest 4 percent in 2008.

Periodically, initiatives such as the machinery that Rove and Mehlman built around President Bush and Dean's 50-state strategy generate headlines, but it is important to put them in perspective. The two staffers that the DNC program put on the ground in each *state* to help build the volunteer base is no more than the number of people working full time to run local party organizations like the Democratic Town Committee in Stamford, Connecticut, or the Somerset County Democratic Party in New Jersey. Some of these local organizations survive with aging members—a few even thrive because of the efforts of talented and dedicated organizers and members—but most seem to continue the decline they have been in for decades. And despite top operatives' recently regained interest in the ground war, campaign organizations and national party organizations have not yet been unable to replace these with any equally effective alternatives. There is no permanent campaign ready to fight the ground war today, nor any interest groups or other allied entities capable of doing it all on a candidate's behalf. Instead, campaign assemblages are built, mobilizing and organizing different elements to target and contact voters at home, at the door or over the phone.

CHAPTER 3

Contacting Voters at Home

Episode 3.1

Since four o'clock on this warm and sunny August afternoon, I have been canvassing with Allen in affluent, suburban Trumbull, Connecticut. He is a college senior doing an internship with Himes for Congress over the summer. We are walking a list with about a hundred targeted voters distributed across roughly eighty households. It will take us something like four hours to knock on every door in a terrain like this. We expect to speak to maybe thirty people. The canvassing director will come back to pick us up around eight.

Three more canvassing teams are working in pairs to "knock through" other parts of the area. We are staying out of some parts of Trumbull to avoid getting the candidate entangled in a primary fight between two well-connected local Democrats who both want a shot at the state Senate.

Allen walks up to a large, well-kept house, looking for signs of life. He rings the bell and waits for about twenty seconds. He pounds on the solid wood door and shouts, "Hello?" Ten seconds later, he sticks a Himes for Congress flyer under a potted plant next to the doorstep and walks back down toward me. As he reaches the road, where I'm waiting, he says, "Not home," and wipes the sweat off of his increasingly sunburned face.

Episode 3.2

I am phone banking with Paula and the other volunteers in Fanwood, New Jersey. Most of us have been on the phones for more than an hour, and the pace is increasingly sluggish. It is around five in the afternoon. Today we are calling women over sixty-five who are registered as Independents. The first hour, I made forty calls and had five contacts. I am on my second hour, and I have lost some pace. I have made fewer than thirty calls and have had only one contact. I feel no particular urge to punch in the number for the voter next on my list.

But I do it. And I sit with the phone in my hand listening to the dial tone while I count toward twenty in my head. After about fifteen seconds, I hear a robotic voice: "The person you have called is not available to take your call at this moment. Your call has been forwarded to an automatic voice-mail service. At the tone, please record your message. When you have finished recording, you may hang up or press one for more options."

I look down on the script in front of me, wait for the tone, then start reading. "Hi, my name is Rasmus. I'm a volunteer with Victory '08. I just wanted to call you to tell you about Linda Stender and the Democratic ticket. Linda Stender believes that the Bush administration has led our country in the wrong direction, and she will fight to get us back on the right track. Linda Stender will work to jump-start our economy and create good, new jobs; stop the war in Iraq and bring our troops home safely and soon; fight for affordable health care for every American; and develop a national energy policy that ends our dependence on foreign oil and brings down the price at the pump. Linda Stender will bring the change that New Jersey families need. If you would like to know more or perhaps to get involved in the campaign, please contact the Victory '08 office at 908-490-1380. This call was paid for by the New Jersey State Democratic Committee and Linda Stender for Congress. It is authorized by Linda Stender for Congress. Thank you, and have a good day."

This takes about forty seconds. I've read it into something like forty voice-mail systems today.

EPISODE 3.3

It is October and late in the game. Linda Stender's opponent has been upping his game recently with a new television ad, and the Republican Congressional Campaign Committee has just sent out an aggressive direct mail piece to potentially undecided voters.

Kevin is on the phones, calling through a list of people who previously have been identified as undecided by other callers or canvassers, or are believed to be so on the basis of statistical analysis of the data available to the campaign. He has been in to "help out" a few times, being, as he puts it, "between things" right now. Given his previous experience working in telemarketing, it is no surprise that he is good on the phones—polite but firm, usually unwavering, and hardworking.

He dials the next person on the list and waits. The second he hears the "Hello?" at the other end, his whole body language changes. He straightens his back, brandishes a dazzling smile, and launches into his spiel: "Good evening, sir. My name is Kevin, and I'm a volunteer calling you on behalf of Linda Stender. She is a—" He stops speaking and hesitates for a second, then holds out the receiver while looking at it. He turns to me and says, "He told me to go fuck myself."

EPISODE 3.4

Charlene and I are canvassing together in the outskirts of Bridgeport, Connecticut. While not quite as depressed as the inner city, the area we are in is still poor, especially by Fairfield County standards. A few houses are vacant, many are for sale, and most are somewhat worse for wear. Though we are nowhere near the end of our list and are supposed to go on until eight-thirty, Charlene has announced that she wants to call it a day at seven-thirty. "Nobody wants to talk later anyway," she says. I know the canvassing director won't approve, but I say nothing. The part-timers seem to work slightly shorter hours with each passing week.

With ten minutes to go, I have a couple of houses left on the street we are on, so I have been rushing things a bit, knocking on doors and leaving after ten seconds or so if I sense no reaction. I have skipped some of the houses that seemed obviously empty to me, though maybe I shouldn't—it is sometimes hard to balance between acting like my fellow canvassers and following staff instructions. I sort of want to finish this row, but I half dread running into a "talker" who will go on forever and make Charlene have to wait for me in the car.

I need not fear. The only person I speak to on this street is a man in his late seventies who has even less time for me than I have for him. I ring the bell next to his open front door and say "hello" as he is watching television in his living room. He turns toward me in his chair without getting up and shouts to me, over the loud chatter of CNN pundits, "What is it?" I speak as loudly as I can without shouting, trying to get through to him while Dr. Sanjay Gupta is making some point in a faraway studio: "Hi, my name is Rasmus. I'm just out walking the streets for the Democratic Party, talking to folks about the fall elections. Have you thought about—" The man interrupts me: "Yeah, yeah, you don't need to read me the whole speech. I'll vote the ticket." He turns away and fidgets with the remote control. I hesitate for a moment, then turn around and walk away. On my PDA I put him down as a "solid Democrat" and a "definite supporter" of the various Democrats running.

EPISODE 3.5

Jim Himes won the August primary easily, but it has taken a little time to turn the whole operation around and orient it toward the general election. Now, after Labor Day, the campaign is trying to catch up and reach the target numbers for calls and knocks.

Greg is a local Democrat who has come in to the Norwalk office to lend a hand. The two of us are now sitting in the volunteer room making calls from some of the many phones available. He has made calls before for other candidates, both local and federal.

He gets a live voter. I cannot hear the other part of the conversation, but here is what I jot down: "Hi, this is Greg. I'm looking to get in touch with Stuart? . . . Hi, Stuart, this is Greg. I'm a local Democrat. We are just making some calls to talk to people about the election in November. . . . No, in NO-vember. . . . Yeah, it is a long time. . . . Well, we have this guy Jim Himes running for Congress. . . . Yeah, Himes. . . . So Jim Himes is running for Congress to restore the American dream and bring change to Washington. Jim wants to ensure that every child gets a quality public school. . . . What's that? . . . Yeah, it does sound good, doesn't it? . . . So do you plan to vote for the Democrat Jim Himes or the Republican Chris Shays for Congress in November? . . . That's good. What about for president, are you going to vote for Barack Obama? . . .

Yeah, it's kind of scary, but we can only hope. . . . Have you thought about any of the local races? . . . Oh, I'm sorry. No, that's okay; I realize you have other things to do. I'm happy you had time to talk to me. . . . No, that's fine. Have a good one, all right? Bye, now."

The conversation lasts about two minutes. Greg writes down that Stuart is a solid Himes supporter and a solid Obama supporter and leaves the remaining questions on his call sheet blank. He sits silently for a couple of seconds, staring straight ahead. Then he dials the next number on his list.

EPISODE 3.6

"Aren't you afraid of that Palin woman?" That is what Janet asks after she has introduced herself to the voter at the other end. She is calling women targeted as undecided by the Linda Stender campaign and has a Stender script in front of her. Janet isn't here for Stender, though, and ignores the script. The moment she stepped through the door to the campaign office, she announced, "I'm here to help Obama!"

It turns out that the voter she is speaking to also has her doubts about the Republican candidate for vice president. Again, I hear only Janet's side of the conversation, which lasts about five minutes. "Oh, I thought it was just me. . . . Yeah! Except she is wrong on all the issues! On choice, and on killing wolves! . . . Yeah, and she's cute, and that's all men see." . . . "I'm really afraid," she says in a somber tone and pauses for a moment. Then she continues: "In fact, I read something that was so scary, when she was mayor, you know, she wanted to ban books! . . . Do you want to hear my strangest theory? Because you live in Clark, too, I'm going to tell you. I think her pregnancy is a cover-up for the cover-up. . . . Yeah, and I'm trying to do something about it. I've come down here to Fanwood to make some phone calls. We're safe here, I mean, Obama will win New Jersey, but I don't know. . . . Maybe the stupid people in this country just vote for the person, and not the issues. . . . Yes it is. . . . No, thank you, thanks for listening. I hope there are more women like us. . . . "Me neither. . . . Well, me neither. Go online and search for the 'glorious diamonds letter'. . . . Okay, I'll let you go now, bye-bye, and thank you. Take care."

Neither Linda Stender nor any of the local candidates or issues come up in this conversation, or in any of the others I hear Janet have.

This is what personalized political communication looks like up close. Episodes like these are likely familiar to anyone who has been part of the field side of an American campaign. For those who have not, they provide a glimpse of what the countless contacts made are actually like. It is easy to lose sight of the texture of this in the face of political operatives and their talk of so-and-so many "knocks" and "calls." In the quantitative terms that campaign staffers favor, individual encounters are all alike and can be recorded in the clear-cut categories used to gather response data for further targeting: "not home," "undecided," "solid Democrat," and so on. But for people like Kevin, Greg, Charlene, and millions more like them, who have taken it upon themselves to serve as media for personalized political communication, there is something more at stake in every attempt to contact a voter. Staffers in both campaigns were puzzled that I continued to take part in both canvassing and phone banking throughout my fieldwork. As one said, "You knock on the door and deliver the script. What's the big deal?" The big deal is what personalized political communication entails for those who are directly involved: uninvited interactions with total strangers. What is at stake here is not simply a chance to deliver a message and gather some information about voters, all on behalf of a campaign, but also the right to assume a certain role while doing so. The challenges involved make it difficult to keep personalized political communication "on message" and make it a draining and sometimes unpleasant experience for those involved.

This chapter moves from the sweeping history of recent ground war efforts to the minute details of a few of the millions of contacts made in 2008 to address the question of how encounters between campaign assemblages and voters play out at the individual level. I argue that a close analysis of interactions between callers and canvassers and the voters they talk to from the "dramaturgical" perspective developed by sociologist Erving Goffman and further elaborated by Arlie Hochschild and Robin Leidner can help us understand why people who are involved in personalized political communication systematically go "off message" (despite staffers' efforts to get them to simply "deliver the script") and why the apparently simple work of contacting voters is seen as stressful by those who are engaged in it. These two points capture key parts of what distinguishes personalized political communication from other kinds of political communication. They also help explain why staffers remain somewhat wary of it despite its instrumental promise and why they face so many challenges in term of organizing and targeting it (the people they painstakingly enroll to talk to voters quickly tire of it, and they appreciate other sides of the encounters than those the staffers emphasize).

PERSONALIZED POLITICAL COMMUNICATION AS INTERACTION

Individual encounters between voters and canvassers or callers, and the interactions that may ensue, represent the point where people can come to mediate between the campaign assemblages they are enrolled in and the portions of the electorate that are targeted. It is at the door and over the phone that a particular staffer, volunteer, or part-timer has a chance to put the "personalized" and the "communication" into "personalized political communication." "Knocks" and "calls" can be generated in large numbers, but unless encounters with voters—like episodes 3.3 to 3.6— are turned into interactions with voters—like episodes 3.4 to 3.6—little has been accomplished. In short: no interaction, no contact.

In this respect, personalized political communication is different from television advertising, direct mail, and many other forms of political communication. Thirty-second television spots, online ads, and printed material all rely on what sociologist John B. Thompson calls "mediated quasi-interaction," in which people interact with the object (television set, digital device, glossy brochure, etc.) that mediates the message, rather than with a subject who serves as a medium.[1] So, too, do the traces left behind—a flyer or a voice-mail message—by the many failed attempts at reaching voters (like episodes 3.1 and 3.2). But when callers and canvassers get through to people, it is a different matter, a matter of live interaction, whether over the phone or at the door. A rule of thumb among campaign staffers is that on average 10 percent of all calls and 30 percent of all knocks result in some form of contact with a voter. I analyze these interactions drawing on the work of Goffman, Hochschild, and Leidner. The approach adopted here brings to light the personal stakes involved in how we present ourselves to others, and is therefore particularly suited to understanding how problematic and stressful practices of personalized political communication often are.

The first idea I adopt from Goffman is the notion that whenever we interact with other people, we are not simply trying to communicate or accomplish something ("please vote for Jim Himes"); we are also playing a role (as someone who is volunteering or working for a candidate).[2] The two aspects are intertwined so that both what we set out to achieve and the very role we purport to play are dependent on how the other reacts. Especially in a brief encounter with a stranger, almost everything of consequence has to be established in the course of the interaction—a fact that is of critical importance here. While it is obvious to campaign staffers that Allen and Charlene were engaged in a persuasion canvass in episodes 3.1 and 3.4 and that Kevin, Greg, and Janet were volunteers making persuasion calls in episodes 3.3, 3.5, and 3.6, what make them so ("persuasion" and "volunteers") must be performed in interactions with voters—"dramatically realized," as Goffman puts it. Kevin's brief and unpleasant encounter in episode 3.3 accomplishes none of this and hence fails to even register as a "contact." (The voter is simply taken down as "Refused.") When someone cold-calls a voter, she may think of herself as a volunteer soliciting support for a certain candidate or party ticket. But for the person picking up, she could be anything—a salesman, a crook, someone who has dialed the wrong number. It is always the person at the other end who has the choice of rejecting (as in episode 3.3), modifying (as in episode 3.4), or accepting (as in episodes 3.5 and 3.6) the role proposed, and thus granting or withholding the canvasser's/caller's right to effectively *be so* and *do so*. This is why the first seconds of an encounter between a canvasser or caller and a voter are so important, (a concept that direct marketing professionals have long been aware off).[3]

The second idea I take from Goffman is his view that encounters and interactions have a "moral" dimension.[4] When people do the "face work" required to establish and maintain roles, they are making a claim on their interlocutors. If I present myself as a volunteer for Jim Himes, my performance entails the implicit suggestion that you ought to accept that role. Depending on the degree to which you defer to my proffered demeanor, matters can then proceed. When Kevin (in episode 3.3) presented himself as a volunteer, he suggested that this role should take precedence over whatever inclinations the person at the other end may have had to think of him simply as a nuisance. The voter chose not to defer, and hence the attempt to instigate an interaction failed. The performance was rejected. This left Kevin without a useful role and thus with no way of accomplishing anything instrumentally useful, and it left the voter with the somewhat amorphous, but among campaign participants roundly despised, role of "the kind of person who swears at people and hangs up on volunteers." He was "technically rude," in Mitchell Duneier's delightful phrase.[5] It is the reluctance to be that kind of person that callers and canvassers rely on (as do telemarketers, door-to-door salesmen, religious proselytizers, and con men). They are engaged in an aggressive use of face work, trying to impose a certain definition of the situation upon unsuspecting voters.

As Goffman underlines throughout his work, most interactions in everyday life are highly conventionalized, based on a ritual respect for peoples' presentation of self and some shared or at least overlapping views of which roles and behaviors are legitimate and which are not.[6] In such situations, most participants will go to great lengths to maintain their own face and avoid anyone else's "lose face" by being denied the role they claim for themselves. The reaction Kevin is confronted with in episode 3.3 would be considered outright unacceptable in most situations. Generally, you just do not tell people to fuck off. It suggests that the encounters that are part of personalized political communications, at least in the United States today, fall under conflicting social conventions. Many voters seem to consider attempts at contacting them an illegitimate invasion of their *privacy*, an infringement on their right to withdraw from interactions with strangers in the sanctity of their own home.[7] For a sizable part of the population, attempts to impose politics upon them seem particularly inappropriate.[8] The official line in campaigns is different, insisting that politics is a *public* issue and that callers and canvassers have a legitimate claim on at least a moment of people's time to talk about it, irrespective of where they find them. Close to election time, when campaigns do their final get-out-the-vote work and the message is short, clear, and less obviously self-interested, people may have a bit more patience with contacts. (One creative volunteer in New Jersey ignored the official get-out-the-vote message and cast his calls in the final days as a service offered to a fellow citizen: "I'm just checking in to make sure you are all set to go and vote. You know how many irregularities there have been in the past, so we're just calling to make sure everything is okay. Do you know where your polling location is?") But most callers and canvassers get at best a guarded reception from people who resent the interruption, are concerned about their privacy, or question the legitimacy of the contact for other reasons.

It is left to those who try to talk to recalcitrant voters to bridge the chasm that sometimes exists between these different views of what is going on. Hochschild's and Leidner's research on the "emotional labor" involved in service industry jobs like waiting tables is useful in understanding why this is often stressful work. At the door and on the phone, those who try to talk to voters make an investment in a role that in turn may be disputed.[9] This is why personalized political communication is, as one volunteer told me, "very personal." Like it or not, the entire situation, including the vocabulary employed, underlines that the voter who refuses a contact is rejecting *you*. The voter Kevin spoke to did not tell Linda Stender, her campaign, or the Democratic Party to fuck off. He told Kevin to fuck off. Veteran callers and canvassers rationalize the experience and tell disheartened compatriots, "It's not you they don't like, it's the call." But everyone feels the sting. "I can't believe he blew me off like that," said one part-timer after several weeks of canvassing. A ruddy union retiree complained on Election Day itself, "I've done this so many times. I thought I had thick skin by now, but this really does wear you down." The experience of losing face, of having one's entreaties and proposed role refused, ranges from mildly disappointing to fairly disturbing, depending on the character of the rejection and on how invested people are in the role, the costs associated with being forced to act out of role, and how strongly they feel about the legitimacy of what they are doing (the difference between what Hochschild calls "surface acting" and "deep acting"). Staffers have very different experiences of their interactions with voters, volunteers often identify strongly with their role and believe in the legitimacy of what they are doing (it is part of what it means to be a "good citizen"), and part-timers are frequently less invested in the whole enterprise (for them it is "just a job"). But everyone is at least somewhat hurt when confronted with a rude voter—and there are many. And all campaigners have to deal with the regular experience of dissonance between the voters' perception of the situation and the expectations of the staffers and the wider campaign that they will make the contact and "deliver the script."

The official line, quoting from one set of canvassing instructions, is that "it is important to follow the script when you get to the door. The campaign has a finely tuned message aimed at persuasion, which will lose its effectiveness if each canvasser delivers something different." Some researchers have noted how political operatives today increasingly aim at "narrowcasting"—that is, tailoring their messages to the perceived needs, wants, and hopes of the target voters.[10] I have seen no evidence that personalized political communication was systematically customized in such a fashion in the campaigns I followed. Although contacts are carefully targeted and scripts and talking points do vary somewhat, the latter are generally standardized and rarely changed, simply because the organizational overhead involved in trying to control and continuously update the messages delivered is well beyond what the staffers in the campaign organizations have the resources to handle. The extensive "codification" and development of communication as a distinct form of expertise that Deborah Cameron has argued pervades many areas of contemporary life have not made great inroads in American politics.[11] Most campaigns do not have the resources required for extensive scripting, testing of messages, and training of messengers—let alone effective tailoring to individual voters or even segments of voters. Instead they try to mass-produce knocks and calls. It is then largely up to individual canvassers and callers themselves to translate these into contacts when they encounter and interact with different voters at the door or on the phone. Examples of a script and some talking points with their "finely tuned message aimed at persuasion" can be seen in figures 3.1 and 3.2. The script is from New Jersey, the talking points are from Connecticut, and both are representative of their genre. In general the sheets given to callers and canvassers only differentiate between "supporters" and "undecideds" and offer a short list of boilerplate talking points on a couple of potentially relevant issues. The messages are not tailored to voter demographics and are not customized on the basis of recent events or anything like that. (Even when Congress was debating President Bush's $700 billion Emergency Economic Stabilization Act in September and October 2008, and more and more voters asked volunteers and part-timers about Himes's and Stender's stances on the bail-out package, the scripts remained unchanged.)

The scripts are, in short, fairly primitive and rarely modified. These canned messages aimed at persuasion of the undecided or mobilization of infrequently voting partisans, combined with numerous questions to

My name is _____ and I am with the New Jersey Democratic State Committee. We are talking with folks about the election here in the 7th District, featuring Linda Stender for US Congress.

Q1: Do you know who you will be voting for in the congressional race is November?

(1) Definitely Voting for Linda Stender (2) Leaning Towards Linda Stender (3) Undecided (4) Leaning Towards State Senator Leonard Lance (5) Definitely Voting State Senator Leonard Lance (6) Other

If undecided about Linda Stender...

Linda Stender and the Democratic ticket will bring the change our families need. In Congress, Linda will end the failed Bush policies and revitalize our economy; bring down gas prices and make America energy independent; provide quality, affordable healthcare; and bring our troops home from Iraq safely and soon.

If a Linda Stender Supporter... GREAT may I sign you up to volunteer with Victory 08? We need volunteers to phone bank, door knock & other activities in support of our Democratic Ticket. (1) Yes...sign me up! (2) Maybe (3) No

If a Linda Stender Supporter... Would you like a Yard Sign?

Q2 In the 2008 General Election for President, do you support Democrat Barack Obama or Republican John McCain?

(1) Definitely Obama (2) Leaning Obama (3) Undecided (4) Leaning McCain (5) Strong McCain (6) Other

Q3 In the general election for U.S. Senate, will you be supporting Democrat Frank Lautenberg or Republican Dick Zimmer?

(1) Definitely Frank Lautenberg (2) Leaning Frank Launtenberg (3) Undecided (4) Leaning Dick Zimmer (5) Definitely Dick Zimmer (6) Other

Q4X3 In this year's election for Union County Freeholder, which 3 of the following candidates do you support? Democrat Angel Estrada, Democrat Rick Proctor, Democrat Nancy Ward, Republican Michael Yabukov, Republican John Russitano, Republican Joseph Franchino?

(1) Angel Estrada (2) Rick Proctor (3) Nancy Ward (4) Undecided (5) Michael Yabukov (6) John Russitano (7) Joseph Franchino (8) Other

Paid for by the New Jersey Democratic State Committee. Authorized by Frank Lautenberg and Linda Stender.

Message: My name is _____ and I am a volunteer with Victory 08.

Linda Stender and the Democratic ticket will bring the change our families need. In Congress, Linda will end the failed Bush policies and revitalize our economy; bring down gas prices and make America energy independent; provide quality, affordable healthcare; and bring our troops home from Iraq safely and soon

If you would like to volunteer, please call the Victory 08 office at ~~(732) 868 – 8023.~~ 908 490 1380

Paid for by the New Jersey Democratic State Committee. Authorized by Linda Stender for Congress.

Paid for by the New Jersey Democratic State Committee. Authorized by Frank Lautenberg and Linda Stender

Figure 3.1. Example of a phone script (from New Jersey).
The script leads with what the campaign staffers consider the most important question in this district—namely, who the voter is inclined to vote for in the race for House of Representatives. It provides a persuasion message for undecided voters, and a list of further ID questions concerning other candidates and issues, all used for targeting purposes.

Jim's Positions

Iraq

- Jim is against the war and supports an immediate withdrawal of US troops.
- SHAYS: Chris Shays has supported the war in Iraq over and over again. Now he's supporting John McCain for President, and McCain says he's ready to stay in Iraq for 100 years.

Economy and Jobs

- Jim believes the Bush economic policy has failed. Jim believes we need a tax policy that encourages creating jobs at home rather than shipping them overseas, and sound regulation that will prevent abuses like those we saw in the sub-prime mortgage crisis. Jim will bring fiscal responsibility back to Washington, and will put his private sector experience to work to improve our economy.
- SHAYS: Chris Shays has supported the failed Bush economic policy down the line. He supported tax cuts in a time of war, took no action when the housing market threatened to collapse, and has passed budgets with huge deficits for years now.

Healthcare

- Jim will work for universal healthcare in Congress and wants to lower the costs of a system that is too expensive and inefficient and believes we can do this through more focus on preventative care and cutting administrative costs.
- SHAYS: Chris Shays opposed universal healthcare until this spring, when it became clear that it was an important issue politically. In fact, Chris Shays is now endorsing a bill he once voted against.

Education

- Jim believes that great schools are the key to making sure that the American dream is available to everyone. Jim opposes No Child Left Behind in its current design. Jim will fully fund No Child Left Behind, and is devoted to finding creative solutions to improve schools in need. As a product of public schools himself, Jim knows just how important a good education is.
- SHAYS: Chris Shays has not voted to fully fund No Child Left Behind

Figure 3.2. **Example of talking points (from Connecticut).**
The talking points are used in conjunction with a script like the phone script from New Jersey. They provide the canvassers with additional information to use in conversations with voters, depending on what the latter seem to care about.

secure "response data" for further targeting, are what callers and canvassers are expected to stick to even as they face the challenge in each encounter of defining the contact as a legitimate interaction rather than an illegitimate invasion of private space. Doing so involves using all the verbal and nonverbal means at one's disposal to establish a role that the voter in turn may dispute. It thus puts something of oneself at stake in every situation. Both in on-site conversations and off-site interviews, everyone involved recounts again and again examples of the real social and personal costs of rejection. In any particular case these experiences might seem trivial, but personalized political communication is pursued on a large scale, so they add up as volunteers place call after call and part-timers knock on door after door. To show how personalized political communication works and what the implications are, I deal first with initial encounters with voters and then examine some opening lines used, three distinct kinds of voter reactions, and a few examples of ensuing interactions. I then turn to the question of how campaigners are prepared to engage in these interactions and why they find them so stressful.

ENCOUNTERING THE VOTERS

In any given encounter with a voter, the caller or canvasser has only one chance to turn the situation into an interaction with recognizable and legitimate, and thus potentially useful, roles. "Knocks" and "calls" do not automatically translate into "contacts," even if people open the door or pick up the phone (and many do not). They have to be translated in situ in an interaction between people who have different perspectives on what is and what should be going on. That is what is at stake in the first seconds. Is this call an acceptable interruption from someone doing their job, a legitimate invitation to talk about politics and public issues from someone doing their civic duty as a citizen, or an illegitimate invasion of someone's privacy? Ought the contacted go easy on the person initiating the contact, engage in a conversation with her, or hang up? Kevin's experience in episode 3.5 above illustrates the complications most forcefully.

With the importance of the encounter and possible subsequent interaction established, let us return to the opening episodes for a closer look at them. Apart from episodes 3.1 and 3.2, where there is nobody at the receiving end, the callers and canvassers in each case try to turn the encounter into an interaction, to put the "personalized" and the "communication" into personalized political communication. If successful, they let the interaction run its course while trying to balance between what they are doing, what the voter will let them do, and what they know the staffers would like them to accomplish along the way. A few basic similarities can be pointed out. First, the caller or canvasser will deliver an opening line, normally identifying himself ("this is Greg") and describing his role as he sees it ("I'm a local Democrat"). Then the voter will react by rejecting ("Go fuck yourself"), modifying ("You don't need to read me the whole speech"), or accepting (as in Greg and Janet's conversations) the definition of the situation offered. If the opening is modified or accepted, an interaction will take place (as in episodes 3.5 and 3.6).

Given the vast number of contacts made, it is impossible to capture the qualitative experience of all of them, but in a sense the most important point has already been made. The nature of the encounters *as interaction* consistently draws communication away from the simple blueprint offered by the scripts and talking points. It is almost impossible to simply "deliver the script." The material that canvassers and callers are expected to follow, however, makes few concessions to this reality. Scripts are written with little sense of probable voter reactions, as if they could simply be delivered verbatim. They may be closely aligned with the overall campaign message as communicated via other platforms—like television and direct mail—but they seem to be written by people with at best a limited understanding of what interactions with voters are actually like, with more focus on what the campaign hopes for than on what it actually looks like at the receiving end. (Some field staffers recognize this and make only limited and selective efforts to get those working with them to stick closely to the written instructions.[12]) Balancing one's own perspective on the situation with that of the voters and the staffers, and maintaining the fragile balance that allows a given interaction among strangers to proceed, rarely leads one back to the script.

OPENING LINES

The first moment of the encounter with the voter is one of the few times where actual interactions and official scripts are roughly similar. Typical scripts go: "My name is _____ and I am with the New Jersey Democratic State Committee," or "Hi, I'm _____ calling for the Jim Himes campaign for Congress." The precise phrasing depends partly on exactly what parts of the campaign assemblage pay how much for the phone lines, vans, and various other forms of equipment that make the calls or knocks possible (making them "paid for," as in episode 3.2, even when no wage is paid to a volunteer), and partly on strategic considerations such as the degree to which senior staffers think the lead candidate should stress party affiliation (as suggested by the quote above about a "finely tuned message").

Actual opening lines I heard used on the phone or at the door did not veer far from the general structure of the script, though they rarely stuck to the precise wording. Consider the following four examples of how people presented themselves and the role they wished to play vis-à-vis the voter. (Opening lines 1 and 2 were delivered by part-timers, 3 and 4 by volunteers.)

1. "Hi, I'm here to represent the Democratic Party. Have you thought about the congressional election this fall, featuring Jim Himes?" (At the door.)
2. "Hi, I'm Charlene. Is Mr. Gordon in?" (woman) "What is this about?" "I'm a Democratic congressional campaigner. I'm here to ask him about the fall elections." (At the door.)
3. "Good evening, my name is Jane. I'm a volunteer with the Democrats. Are you Mr. Rodriguez?" (At the door.)
4. "Hello, Susan, this is Miriam. I live on Oak Road in Easton with my husband. I just wanted to talk to you for a few minutes about the fall elections. I'm a volunteer for Senator Obama." (On the phone.)

There are some overlaps in how they each attempt to initiate interaction and establish their role. Many use an informal first name (and volunteers generally their actual first name) to identify themselves. Some address the voter by name, too, sometimes by last name (without telling how they know—the campaigns have this information from voter files). There are also some noticeable differences when it comes to establishing their role. Part-timers tend to stress their task ("I'm here to represent") or their job ("I'm a Democratic congressional campaigner"), suggesting widespread surface acting. Volunteers often stress their role, too, but in ways that suggest a stronger identification with it, and thus deeper acting ("I'm a volunteer for" or "with" is endemic). When discrepancies between scripts and actual opening lines exist, volunteers normally say what they think they are doing ("I'm volunteering for Senator Obama") rather than what the staffers would like them to say they are doing ("I'm _____ calling for the Jim Himes campaign for Congress").

The double move is clear, opening lines are about minimizing the strangeness of the encounter by making oneself as familiar to the voter as possible and by offering a meaningful role that would legitimate the call or the knock. "This is who I am; this is what I do." (And thus, in line with Goffman's reasoning, implicitly, you *ought* to recognize me as such, and *should* accept the legitimacy of this interaction.) Sometimes people identify themselves beyond simply using a first name by mentioning where they live, where they are calling from, or emphasizing something else they might have in common with the voter they are talking to (gender, hometown, or some other imagined affinity). On the phone, few means but words are available, but at the door, a whole plethora of opportunities present themselves for those with the instinct and will to pursue them. The canvasser can dress up a bit, wear stickers signaling her role, present a friendly façade as she walks up toward the door, wave and smile if someone can be seen from the road (which reduces not only the strangeness of the situation but also the element of surprise that is unavoidable with an unexpected phone call), and maybe ask an innocent question or make a remark about something to strike up conversation ("Is that your car?" "Nice house!" "Those roses are beautiful," etc.)—all the little things we do every day to ease interactions with other people. A smile and a collared shirt is hardly enough to overcome prejudices about race (or gender or class or some such), or even to counter the frequent desire to simply be left alone in privacy, but these are at least steps canvassers can take to try to ensure that the encounter moves beyond the opening gambit.

VOTER REACTIONS

While opening lines can be scripted and often turn out to be delivered in something like their scripted form, people's reactions are beyond staff control. And they vary in important ways. The voters have the upper hand, with three distinct options: (1) they can reject the entreaties made and bring the encounter to an end with no further interaction; (2) they can modify the terms of the encounter by explicitly or implicitly proposing different roles or rules; or (3) they can simply accept the proposition made and go along.

Rejection

Over the phone, people often simply hang up. At the door, people occasionally just close it. Such nonverbal rejections are sometimes supplemented with a little comment like in episode 3.3, or others like it: "How dare you!" (hangs up); "That you have the gall to disturb me at home!" (hangs up); "You guys have some balls to come here and knock on my door!" (shuts the door). Such rather harsh rejections underline how salient the convention of privacy is. Sometimes they are softened with an excuse suggesting that under other conditions the voter might have accepted some version of the proposed interaction: "Look, this is not a good time"; "You know what, I'm in the middle of something"; "I'm actually about to leave. Can you come back later?" Either way, the encounter is over, no interaction ensues. Though a trace may be left in people's memory and on voice mail or in the form of a flyer, the abortive contact does not result in a personal conversation communicating a message on behalf of the campaign, nor does it produce any of the response data that staffers want for targeting purposes. The call or knock is generally recorded as if the voter was "Not home," unless the rejection was extremely harsh, in which case it is taken down as "Refused."

Modification

The voter might instead suggest that interaction can occur, but on terms other than those suggested by the opening. It is rare that voters reject the personal identity people claim, but it does happen that part-timers and volunteers are mistaken for automated robocalls (hence some people's penchant for introducing themselves as, well, people—"Hi, I'm Robin, a live person calling you for Linda Stender"). A more common modification is to challenge either the role suggested or to more or less explicitly stipulate the conditions under which interaction may continue. Consider a few examples:

1. "Is this some kind of survey? I don't do surveys."
2. "Yeah, I'm going to vote for him. Anything else?"
3. "Out earning a quick buck, are you?"
4. "Ah, out counting the votes?"
5. "Make it brief."
6. "What do you want?"
7. "I'm not a Democrat!"
8. "You know, I'm not even sure I'm registered to vote."

In reactions 1 and 2, as in episode 3.4 above, the voters take control by jumping to what they think might be the purpose of the contact. In reactions 3 and 4 they offer a role that does not correspond to what has been suggested in the opening lines. In reactions 5 and 6 the voters make it clear that time is likely to be limited. In reactions 7 and 8, they question whether they really should have been contacted at all.

Faced with such reactions, callers or canvassers usually accept the voter's definition of the situation and typically try to accomplish just a few potentially useful things quickly, maybe asking one ID question or saying one good thing about the candidate, and then move on. ("ID question" is the staff term for the questions in the script about where the voter stands on various candidates and issues. See figure 3.1.) When this happens, the discrepancies between what staffers prioritize and what matters to part-timers and volunteers becomes manifest. Volunteers prioritize whatever they themselves care most about, whether it is an issue or a candidate. Again, this may not correspond to what staffers are most interested in. Many of the conversations I observed in Connecticut and New Jersey were about Barack Obama rather than about Jim Himes or Linda Stender, though officially the latter were the number-one priority races in these competitive House districts in otherwise solidly blue (Democratic) states. Especially with volunteers, presidential candidates and national issues seem to be emphasized at the expense of local and even congressional candidates. Part-timers generally stick to the easy questions: "Who are you going to vote for in the presidential election?" Or they deliver a line memorized from their script: "I hope you'll keep in mind that Linda Stender will fight for good jobs when you vote in November." Many staffers are well aware of this selectivity and what it means for both the message delivered and the information gathered, but, as one staffer put it, "It's better than nothing." Luis, the canvassing director in one of the campaigns, inadvertently echoes Marshall McLuhan's famous quip that the medium is the message when he says, "Maybe they'll remember that nice young man who came to their door when they finally go vote." (They might, and being there in the first place surely matters, but all research suggests that the nature of the interaction and the character of the person who makes the call or knocks on the door matters too.[13])

Acceptance

Sometimes voters just accept the roles offered and let the person making the contact go ahead. Greg's brief conversation with Stuart in episode 3.5 might well be the most typical form of interaction between canvassers and callers and the people they contact: an initial acceptance followed by a short exchange eventually cut short by the voter. In rare cases people may even encourage longer conversations. Here are a few sample responses:

1. "Oh, hi."
2. "How are you doing?"
3. "I'm glad to see somebody is knocking on doors for him!"
4. "I thought you guys would never come around."

Faced with reactions like 1 and 2, part-timers generally stick to the script and try to get as much done as possible before they overstay their welcome, or until they are done and can move on. What volunteers do and say depends on who exactly they think they are volunteering for and how comfortable they feel with the script they have. In cases like 3 and 4, callers and canvassers often respond with a nicety, part-timers again typically stick to the script, while volunteers often go for a longer conversation when they sense that the voters they are talking to don't mind that.

ENSUING INTERACTIONS

Even in encounters where the voters accept the opening line and recognize the caller or canvasser as a person (as opposed to a robocall) and as someone volunteering or working for a political cause or candidate, the ensuing interactions rarely follow the basic blueprint suggested by the official staff line (knock on the door, deliver the script). This is even more so in encounters where the voter has modified the definition of the situation and, of course, in cases where the opening line is simply rejected. As stated earlier, where exactly interactions go after the opening seconds can vary widely and cannot be summed up easily (openings are generally similar, reactions can be captured by the three basic options of acceptance, modification, and reaction, but what follows differs). A few more episodes from my fieldwork demonstrate why it is so hard to follow a script closely; the problem is that doing so too rigidly puts at risk the temporary compromise between canvasser and canvassed, caller and called, that any interaction is premised upon. Beyond the basic tension between privacy and public-ness, a straight-faced delivery of a canned message in itself seems to strike many people as a violation of social norms. In each of the following three episodes canvassers go to great lengths to stay on message, yet their interactions with voters complicate matters and ultimately put an end to the encounter well before they have made it through all their talking points and questions.

EPISODE 3.7

It is getting dark, so it is probably a good thing that Mark has just one door left. We should stop soon and get back to the office anyway. I have knocked through my list, so I join him as he rings the bell on the four-unit apartment building we are in front of. A woman around forty opens the door. Mark asks, "Is Mr. O'Neill in?" "What is this about?" she asks. "Sorry, my name is Mark. I'm a volunteer with Linda Stender's campaign for Congress. I'm here to ask him about the fall election. Do you happen to live here, ma'am?" She shakes her head. "No, I'm his caregiver. Let me ask him if he's interested."

The woman disappears for a minute and then returns with a man around eighty, who walks with a cane and drags an oxygen tank on wheels along with him. He is wearing a worn bathrobe and slippers with holes in them. He smiles a toothless smile at us and asks in a surprisingly firm voice, "What can I do for you guys?" Mark introduces himself: "Good evening, Mr. O'Neill. I'm Mark. I'm here on behalf of Linda Stender. I work on her campaign for Congress. I was wondering if you have made up your mind as to who you will vote for in the fall election?" O'Neill laughs. "What kind of question is that? Of course I have." He smiles and looks at Mark, who hesitates and then asks, "Do you mind sharing that with me?" O'Neill coughs and says, "I'll be voting for that young man, Mr. Obama!" Mark smiles. He asks, "What about for Congress? Do you know who you will be voting for?" O'Neill pauses and then looks at Mark. "Well, I don't know. Are you thinking of anyone in particular?" He smiles again. Mark clears his throat and says, "Well, Linda Stender is running to get our country back on the right track after eight years with George Bush—"

O'Neill interrupts him. "Is she a Democrat?" Mark pauses for a second, then says, "Yes, sir, she is." O'Neill says, "Then I'll probably vote for her." "Thanks, I'm mighty happy to hear that, sir," Mark says, and continues: "Have you thought about the freeholder races?" O'Neill leans against the door frame and waves his hand in front of him while clutching the metal frame that holds the oxygen tank, and says, "Look, I can't be bothered to go through every one of them. I usually vote for the whole ticket, as long as they're not crooks." Mark grins and nods. "That's what we like to hear, sir." The caregiver starts tapping her fingers on the wall. O'Neill says, "I think she thinks I should get back to my chair. Thanks for stopping by. I don't get to talk to many young people these days." He chuckles. The caregiver shoots us a look. Mark says, "Thanks, Mr. O'Neill. We appreciate your support. You have a good day too." The caregiver helps O'Neill turn around and then closes the door.

Notice here that even though O'Neill accepts the role that Mark presents, and is very patient, he still changes the course of the interaction before Mark is even halfway through the many questions in his script. Mark sticks to the script as far as he can, but even with a conversational partner who plays along, he is prompted to mention Stender's party affiliation (something the campaign has decided to downplay, since the district she is running in retains a slight Republican bent), and he does not get a chance to deliver any of his talking points.

EPISODE 3.8

As Allen and I approach a two-story house in Trumbull, he shouts to a young man washing an old car in the driveway: "Hey, would you happen to be Daniel Vieira?" The young man looks up and says, "Yeah. Hi. What can I do for you guys?" Allen walks up and offers his hand. Daniel hesitates a second, then dries his hand with a towel and shakes hands with both of us as Allen says, "Hi, Daniel. My name is Allen. I'm with the Democratic Party here in the state. I'm a volunteer for Jim Himes. We're just walking the neighborhood talking to folks about the fall election." I introduce myself, too, as a volunteer. Daniel says, "That sounds like good exercise." He pauses, then takes up the sponge again and resumes scrubbing.

There is a moment of silence. Then Daniel says, "I'm not even sure I'm registered to vote." Allen replies, "Well, that's the kind of thing we're checking up on. Let me look you up." Since Daniel is on our list, we know he must be registered to vote, but Allen takes out his PDA and pretends to look for information for a few seconds, then says, "You should be good to go." Daniel does not say anything. Allen pauses and then asks, "You live here with your parents?" Daniel says, "Yeah, I just moved back here." Allen waits a second, then asks, "Are you following the presidential election much?" Daniel responds, "Well, I take a class on politics, so I sort of have to." Allen says nothing. After a few seconds,

Daniel says, "I'm at Housatonic [Community College]." Allen says, "That's cool. Have you thought about who you are going to vote for?" "Nah, I don't know, man." Allen waits for a second, then asks, "What about the congressional election, have you thought about that?" Daniel puts the sponge down and looks at us. He says, "You know what? I don't care that much, frankly." There is a moment's pause, then Allen holds out a Jim Himes for Congress flyer. "Well, I have a little piece here with information about Jim Himes, the Democratic candidate here in our district. You should check it out." Daniel says, "Cool, man, you can just leave it here." Allen asks him, "Any particular issues you care about?" Daniel says, "Not really," and resumes scrubbing the car.

I expect Allen to give up, but he looks at me and then turns to Daniel again. "So you don't really care about health care, about the economy, about the war in Iraq?" Daniel responds—and there is a slight edge to his voice that wasn't there before—"You know what? I just came back from the Marines. I'm just happy I wasn't sent over there, okay? And I hope I don't have to go back. I just want to go to school, man." He looks at us. Daniel puts down the sponge and takes up the towel, dries his hands, and starts polishing the car. He says, in a more mellow tone, "You know, I just don't care much. But thanks for the folder, and thanks for stopping by." Allen looks at me, then looks at Daniel and says, "No, thanks for *your* time, man. Appreciate it. If you have any questions or anything, feel free to call the office. The number is on the flyer." Daniel says, "No, it's all right, man. You have a good one." He keeps polishing the car. Allen and I leave. We have been there for a couple of minutes.

Vieira is not as easy as O'Neill. He makes several interventions to define the terms of the interaction ("I'm not sure I'm registered to vote," "I don't care that much"). Even though Allen goes to considerable lengths to both maintain the conversation and elicit responses to the questions he is supposed to ask, he only gets in three questions (about the presidential election, the congressional race, and what issues Vieira cares about). In most situations like this, a part-timer like Charlene would have been satisfied with just one answer to make the encounter count as a contact, but Allen is much more persistent. Yet he leaves several questions from the script unasked (party identification and several state-level and local races), and probably wisely so. Even given the information elicited, Vieira's responses remain to be interpreted. Is he, for example, "undecided" about the congressional election or simply uninterested? There is not an official category for the latter. (Ironically, for reasons I explain in chapter 5, voters like Vieira are particularly likely to be contacted again in short order.) The tensions between Allen trying to accomplish what he is meant to in this case (deliver a message and elicit information) and what he needs to do in order to achieve his goal (maintain a role and keep the interaction going) are palpable throughout the conversation.

EPISODE 3.9

I am wandering around our turf looking for Charlene so that we can walk back to the car and drive it to the next couple of blocks. She likes to keep it close, especially when we are in Bridgeport. Moving it once in a while also creates an occasion to sit down for a minute to relax and have something to drink.

She turns out to be talking to a voter. I hear the voices before I turn the corner and see the scene. Charlene is speaking: "But, ma'am, please, this will only take a few seconds more. What about for state Senate? Do you lean toward supporting Anthony Musto or Rob Russo?" A woman shouts, "Go away!" Now I can see them. Charlene is standing on the lawn in front of a small two-story house. An old woman with wild white hair is leaning out of a window on the second floor. She is gesturing toward Charlene, who stands with her clipboard in front of her, looking down at her script. She asks, "For state assembly, then, will you vote for Chris Caruso or Joseph Minutolo?" The woman yells, "Get off my lawn!" and then slams her window shut.

Charlene looks up at the window, then turns toward me and shakes her head. She walks out to join me on the paved sidewalk and says, "I don't understand why they give us all these questions when nobody wants to answer them anyway."

This example is extreme in Charlene's insistence on running through the questions in her script. She was, like other paid canvassers, occasionally rigid to the verge of being spiteful in her loyalty to the official line and the formal instructions given, even when she personally thought they made no sense. Even in this case she does not get through all the questions. I did not witness the first part of the conversation, so I cannot say how the situation turned so baroque. But Charlene's comment to me as we left clearly underlines the fact that she blames the staffers for the result—it is, after all, "they" who insisted that she ask all these questions, though "nobody wants to answer them anyway."

That is one challenge part-timers face. Another is voters who are actually all too comfortable with making conversation (such people are often called "talkers"). Such encounters are time-consuming, and they run the risk of exposing the caller's or canvasser's limited knowledge of a candidate's past or positions. One paid canvasser formulated it quite clearly: "One thing I don't like about talkers is that they ask a lot of questions." If you have successfully claimed the role as someone working for Jim Himes, it is embarrassing (and probably counterproductive, at least in terms of persuasion) to be revealed as ignorant about what he claims to stand for. The problem is most pronounced with part-timers, who rarely care or know much about politics and generally hate discussing policy. Volunteers are usually at least knowledgeable about the candidate or cause that drew them to the campaign in the first place. But they, too, face occasional challenges and embarrassments. Most would confess to not knowing the names of even long-serving local politicians in the state legislatures, let alone what they stood for, or who people further down the ballot might be or what they believe in. Some voters have no qualms about calling people out on this: "You really don't know anything about this, do you?" "Oh, so you want me to vote for Himes, but you don't know what he stands for? That's very helpful." (And numerous variations of such responses.) It is hard to imagine that these incidents leave voters with a good impression, and the callers and canvassers themselves certainly dislike them.

The dynamics of the interactions themselves tend to veer away from the plotted course, truncating contacts and interrupting attempts to deliver the "finely tuned message" staffers talk about. (The same happens in tele-marketing.[14]) This is so even in situations like episode 3.7, with Mark and Mr. O'Neill, where those making the contact try hard to stick to the script, and those contacted largely accept the roles involved. Once interaction commences, most people answer a few questions but not a lot. They may have questions of their own. Very few are willing to listen to long chunks of a scripted message. Some people have patience for longer conversations, such as the one that Janet had with a voter in episode 3.6, but these remain a minority and don't fit well with the staff's instrumental perspective on contacts. Consider again a few bits of what Janet says to the voter she is talking to. She claims that Sarah Palin is "cute, and that's all men see." She suggests that the governor is involved in some untoward cover-up for her teenage daughter's pregnancy. She explicitly paints those who vote for the Republican Party as "stupid." This is not the official party or campaign line. She is way off message. And she not only ignores the script and every talking point she has been given, but she also neglects to even mention Linda Stender, the candidate for Congress, or any other New Jersey–based politician. From a staff point of view, Janet is out of control.[15]

PREPARING TO BE A MEDIUM

It is unclear how important control and message discipline really is when it comes to the instrumental effectiveness of personalized political communication. Like other forms of communication, personalized political communication involves much more than words, and it includes a wider range of nonverbal elements such as commitment and attitude (which are probably more effectively communicated in person than in any other way) and the "embodied symbols" that we carry as people see us—whether we like it or not—as members of a certain race, gender, and social class. Close attention to how actual encounters unfold suggests they are often stressful and fragile interactions and rarely go according to the plan. This may not matter much in terms of their impact. We do not know for sure when personalized political communication works, why it works, which dimensions of it matter most—the substance of the conversation, their live nature, the symbolic overtones, that someone would single you out like that. Its effectiveness could be attributed to any number of factors alone or in combination. Political operatives have their own folk theories on what works and what does not. They are reluctant, for example, to send black and Latino canvassers to canvass in white neighborhoods, arguing that it "sends the wrong message." Here is how Nelson, who is not white himself and who worked as the canvassing director in one of the districts, explains the implications this has for hiring practices:

EPISODE 3.10

"Frankly, I need more canvassers, and I especially need more white canvassers." I ask him what he means by that. "You know what I mean." I somewhat disingenuously protest my innocence, and Nelson continues. "You've seen Bobby, who interned here over the summer? Young black kid. You remember how he used to dress? Shorts, basketball jerseys. He's a nice guy, a decent young man, and a college student. But if someone in Fairfield sees him at the door like that, you know, I think it's fair to say that they are less likely to open than if you were at their door."

We both pause for a moment. Then he continues, while shuffling around a stack of walk packets. "Remember that kid who used to help me cut turf?" "Alex?" "Yeah, Alex. He was always wearing jeans, a T-shirt, sneakers. Very relaxed, very casual. But he was white. It just screams 'college kid.' I was sending a bunch of interns to canvass in Fairfield. All but Bobby were white. All were wearing rather casual outfits. You know, I try to be sensitive around these issues, but I also consider myself a fairly good judge of people and their reactions. And sometimes you just have to intervene. So I try to make sure that I send out the white kids first, to get Bobby one-on-one. Though of course Alex and one of the others come back to pick something up. But so I ask him, 'Bobby, would you mind wearing a shirt with a collar today?' And he's like, 'What do you mean?' And I'm like, 'I'm just asking you, would you mind wearing a shirt with a collar today?'" Nelson touches his own collar. "And he's like, 'What are you talking about?' So I go, 'What size do you wear?' and he says, 'Extra large,' so I'm like, 'Good, I have one in my car. Let me get you a shirt.' So I run down to my car and take one of my shirts and give it to him.

"Of course, he was a little angry about that whole incident, and I understand him. He's the only kid I asked to dress up like that, and though I tried to make sure it wouldn't be like that, we ended up having that conversation in front of other people. But what can you do? You need to face the facts." He concludes by saying, "Let's just say we don't go out of our way to hire more black canvassers."

The basic idea behind this form of institutionalized racism is that contacts are more effective the more people have in common. (How one determines what counts as commonality is left vague, but race is by far the most frequent subject of conversation.) There has been only a limited amount of research on the importance of who the messenger is, and the findings remain mixed.[16] It seems that part of the importance lies in whether the encounters become interactions at all, especially at the door. Focus group research suggests that some people may be particularly unlikely to welcome a minority canvasser and that conversations across age, class, gender, and race boundaries may be more complicated than others.[17]

When interactions unfold beyond the initial steps of opening lines and voter reactions, contacts also communicate something else even more difficult to measure—both for social scientists and for political operatives evaluating their own efforts. Staffers talk about the importance of "enthusiasm" and "authenticity," characteristics they attribute to volunteers more than to part-timers. (Of course, the hospitality industry and others would probably argue that such characteristics, too, can be manufactured.) Experimental researchers have tried to get at this concept also, stressing the potential importance of hard-to-quantify variables like the "tone" of conversations, whether it is "boilerplate" or "chatty" and whether it is delivered by an engaged volunteer or a more detached paid person. Again, the evidence is somewhat mixed, with a provisional consensus that tightly scripted conversations generally seem less effective than those that are more free-flowing.[18] It seems plausible that a mutually satisfying interaction leaves a better impression with the voter than a stilted one in which the caller or canvasser sticks closely to the script and talking points. As with many forms of political communication, it is exceedingly difficult to identify the relative importance of different components in influencing voting behavior. What is clear is that personalized political communication cannot be reduced to the message (the script) or the medium (the fact that a person is conveying it), but involves an element of interaction realized only in actual encounters between callers or canvassers and the voters they talk to.

Despite this, campaign staffers in theory put considerable emphasis on message control. Individual staffers sometimes downplay this control when they are around volunteers and part-timers, but the official line is clear and focused on staying "on message." In practice, the perpetually overworked staffers rarely prioritize training and motivating the volunteer and part-time callers and canvassers. A quick pep talk now and then is usually what is on offer. The kind of ongoing quality control and coaching common in telemarketing, sales, and service work are entirely absent. Staffers' main efforts at maintaining control over the campaign message are the ubiquitous scripts and talking points that are handed to everyone, along with the introductory training sessions that some volunteers and almost all part-timers are asked to take part in. (In general, campaigns put little emphasis on training, but most people on payroll are put through at least a short orientation on voter contact.) A few training sessions last a couple of hours when a senior staffer or an outside field consultant takes the time to train new field organizers or a large group of paid part-timers. But the most common kind of training takes the form of a short informal session conducted in the campaign office, usually by a junior staffer and involving a couple of volunteers and/or part-timers. (Many volunteers are never trained but are just asked to read the script and talking points before they start making phone calls.) The training sessions are almost exclusively focused on the content of the script and the talking points, and despite the role-playing exercises involved, they bear little resemblance to actual encounters with voters.

EPISODE 3.11

Laura has agreed to help the canvassing director of the Jim Himes campaign by training two of his newly hired part-timers alongside two new volunteers she has signed up to phone bank from the office. She is one of the few field organizers who regularly try to train volunteers. Laura has let me sit in on the session provided I agree to play voter when we do the role-playing.

Lizzie and James have signed on to do some paid canvassing a few times a week for the campaign. Both are African American high school seniors from a nearby school. Barbara and Michelle, two white women in their fifties, are here to volunteer. Barbara is a local schoolteacher, Michelle is a housewife. Both say they have phone banked before. Michelle explains that her husband is an active member of the Communications Workers of America. "We always end up in some dingy office making calls before the election is over," she says.

Laura asks us to read the script and the talking points first. She returns a few minutes later and explains that she'll start by asking us a few questions to make sure we are "on message" and that we will then practice contacts through a role-playing exercise in which one person plays the voter.

She starts out by asking Lizzie, "What is Jim's position on the Iraq war?" There is a moment of silence. Lizzie looks down. Laura repeats the question: "What is Jim's position on the war?" Lizzie hesitates, then says, "I guess he is against it?" Laura points at the talking point outlining Himes's position in a paragraph and asks, "What does that mean more specifically?" Lizzie looks at the script and asks, "What does 'withdrawal' mean?" Laura pauses for a moment, then changes track. "Okay, do you know who Jim Himes is?" Lizzie says, "No." Laura sighs audibly. She then spends a few minutes outlining Himes's background, explaining that he is running for Congress, what that is and why it is important, and then asks Lizzie to make sure to read the script and the talking points again later, "and maybe look at the website too," and to come back if she has any questions. She looks at the rest of us and asks if there are any questions. There aren't.

We then start the role-playing. Laura asks Michelle if she is okay with the two of them doing one round in front of everyone else before we break out and practice in pairs. Michelle nods. Laura plays the canvasser, knocking on an imaginary door, and Michelle plays the voter, responding, "Yes?" "Hello, my name is Laura. I'm a volunteer with Jim Himes's campaign for Congress. Can I ask you, will you vote for the Democrat Jim Himes for Congress this fall?" Michelle says, "Yes!" The rest of us burst out laughing, and Laura blurts out, "You are supposed to act as if you are undecided!" They repeat the exercise, and this time Michelle says, "I don't know. Can you tell me a little bit more about him?" Laura delivers a few of the talking points, and Michelle says, "That sounds good. I think I'll vote for him." Laura turns to the rest of us and says, "What I want you to do is to work with this in pairs, alternating, so that all of you get to try out the script in practice. Those playing the voters should pretend they are undecided."

I play voter a couple of times to Barbara as the caller. Even though I follow Laura's instructions and act as an unusually patient and polite undecided voter, Barbara is visibly uncomfortable with the exercise, reading whole blocks from the script verbatim, stumbling over words, and sometimes starting over on whole paragraphs. She says, "This is a little stilted, isn't it?"

Role-playing sessions are almost entirely focused on memorization of scripts and talking points, and while they may familiarize callers and canvassers with the idea of having conversations with voters, they do little to prepare them for the actual interactions they will have. Virtually no voters are as docile as the people who play them in role-playing exercises. In the campaign offices, those who role-play abide by the generalized basic ritual respect for others that Goffman talks about, taking care not to challenge the roles they perform or their right to speak. But in conversations with voters, the tensions between the convention of privacy and the convention of public-ness cast the whole encounter in a different light.

Of course, formal training is not the only way people learn how to engage with voters. Volunteers and part-timers talk among themselves, sharing tips and offering advice. Some staffers play a willing part in these informal conversations, telling people to ignore the official instructions and formal training and "do whatever works for you." Jack, the volunteer coordinator in New Jersey, often repeated the line "It's ninety percent about being nice" when he introduced volunteers to phone banking. This is probably more precise than the official campaign line with its emphasis on message control, but the problem is that cold-calling total strangers to talk about politics is not a traditional part of "being nice."

It is worthwhile here to briefly compare how campaigns prepare people to engage in personalized political communication with how some businesses and civil society associations train people to mediate between these organizations and their target audiences. On the one hand, there are attempts by various companies in what Robin Leidner calls the "interactive service industries" to routinize encounters between employees and customers.[19] One approach is to script every element of the employee's behavior (standardized surface acting is common in, for instance, the retail or fast food industries). Another is a more fundamental attempt to shape an employee's very sense of self (instrumentally cultivated deep acting is used in direct sales in high-margin industries like insurance and pharmaceutical products). Many marketing researchers argue that standardization is rarely the most effective approach to interactions with customers but recognize that the high organizational overhead that comes with training and ongoing coaching may still make it efficient in labor-intensive, low-margin, high-volume businesses like McDonald's.[20] While there are affinities between the standardization approach used by the fast-food industry and how campaigns train volunteers and part-timers to talk to voters, it is notable that campaigns monitor and coach those involved to a much lesser extent than burger chains do, and that staffers have far less authority over those involved than a manager has over employees (as we shall see in the next chapter). One exasperated part-timer complained, "This is so poorly organized compared to my last job [at McDonald's]."

On the other hand, some civil society associations like religious and civil rights movements have tried to cultivate a systematic approach to personalized communication that is centered not on scripted routines but on individual narratives (of conversion, of becoming conscious of the grievance a certain movement is trying to address, etc.). There is a rich tradition of "practiced storytelling" in many movements of various sorts (often used for recruitment and for consciousness-raising). This approach was at least partially adopted by the 2008 Obama campaign, where training, at least in the so-called Camp Obama series, included exercises in which individual participants were encouraged to develop their own pitch based on the history of their own involvement in the campaign.[21] Seen in an instrumental light, such an approach is a clear example of systematic attempts to leverage the nonverbal dimensions of personalized communication to greater effect, sacrificing an element of message control to cultivate both people's experience of authenticity and enthusiasm and their ability to share it with voters.

In a sense what most campaigns seem to have is neither quite the scripted routines that interactive service organizations continually force upon their employees nor the individualized narratives of some social movements. Rather, there is an ongoing disjoint between the official demands that callers and canvassers "deliver the script" and then their de facto reliance on their own variable skills—whether one thinks of that as ethnomethodological competence, interpersonal intelligence, or a form of practical expertise—in talking to strangers and in creating a chance to make a case for their candidate, and to solicit at least a few useful responses to the various identification questions they are supposed to ask.

THE STRESS OF BEING A MEDIUM

Canvassing voters and working the phones is widely seen as stressful. Almost everyone seems to be in agreement on this. One staffer remarked, "Honestly, I hate making phone calls." Some volunteers, clearly anticipating what they will be asked to do, arrive at campaign offices announcing, "I don't do phones, and I don't do doors, but I'll do anything else I can to help." (This is quite a headache for staffers who need help with "doing" phones and doors more than they need help with anything else.) Other volunteers are more stoic: "I don't like this, but if that's what I can do to help, so be it." Part-timers voice their concerns too: "I don't know how long I can continue doing this" (a remarkable verdict on a part-time job that will last at most two months). During my fieldwork I have seen everyone from senior staffers supervising dedicated volunteers to the most conscientiously loyal part-timers shirk from the job at hand. Some people fake phone calls by punching in imaginary numbers and holding the receiver while the error message sounds at the other end. Dozens admitted in private conversations to not actually knocking doors they have walked up to and to sometimes fabricating response data about contacts that did not take place. No one stands by such behavior, but most of those who admitted to it explain it with reference to the wear and tear of seemingly endless numbers of often unpleasant conversations with voters. This is what most of those involved found most draining, uncomfortable, and ultimately stressful about personalized political communication. Not the hours spent on the phone or walking the streets, but the interactions themselves. (This helps explain why people strongly dislike productivity-enhancing technologies like auto-dialing systems for phone banking. Most people are reluctant to make calls for more than an hour or two at the normal rate of thirty or so calls an hour. Computerized systems can ramp that up to a hundred or more, making the work even more taxing.)

The stress that people feel surely has multiple roots. Some battle a sense of futility, despite staffers' protestations to the contrary: "Personal contacts have been shown to be one of the most effective ways of influencing voters!" As made clear, much research suggests that staffers are right, and yet people wonder, "Why are we doing this?" "Does this make any difference?" Brought up on mass-mediated politics, it may be counterintuitive even to the people involved that talking to people one at a time may actually add up in a demonstrably effective way. Others complain of the tedious work involved: "I'm soo bored. . . ." "One more phone call and I'm going to shoot myself!" And though the interactions with voters are rarely the same, the work of contacting them surely is repetitive and a long way from the drama some news coverage and fictionalized accounts suggest surrounds politics. As one college intern put it, "I didn't realize how much hard work goes into campaigns!"

But many things in life are potentially futile, somewhat tedious, and decidedly undramatic. I would suggest that the most important source of stress comes from the encounters themselves, from the serial interactions with voters. This is what the dramaturgical perspective adopted here helps elucidate. Personalized political communication involves someone putting himself on the line every time. For every one of the countless contacts recorded, someone has made a performance—and risked rejection, faced the challenge of negotiating between conflicting conventions with differing views of what ought to happen, and tried to represent herself in a manner that is personally satisfying, acceptable to the voter, and useful for the campaign. And almost everyone involved at this level recognizes how tricky the performance is. "I would hang up on myself too," says one volunteer, capturing the conflict between norms of privacy and norms of public-ness in one poignant and self-reflexive sentence. And yet most campaign workers insist on the basic ritual respect for other people that personalized political communication tries to leverage for the campaign's instrumental purposes. "People don't have to be so rude."

Different people feel the stress of being a medium to different degrees and in somewhat different ways. No clear distinctions can be made, but some broad differences are suggested. The volunteers who actually buckle up and keep on making calls and knocking on doors are often people who are particularly invested in the project of winning the election; they are also often people who hold a certain and highly normative understanding of what they are doing and what it means. They are not only partisans but *citizens*, and they think of what they are doing as something that is *good* (and not simply useful). They are particularly disappointed when voters blow them off: "Don't they realize how important this is? Don't they at least see why I'm doing this?" They—the voters—rarely do. These people are engaged in what Hochschild calls "deep acting" and identify strongly with the role they put forward in interactions. Many staffers feel like this too. Part-timers, on the other hand, are more likely to engage in "surface acting." "It's just a job" is a refrain I heard numerous times. No one likes being cut off or turned away, but a certain distance from what one is doing helps soften the blow. The particular problem that part-timers face is that they make more contacts than almost anyone else, and thus though many of them may feel the sting of each individual rejection or brisk modification less than particularly idealistic staffers and volunteers, they experience it more often. And their limited engagement can turn into outright detachment when confronted with the more unpleasant reactions: "I'm just not getting paid enough to deal with this."

Everyone involved is continually misrecognized when contacts go awry. People playing a role as a good citizen volunteering for a cause they believe in are brusquely asked to "tell your boss we don't want you to call here." Part-timers maintaining a certain distance from the campaign they work for are held personally accountable for their actions: "I can't believe you dare come and disturb me at home!" And voters who are probably just trying to uphold a right to privacy that they sincerely believe in are judged harshly by their spurned interlocutors: "What a fucking asshole!" (to take a line from one particularly incensed volunteer after a call was rejected in no uncertain terms).

The last quote is just one of many and often rather salty examples I have of the backstage venting of frustrations, out of earshot of voters. Some people fantasized about calling particularly rude voters back, one volunteer suggesting this as an opening question: "What the hell do you think you're doing, talking to me like that?" Off the phones and away from the doors, the polite use of "sir" and "ma'am" that dot interactions with voters is often replaced by far less respectful terms, of which "idiot" seems to be the most common and certainly the least offensive. Just as supermarket cashiers rarely hold customers in high regard because they see them at their worst, callers and canvassers often despair at the state, civic virtues, and manners of the American electorate. An additional significant example of such backstage venting is the frequent complaint among volunteers and part-timers about the staffers' apparent absence from the front line of the ground war. Volunteers would often grumble among themselves about this; in the words of one: "If this [making phone calls] is so important, why aren't *they* doing it?" A part-timer expressed a parallel sentiment: "Until I see them out here knocking on some fucking doors, I'm not going to take all their talk all that seriously." (Most junior staffers in fact make thousands of door knocks and phone calls themselves, but often in the summer, before volunteers start coming in significant numbers and before part-timers are recruited. When volunteers and part-timers start to get involved, the field organizers generally transition to a team leader role rather than doing canvassing and phone banking themselves.)

People deal with the ongoing wear and tear of the work in different ways, empathizing with voters to try to be understanding of their reactions, distancing themselves from the role that has been rejected, and generally abandoning stilted scripts in favor of their own social competence in attempts to navigate these interactions. The irony here is that many of the things that make a contact less frustrating for the caller or canvasser also in some ways make it less clearly useful for the campaign. An interaction that is either entirely detached or entirely relaxed is not well suited to deliver a scripted message or to gather the information that campaigns need for their targeting efforts. (However, such interactions might still increase turnout and/or support among targeted voters. As pointed out earlier, we do not know how important the actual substance of conversations is in producing the immediate effects of personalized political communication. The very turning up on someone's doorstep, the fact of the phone call, the impression it makes, the enthusiasm expressed—or not expressed—may say more than words.) Asked to describe what a "good contact" is like, staffers often underlined instrumental factors: "It's when we reach someone who might not vote otherwise. Or convince someone to vote for Jim. That's a good contact." But volunteers and part-timers put more emphasis on their own experience. "A good contact?" Janet, a volunteer, said, "It's when I get a chance to have a serious conversation with a reasonable person." "Reasonable person" here often means someone who agrees, not the most important targets from a staff point of view. Charlene's take is different. When I asked her to describe a good contact, she replied, "No drama, please. That's a good contact." This is the stance of most of the part-timers I spoke with.

* * *

In this chapter I have highlighted the interactions that are part and parcel of turning the millions of knocks and calls generated every election cycle into actual contacts that might move or mobilize people. It is difficult to convey at the same time the sheer number and repetitiveness of encounters with voters and how each one remains problematic, singular, in a sense a unique experience for the person mediating between the campaign assemblage and its targets. But it is necessary to understand this idea to realize both what it takes to put the "personalized" and the "communication" into personalized political communication and why those who do so find the work so stressful. This is what the dramaturgical perspective of Goffman, Hochschild, and Leidner helps us see, just as close attention to the details of actual encounters with voters shows why callers and canvassers systematically go off message. The element of interaction distinguishes personalized political communication from other forms of political communication, like television sports, online ads, and direct mail. Callers and canvassers carry with them scripts that are aligned with the overall campaign message and more or less (often less) "finely tuned" for persuasion, for getting out the vote, and for data-gathering purposes. But staffers are not in a position to tailor or customize the actual conversations to serve their own instrumental ends. Personalized political communication is entirely dependent on the ability of volunteers and part-timers to establish their roles as such and convey a message to—but also share their own convictions with—voters who have the upper hand in each encounter.

The instrumental impact of calls and knocks may well lie in their nature of live interactions, but this very same feature also presents control-oriented staffers with challenges distinct to the use of people as media. Herein lies both the power and the problems of personalized political communication. The numerous hours of hard work it takes and the stress that accompany it help explain why staffers cannot do it all themselves and why they rarely manage to mobilize enough volunteers to do it for them. This is part of the reason campaign assemblages have to involve a much wider set of elements, ranging from organized allies, to individual volunteers, to temporarily hired part-timers. The next chapter deals with how all of these people are organized. If personalized political communication were less important, less labor-intensive, and less stressful, it might be much simpler, something campaigns could pursue through the plug-and-play means that dominate some other areas of political communication (where campaigns can simply buy all they need) or leave for grassroots activists to play around with on their own (a quaint relic from yesteryears' elections). But it is not. Each encounter, each interaction, from a few seconds to sometimes long and wide-ranging conversations with voters, speaks to this fundamental fact.

CHAPTER 4

Organizing Campaign Assemblages

EPISODE 4.1

The campaign manager and the canvassing director are sipping beers late at night, watching a ballgame and talking about the field effort. "Like all campaigns," the campaign manager says, "this is in the end an enterprise run by two or three adults and a bunch of kids." He continues: "What you and I are doing is like industrial engineering. It's about keeping people in line and finding ways to contact more people in less time at a lower cost, whether that means covering more turf by finding better ways to walk the streets, ways of increasing the contact rate, or whatever it takes." The canvassing director nods, his eyes glued to the screen.

EPISODE 4.2

It's late Saturday night, three days until the election. I'm in the Bridgeport office when the field director arrives. As he walks in, he pulls off his headset and asks how things are going. The answer comes not from the young field organizer nominally responsible for the area but from a man I will call Jorge.

Technically, Jorge works for a local elected official and has no formal role in the campaign. But he has worked close to full time as a staffer to coordinate the ground effort in this crucial city for the last few days. He says, "Pretty good. The paid program is working, people show up, and we knock the doors and call through the universe afterward with them. The volunteer program has been doing okay, though it is not impressive." He adds, "I think AFSCME [American Federation of State County and Municipal Employees] will send some folks later."

The field director asks, "What about the locals?" Jorge says, "We're flying blind in [state senator] Ed [Gomes]'s district. We just have to trust that they are doing the work. [State Representative Andres] Ayala's people have been good. They are offering us help; they have already called through their lists so many times by now." Jorge asks the field director how the rest are doing. "The Norwalk paid canvass is doing okay," the director answers, "but there have been some problems with the volunteer operation. Apparently they've pissed off some African American community leader, so she got up and left and took fifteen people with her." Jorge says, "That's not cool." The field director responds, "They don't know what the fuck they are doing," puts his headset back on, and calls the Stamford office for an update.

EPISODE 4.3

This Sunday a volunteer canvass will be going door-to-door in Summit, New Jersey. The staging location is the home of a local city council candidate, Laura. In contrast to many of her peers, she has been working quite closely with the campaign staff. I arrive with Rick, who has taken a semester off from college to work as a field organizer for the coordinated campaign. He has put together ten walk packets for the day, each containing some Linda Stender flyers, a Stender script and some talking points, plus a walk sheet with the names and addresses of about fifty targeted voters. Laura is in the script, too, but she is number four, after Obama, Stender, and the county freeholder candidates, reflecting her low priority in the eyes of state party and campaign staffers.

Six people are waiting for us at the house. One is the local candidate herself. Four more, all in their forties or fifties, introduce themselves as her friends. Then there is Dave, a high school intern with the Stender campaign who has been commandeered to walk door-to-door with us today. Rick has the names of two Stender volunteers who are supposed to come. They never show.

The rest of us stand around and chat for about fifteen minutes while he is trying to get in touch with them. Then Laura finally loses her patience and announces, "Let's get going." Rick says, "Yeah, you're right." He begins to explain how we are supposed to use the scripts and walk lists that he has brought along. One of Laura's friends, a stately silver-haired man in his late fifties, cuts Rick off mid-sentence after less than a minute and says to the group, "You all know Laura and what she stands for. I want you to know that we have been well received over the past weekends. I expect the same today. Now let's go knock some doors." Laura nods, then thanks us for coming, and explains, "It was a close race last time. If we can get all the Democrats out this time, I think we can do it. I really appreciate your help."

After this the volunteers start picking up some additional literature about Laura to supplement the Stender material Rick has provided. People begin to leave. Rick raises his voice and says, as they walk out, "Yes, thank you everyone for helping out. This kind of work, volunteers hitting the streets, will be decisive in getting Linda elected." He starts to talk more about Stender's fund-raising advantage over her opponent but then interrupts himself, saying, "Oh, yeah, I should probably get everybody's cell number. Please, just call me if there is anything you need. And remember to return the [walk] sheets. They are important to us." By now, everyone but Laura, Dave, and I has left.

EPISODE 4.4

Lucia, a woman in her early forties, has been one of the most energetic volunteers on the Himes campaign. After she quit her job in corporate marketing and set up her own business a few years ago, she found herself with "a lot of time on [her] hands." Initially she got involved in the campaign because she liked Obama. But she ended up helping with the congressional campaign instead, because it was "more fun." "There is more going on," she explains.

As we drive to an evening event in Stamford, she says, "I get the sense that this is really badly organized. It's so old-fashioned, I mean, if you compare it to my old job." She complains about the internal "maneuvering" and adds that the main office in Bridgeport is unresponsive, unhelpful, and uninterested in helping out in the town where she lives. She says, "That's why I'm happy I'm a volunteer. I can do what I want and then leave when they [the staffers] start fighting." She complains, "There are so many egos in politics, and you have to stroke each and every one of them." She laughs.

I ask her for an example, and she says, "There is this woman who is supposedly running the ward where I live for the [Democratic] Town Committee. She's like—what is it they call it?—a district leader? And she doesn't get much done. And I think she's afraid of me, because I do. So I organized a voter registration drive downtown, and we registered thirty-eight new people in two hours. And I didn't tell her, so she complains to the Himes campaign and the town chair, and then the Himes people are like, 'we are a campaign, we don't do voter registration,' and they start trying to boss me around. But I don't like making those calls and knocking those doors for them. They can do that shit themselves, you know what I mean? I want to do something special. I want to be the cherry on the top."

EPISODE 4.5

"Sometimes you do wonder," Donald says, "do they even know what's going on?" A man in his early fifties, with a graduate degree and experience in management consulting, he has an unusual—though by no means unique—background for a part-timer, knocking on doors six days a week for ten dollars an hour. "I'm just trying to make rent," he says by way of explanation as to why he is here. He adds that he is still looking for new jobs in the consultancy world, where he has worked as a freelancer for about twenty years. "It's difficult right now. I'm glad my wife has a job."

I ask Donald about his sense of the campaign organization, and his response is as swift as it is clear, delivered without hesitation: "Anarchy." He pauses for dramatic effect and then continues: "A lot of kids running something they can't control." I ask him for an example. "Look, when I applied for this job, I called them, spoke to one person, never heard anything, called back, left a couple of messages, and got a sense that the guy was almost trying to avoid me. Then I learned someone else was in charge of the canvassing and called her, and then it was suddenly someone else, and I finally got a hold of him."

Asked if this is perhaps just one incident or whether he can think of other examples, he says, "How much time do you have? I realize I see this from the floor up, but sometimes I wonder, is there a plan? What is it? Do they know what they are doing? Do they evaluate and learn from their mistakes? That's not clear to me." I press him for concrete details, and he says, "In most jobs I've worked in, management is aiming at consistency and structure. But here we improvise. Oh, boy, do we improvise. What is the candidate's position on abortion? Nobody knows, so we'll make something up. Where does the candidate stand on the bailout package? Nobody knows; there we go again. What does the candidate think of same-sex marriage? Nobody knows. And we are out knocking on doors every day, talking to voters, and we need answers, and we don't get them, nor briefings, and only very little training. It does not strike me as very professional."

Contacting hundreds of thousands of voters in person involves thousands of hours of work by hundreds of people. A few work full time as campaign staffers, others are mobilized via allied organizations, and many join as individual volunteers or paid part-timers. All of these people want to win. But they rarely agree on how to win, who should do what to win, or even on why winning is important. Elections are curious affairs, ambiguous—they mean all things to all people—and yet they are clear in their deadlines, mechanics, and mathematics. You win or lose on the first Tuesday of November, in a given district, by getting (or not getting) at least one more vote than your opponent. It is that simple—and yet so complex. Candidates, party officials, and people from various allies have additional aspirations and are sometimes at odds, just as the staffers, volunteers, and part-timers involved in the ground war are after goals other than victory: they want to pursue a career, be part of something meaningful that might make a difference, they want to make a living—and sometimes all three at once. As a consequence of the combination of elements enrolled, campaign assemblages are deeply heterogeneous.

This diversity is both an asset and a liability. It is an asset in competitive races because diversity is a necessary outcome of the mobilization of the allies, volunteers, and part-timers who do most of the work involved in contacting voters at home and over the phone. Without these people and their time and effort, the staffers running the campaign organizations at the core of each campaign assemblage would fall far short of having the resources required for an effective field effort. (Even extraordinarily wealthy candidates like New York City mayor Michael Bloomberg or New Jersey governor Jon Corzine and phenomenally successful fund-raisers like George W. Bush or Barack Obama have relied heavily on allies, volunteers, and part-timers for personalized political communication.) But diversity is also a liability, because it entails friction as different elements of the campaign pull in different directions and spend valuable time searching for ways to work together. In this chapter I analyze how the diverse elements enrolled in campaign assemblages organize their pursuit of the shared ground war project. I argue that to understand this, we need to distinguish analytically between (1) the hierarchical campaign organization that staffers populate, (2) the wider network of allies involved in the assemblage, and (3) the ambiguous relations that exist at the interface between the staffers and the volunteers and part-timers who are mobilized to serve as media for personalized political communication. Analysis of these three facets shows how campaigns operate at numerous fractious intersections: between old hierarchical forms of campaign organizing and campaign practices premised on new technologically assisted forms of popular involvement; between temporary entities and permanent players; between national and local organizations; and between self-avowed professional operatives with a vocational interest in politics and the civically motivated volunteers and financially motivated part-timers with whom they work. Field campaigns in competitive districts are neither the kind of "grassroots politics" that some romantics long for nor the thoroughly professionalized operations that some other parts of politics are. Even in well-funded races for federal office, the ground war is pursued in practice by a highly heterogeneous set of actors working in (sometimes tenuous) concert, dominated by no single set of actors or one mode of operation, but deeply dependent on the many different elements involved. The analytical distinction between campaign *organizations* and wider campaign *assemblages* serves to capture these dynamics.

CAMPAIGN ORGANIZATIONS AND CAMPAIGN ASSEMBLAGES

The social sciences have produced a rich literature on organizations and how they work, in politics and elsewhere. A classic view, in sociology associated with Max Weber and in political science with his student Robert Michels, conceives of organizations theoretically as entities operating as means to an end.[1] The paradigmatic example of this "logic of efficacy" is the ideal-typical bureaucracy or assembly-line factory, a distinct unit characterized by clear hierarchy, impersonal rules, and a permanent division of labor. In government such organizations supposedly ensure efficient administration and delivery of services; in business they organize cost-effective mass production. More recent work has problematized both the notion that organizations can be understood theoretically simply as more or less effective tools and the idea that, empirically speaking, bureaucratic organizations are the dominant form. A number of theorists have highlighted how organizations embody not only a logic of efficiency but also multiple "logics of appropriateness," shaped as they are by inherited norms, legitimized repertoires, and normalized technologies and tools.[2] Empirical analyses have identified a number of organizational forms beyond the classic bureaucracy or assembly line, mixing or replacing hierarchy, rules, and the division of labor with other traits and operating as "network enterprises."[3] In some cases these developments go hand in hand with exciting new opportunities and what have been called "flexible specialization."[4] In others new organizational forms have been paired with widespread de-skilling and increasingly precarious employment—as in the service and retail industries.[5]

Campaign organizations can be thought of as distinct entities organized along these lines, with some bureaucratic traits and shaped by both the explicit aim of efficacy and the implicit reliance on routines. They are made up of those who work full time—for pay or other reasons—for a given candidate. In the last several decades the number of full-time staffers involved in campaign organizations has increased, as has the use of outside consultants for specialized services in areas like direct mail, polling, and media buys.[6] This, and the gradual general import of techniques and technologies from the corporate world, has led many to conclude that American politics has become "professionalized."[7] But, as I have made clear from the outset, campaigns should not be reduced to campaign organizations or the handful of consultants with whom they contract. Just as some sociologists talk about how "meta-corporations" go beyond the individual firm, political scientists maintain a distinction between "party networks" and individual party organizations, and social movement scholars distinguish between broader social movements and more concrete social movement organizations,[8] we should think of elections as involving wider campaign assemblages of heterogeneous elements engaged in concerted action. Campaign organizations are at the core of these; they are distinct entities defined by a boundary between inside and outside, a line that is clear to those within, and one that can be observed by researchers. They are what staffers usually talk about when they talk about "the campaign," and they are often at the crux of the less labor-intensive and more capital-intensive air wars and mail efforts.

But they are only one part of the field effort. As Election Day approaches, wider *campaign assemblages* are put together, collections of elements that are less clear-cut than the campaign organizations themselves. Analytically, I define campaign assemblages as those involved at any given point in time in the shared project of winning a particular district. They encompass what allies, volunteers, and part-timers usually mean when they talk about "the campaign" (many of these refer to the campaign organizations in a more specific way, such as "the Himes people," "the Stender office," "the coordinated campaign," and so on). Campaign assemblages include the campaign organizations but go beyond them in two ways. First, they include a wider network of allies, many of whom, most notably party organizations and interest groups, are *themselves* distinct organizations—more or less bureaucratic—and only get involved in the electoral project in a partial way and on a temporary basis. Second, campaign assemblages include communities of individual volunteers and part-timers who join the campaign but are not fully integrated into the campaign organization. The field operation, the time-consuming and complicated process of contacting large numbers of voters at home one at a time, would not be possible without the help of allies, volunteers, and part-timers.

Figure 4.1 offers a schematic illustration of what were some of the most important elements of the campaign assemblage in Connecticut's 4th district in October. In the center is the hierarchical campaign organization, around it the network of allies (and consultants involved on a market basis), and partially overlapping with it are the two communities of volunteers and part-timers (which are not entirely distinct, since people sometimes migrate from one to the other, usually from volunteering to working part-time). Campaign assemblages are organized in a contingent, modular, and dynamic fashion, so they evolve over time as more elements are enrolled (and a few fall away). The campaign is not the same in May or August as it is in October. In analyzing the three highlighted facets of how they are organized, I rely on the extensive existing literature that deals with some of the different elements involved (campaign organizations, parties, interest groups, activists, etc.). But my primary focus here is on how those involved organize their interactions, the "dance" between them that my participant-observation gives me unique ethnographic data on and that political scientists have noted is rarely studied.[9]

To understand how these different elements pursue their common project, I draw on a somewhat stylized set of distinctions between distinct forms of organizing, developed by the sociologist Walter W. Powell.[10] He argues that one can distinguish between hierarchies, networks, and markets as different ways of organizing action in concert.[11] I use his typology here to formalize some of the differences between the campaign organization; the network of allies around it; and the interface between staffers, volunteers, and part-timers. According to Powell, relations between elements that are dependent on one another and that coordinate through structures of authority can be described as organized by a *hierarchy*. As long as they are in place, hierarchical relations are typically characterized by their reliability and the ability to hold people accountable for their actions. I do what you say, because you are my boss. When action is organized in a hierarchical fashion, friction typically takes the form of inactivity or outright disobedience. The internal workings of both campaign organizations and many of their allies can be seen as predominantly hierarchical. Relations between elements that are interdependent and coordinate through negotiation and exchange Powell describes as being organized in a *network*. I do this, and you do that, because we have come to agree that we have a shared interest in it. Networks are

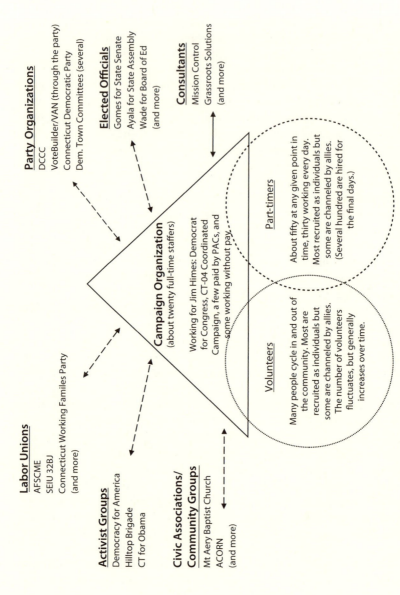

Labor Unions
AFSCME
SEIU 32BJ
Connecticut Working Families Party
(and more)

Activist Groups
Democracy for America
Hilltop Brigade
CT for Obama

Civic Associations/ Community Groups
Mt Aery Baptist Church
ACORN
(and more)

Party Organizations
DCCC
VoteBuilder/VAN (through the party)
Connecticut Democratic Party
Dem. Town Committees (several)

Elected Officials
Gomes for State Senate
Ayala for State Assembly
Wade for Board of Ed
(and more)

Consultants
Mission Control
Grassroots Solutions
(and more)

Campaign Organization
(about twenty full-time staffers)

Working for Jim Himes: Democrat for Congress, CT-04 Coordinated Campaign, a few paid by PACs, and some working without pay.

Part-timers

About fifty at any given point in time, thirty working every day. Most recruited as individuals but some are channeled by allies. (Several hundred are hired for the final days.)

Volunteers

Many people cycle in and out of the community. Most are recruited as individuals but some are channeled by allies. The number of volunteers fluctuates, but generally increases over time.

Figure 4.1. Schematic illustration of the campaign assemblage in Connecticut's 4th district in October.

generally fairly flexible, facilitate the exchange of intangible assets, and over time may lead to the development of some level of trust and shared supplemental identity (such as "the Democratic coalition," which, at least at election time, routinely includes many otherwise disparate interest groups). In networks friction often takes the form of more or less willful misunderstandings or the waste of time associated with fruitless or even insincere negotiations. In campaigns the relations between the campaign organization and its allies are, broadly speaking, network relations, as are, in a more ambiguous sense, the relations between staffers and volunteers. Finally, relations between elements that are independent of one another and that coordinate through prices paid for services rendered can be described as organized by a *market*. I do what we have agreed I will, because you pay me for it (and anything else will cost you extra). As long as supply and demand exists, Powell suggests, such relations are characterized by their high flexibility and a low level of mutual commitment and organizational overhead. (Importantly, there are things that you cannot buy, such as volunteers.) Friction here typically takes the form of disagreement over specifications of what exactly has been sold and bought. In elections consultant services are the clearest examples of market organizing, but, in a more ambiguous way, part-timers are tied into the assemblage in such a fashion too.

These different forms of organizing are ideal types, and categorization alone is no substitute for analysis. But the typology is useful here because it helps sort out the diversity at hand—through Powell's lens, campaigns can be recognized as assemblages where very different forms of organizing intersect and where disparate elements coexist and act in concert even as conflict and confusion abound. The campaign manager quoted in episode 4.1 is above the canvassing director in a hierarchy, but the relations between the campaign organizations built around Jim Himes and the various allies mentioned in episode 4.2 (local elected officials, labor unions, and community groups) are based on negotiation and often exchange, and volunteers like those in Summit in episode 4.3 and Lucia in episode 4.4, and part-timers like Donald in episode 4.5, have more ambivalent relations to the staffers than the opening quip about "industrial engineering" suggests.

In the next part of this chapter I examine the campaign organizations at the core of each assemblage, the compound entities that the staffers work for. I identify their hierarchical character, temporary nature, and the homogenous professional identity cultivated in them as their key traits. Then I inspect the relations between this core and the network of allies around it, paying particular attention to efforts to organize all major Democratic Party efforts in a given district. In contrast to the clearly demarcated campaign organization, the allies around it constitute a negotiated network of elements that have recurrent interactions with one another, and where a heterogeneous form of professionalism reigns. Finally, I scrutinize the interface between the staffers in the campaign organization and the communities of volunteers and part-timers who they work with to make the actual phone calls and door knocks for the assemblage. This setting is characterized by ambivalent relations between the communities involved, relations that are individually established and embrace very different communities.

THE CAMPAIGN ORGANIZATION

At the core of every campaign assemblage is a campaign organization. Sometimes it is identical to a given candidate's own paid campaign staff, but in competitive elections like in Connecticut's 4th congressional district and New Jersey's 7th congressional district, where I did my research, it is a compound of several elements. It includes both different formal entities with their own, legally separate, staff, and people working full time as staffers but informally and without pay. The campaign organization built around Jim Himes, for example, included not only the staffers working for the entity called Jim Himes: Democrat for Congress, but also those employed by the CT-04 Coordinated Campaign (the party's electoral effort in the district, co-funded by the Himes campaign, the state party, some local candidates, and the DCCC) and several people working full time as staffers without being on payroll (building their resume, angling for a job, trying something new). Additional staffers joined the campaign organization very late, on official or unofficial leave from jobs elsewhere, typically from allies like Democratic Party organizations or friendly elected officials. Staffers frequently and easily move from one position to another within the organization, being informally on board one month, employed by the candidate the next, then on the party's payroll, and so on. As one staffer remarked, "The distinction between the [candidate] campaign and the coordinated campaign matters more to the lawyers than it does to us." What are quite different formal entities from a compliance and fund-raising perspective are often informally interwoven on the ground.

Irrespective of the details of their employment, all the people in the campaign organization are staffers, parts of one community with a hierarchy that spans the various legal entities involved, shares a set of formal and informal rules, and is arranged around a single division of labor. The different entities involved are formed to supplement each other, and field in particular is often left mostly to the coordinated campaign in competitive races. The campaign organization built around the candidate for the top contested office in a given area is usually the most fully articulated and the one that the coordinated campaign is primarily meant to help. A down-ballot campaign may not have a field staff at all if an up-ballot campaign has a particularly strong ground operation in place. (In 2008 many Democratic candidates for Congress running in battleground states did not need to worry about getting out the vote, on account of the Obama campaign's impressive field program.) In a few cases candidate fund-raising may be so sluggish that other entities with an interest in the race actually make up most of the campaign organization itself. (In recent years the national parties and campaign committees have played an increasingly active and hands-on role in many congressional and down-ballot elections.[12])

There is a clear boundary between the campaign organization (compounded and complicated as it sometimes is) and the rest of the campaign assemblage. Allies are not part of the campaign organization, neither are volunteers or part-timers. A snapshot of a campaign organization in the fall of an election year looks like an efficiency-oriented Weberian bureaucracy in several ways, organized as it is in what Powell would characterize as a hierarchical fashion and in full pursuit of the shared goal of victory. (Campaigns seem largely untouched by broader movements toward network organizing, project-based teamwork, and flexible specialization, although more technical functions like direct mail, polling, media buys, and targeting are generally outsourced to consultants.) The inner workings of campaign organizations are important to understand because they command substantial resources of their own (often millions of dollars in competitive races for federal or statewide office); because they constitute the core of the wider assemblage, a hub to which all allies and others relate; and finally because they are where the staffers' professional identity is cultivated, their community of practice defined. I discuss three key traits of campaign organizations here—namely, their *hierarchical character*, their *temporary nature*, and the *homogenous professional identity* cultivated within them.

Each campaign organization is arranged as a hierarchy. The campaign manager is in charge, the next level is made up of directors (finance director, field director, communications director or campaign spokesperson, etc.), and under them are intermediary and junior staffers. (Figure 4.2 shows the organization chart for the field effort in Connecticut's 4th congressional district. Notice that the volunteers who made most of the phone calls and knocked on tens of thousands of doors were not considered part of the campaign organization. I will return to the fact that part-timers were included [the boxes marked "canvasser."]) When fully articulated in the fall, both the Connecticut and New Jersey campaign organizations involved around twenty full-time staffers (some paid by the candidate, some by party organizations or political action committees, and some unpaid). More than half of these people worked in field, the rest in finance, scheduling, and communications. Authority was centralized at the top, with, as the campaign manager quoted in episode 4.1 suggests, "two or three adults" in charge. Staffers older than thirty were few and far between. As previously noted, hierarchical authority in campaign organizations is not always obeyed—there is certainly no shortage of subordinates stonewalling or scheming against their superiors—but formally a chain of command is in place. While it was rarely put so bluntly in my experience, this reality shines through the frequent hazy talk of everyone being "on the same team," as junior staffers complain that they do not feel authorized to make even the most banal decisions. I witnessed field organizers calling their field or canvassing directors or even the campaign manager to ask whether they could spend twenty dollars on pizza for volunteers, and sometimes they were close to paralysis because they were "waiting for orders." Both senior and junior staffers recognize that the hierarchical structure is inflexible. But as one field director explains, the flip side is "that we can keep everything under control and get some stuff done."

"Control" and "productivity" are keywords that the senior staffers who run campaign organizations repeat endlessly. Control is understood as the authority to define the division of labor and as message control—over what, when, and how the campaign communicates with voters. (Chapter 3 has already dealt with some of the difficulties that staffers confront when it comes to people going "off message" in interactions with voters.) Productivity is understood exclusively in terms of quantity, meaning the number of phone calls and door knocks made. From a senior staff point of view, an efficient campaign organization is one that works along the lines of a Weberian bureaucracy and Powell's stylized hierarchy, where a clear chain of command and a functional division of labor allow for reliable, routinized, effective mass production.[13] Here is how one field director explains the setup—sometimes described as "the playbook"—in a language reminiscent of that used by the campaign manager quoted in episode 4.1:

EPISODE 4.6
John and I are talking about his work as we drive back to the campaign office after a rally in front of a local cable channel hosting a candidate forum. He says, "What a lot of the kids who join campaigns don't realize is that this is not like on TV. Most of what we do is intensely practical and essentially logistical. This is not *The West Wing*. That's the first thing they have to understand. It's about wanting to hit *these* [he slams his fist on the steering wheel to mark the cadence] thirty thousand doors over *these* three weekends with *this* message." He continues: "Some of the field organizers have been making fun of me when

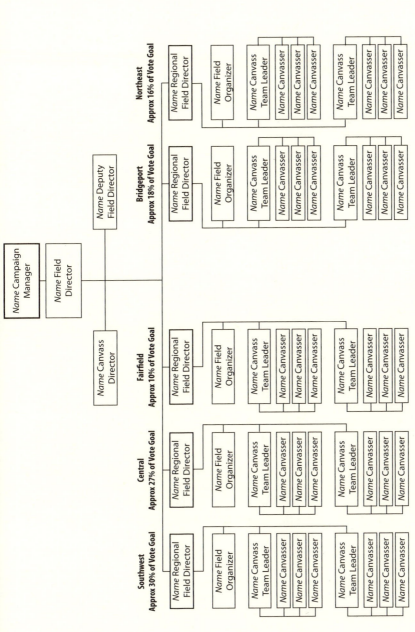

Figure 4.2. Organization chart for the field program in Connecticut's 4th district.
Three things stand out: (1) the clear hierarchy, (2) the absence of distinctions between staffers paid by the candidate campaign and staffers paid by the coordinated campaign (legally separate entities), and (3) the inclusion of the part-timers—but not volunteers—in the chart.

I say that; they think I'm not working myself. What they don't understand is that *my* job [the wheel takes another thumping] is making sure that everybody else is doing *their* job."

I ask him how he keeps track of that, and he says, "I try to focus on the metrics. Are we getting the IDs we need, making enough calls, knocking enough doors—you know, are we on track? Field has really expanded so much, become so labor intensive, there is so much going on. We are trying to hit really big universes these days, so you have to keep track of everything. You can't just hope for the best or do it in the last minute. You have to plan months in advance, backward from Election Day, and keep tabs on everything. Okay, this is our vote goal, this will be our GOTV universe, this will be our persuasion universe, this is how many times we want to hit them, this is how many calls and knocks we need to make." He opens the window and lights a cigarette. Then he says, "So I don't want people who want to be speechwriters and what have you. I want people who can work."

The "people who can work" are the field organizers, junior staffers who make up most of the full-time personnel by the end of election. They are at the bottom of the campaign organization's hierarchy, expected to do what they are told, to accept their role and stick to the tasks assigned. Field directors like John prefer hierarchical organizing because they think it works (in terms of control and productivity), because it is "how these things are done" (it is what their colleagues and allies consider appropriate), and because it is unclear what the alternative is—and an election is no time to experiment. The consequence is a concentration of authority and expertise in the hands of the few senior staffers (and outside consultants), while the junior staffers are left with the important but undistinguished work of contacting voters, mobilizing people for phone banking, and organizing canvassing teams. Most come to it with different expectations (hence the aside in episode 4.5: "This is not like on TV."), little experience, and will work pretty much nonstop on this for a couple of months without much in terms of systematic training.

Campaign organizations are temporary entities, and this permeates everything that is done. It makes them different from many other organizations, bureaucratic or not. Months in advance, staffers keep track of exactly how many days are left until Election Day. Calendars, timelines, and timely reminders are everywhere in the campaign offices. A central idea in the social science literature is that most organizations are primarily oriented toward their own survival and only secondarily toward their professed purpose.[14] Campaign organizations, however, have a final deadline that is as clear and ever-present as the goal: "We are here to win on November 4th." After that, it's over.

The temporary character helps explain why senior staffers construe control and productivity very narrowly and make basically no investments in organizational and technological infrastructure or human capital. They will arrive in a district and work with what is at hand. When staffers engage in what they themselves sometimes disparagingly call "electoral strip mining," it is not because they *think* it works, it is because of *where* they work. As they struggle to mobilize the allies, volunteers, and part-timers they need for their field program, campaign operatives themselves complain that *someone* ought to engage in "base building," but they do not see this as their job. As one campaign manager explained, "It's unreasonable to ask us to do the party's work." (Confronted with the quote, the executive director of a state party retorted, "Right now they want our money for canvassers, mail, and whatnot; two years from now they will complain we didn't spend it on organizing. You can't have it both ways.")

Just as temporary campaign organizations do not prioritize base-building, they are not particularly focused on human resources. "I'm not a big fan of [training]," says one field director, and continues: "We obviously did have some orientation initially, but again, it's not rocket science. It's common sense. It's a waste of valuable time to have daylong seminars talking about common sense." His colleague in the other campaign supports the point: "Everybody can do ninety percent of what [field organizers] do. The rest is on a need-to-know basis. They just have to ask." Of course, junior staffers rarely ask—and rarely have an opportunity to in their busy everyday work life. In the absence of systematic training (something many field organizers express a desire for), and with little information filtering down to them, junior staffers try to divine the meaning of their work from the orders they receive, experiment on their own to find ways of working that actually get results, and rely on informal learning through the rich oral tradition of campaign lore kept alive over pizza and beer late at night. Campaigning is something staffers learn about in practice, on the job, or as in an old-fashioned apprenticeship. It is a form of training that many recent college graduates have a hard time appreciating, and it is not one commonly associated with professionalization.

But those who are serious about pursuing a career working in politics will have to learn to live with this—and something else that also flows from the temporary character of campaign organizations: the knowledge that their current job will last only a few months. From their first day on the campaign, staffers talked about where their position fits in their own personal trajectory. For junior staffers it is often a first step toward a career working in politics or something they wanted to try before going to graduate school. For more intermediary or senior staffers a campaign job is ideally a step up the ladder or toward something else—jobs with allies, consultants, or perhaps on the candidate's legislative or district staff should he or she win.

This communal eye toward the future is just one part of the homogenous professional identity cultivated in campaign organizations. Politics is not the domain of a profession in the sense that medicine or the law is, but campaign organizations are dominated by staffers who are professionals in a broader sense of the word: white-collar employees who want to pursue a career, who share an occupational identity and a set of values, and who claim a set of at least partially distinct competences. Campaign staffers, political consultants, and policy aides all identify as parts of this larger group, even though many do not remain in it for life. (Campaign work in particular is stressful, demanding, and, for most involved, not particularly well paid. A field organizer typically makes about two thousand dollars a month while putting in sixty to seventy hours and sometimes more—effectively working for a lower hourly wage than the part-timers.)

The professional identity that staffers claim for themselves is partially defined in contrast to the volunteers and part-timers involved. "I may look young to them," says a twenty-eight-year-old canvassing director, "but I've worked on campaigns for three years now. I'm not a weekend warrior. I'm a professional." This identity is not so much tied to specialized expertise as it is tied to people's position in the campaign organization. Staffers with only a few weeks of experience maintain the same strong (or even stronger) distinctions between themselves and others as grizzled veterans do, and their interactions with others often reflect the sense that they are just *different*. Despite the senior staffers' view that most people can do most of what the field organizers do—even volunteers who have been involved in dozens of campaigns, or part-timers who have canvassed several cycles in a row are considered different—they are not *professionals*. The rapid development of a professional identity is particularly striking when followed in real time as junior staffers are hired over the summer. Rick, who appears in episode 4.3, was initially a summer intern. He spent much time in the office talking about policy, current affairs, and political history with anyone who cared to discuss such topics. From the moment he was hired as a field organizer, his whole office persona changed. He adopted the staff jargon of "bodies," "calls," and "knocks," and abbreviations like "GOTV," "D-trip," "VAN," and the like; stopped socializing beyond the staff community; and proudly proclaimed to me after a few weeks, "I'm a professional campaigner now." And he was, in the sense the word "professional" has among staffers, a young member of their close-knit community of what in the more male-bonding-inspired moments is called "brotherly love."[15]

The professional identity cultivated in campaign organizations not only distinguishes the staffers from others in the assemblage but is also used to explain the motivations and importance of what they do. Career concerns are not alone here. Staffers extol the "kick" they get out of their work and the opportunity to "make a difference" (what social scientists sometimes call "intrinsic" and "purposive" incentives). Most are college-educated and could probably find better-paying and less time-consuming jobs elsewhere, but politics is their *vocation*; it is not just another job. Even after just a few weeks on the campaign—well before they had tried either winning or losing—junior staffers like Rick would repeat the common claim that "there are no highs as high as winning a campaign and no lows as low as losing." All the staffers I met were highly partisan; even the most cynical ones expressed an often profound distaste for all things Republican. They also all believed that their work made a difference, that victory matters, and that their work could help bring it about (I agree that it does). All senior staffers have stories to tell about candidates who lost narrowly but would have won with a better field operation (or fund-raising, or advertisements, etc., depending on who you talk to). Most everyone recognizes intellectually that the vast majority of American elections are decided by districting, demographics, and events well beyond the control of any one campaign, but in competitive elections like those I followed, races that are pronounced "winnable," calling them that means staffers think *they* can win by doing a good job.

Field organizers find themselves in a curious position when it comes to their professional identity. They are at the bottom of the staff hierarchy (and are sometimes jokingly referred to as "field rats" or "field scum"). They operate at the boundary that marks the campaign organization as distinct from the wider assemblage, in frequent interaction with people who are crucial for its failure or success, but not part of it, and not beholden to the instrumental perspective that dominates it. Not only does most of their own work—menial stuff like assembling walk packets, driving people to and fro, entering data—sometimes jar with their self-conception as professionals (though some do take a special pride in their willingness to do the "dirty work" that no one else wants). The problem is, as one field organizer put it, that "field doesn't lead anywhere." For most, it is more like an entry ticket or a rite of passage, after which a real career can start. Many of the people they interact with in the course of field organizing also directly or indirectly challenge their professional identity. A twenty-two-year-old who has gone straight from college to a job knocking on doors all day might not strike an experienced union organizer or a fifty-year-old volunteer with an advanced graduate degree and several elections under her belt as the epitome of a "professional," or even someone in a position of authority, hierarchical or otherwise.

THE NETWORK OF ALLIES

Within the campaign organization itself, orders are given and followed on the basis of who gives them. Outside the organization things function differently. Even as many of the most important allies, from party organizations over labor unions to politically involved congregations, are themselves at least partially hierarchically organized; their involvement in the assemblage and the commitment to the electoral project that defines it are subject to ongoing negotiation rather than clear-cut control.

The network of allies that form around a campaign organization is uneven and often discontinuous—parts of the labor movement here, a cluster of activist groups there, a civic association elsewhere. Figure 4.1 shows a selection of the many that were active in the summer and fall in Connecticut's 4th congressional district, including party organizations (ranging from the DCCC in Washington, D.C., to the Connecticut Democratic Party in Hartford, to several Democratic Town Committees) and elected officials (from the state and local level; e.g., Gomes for State Senate, Wade for Board of Education). As the extensive literature on the participation of interest groups, civic associations, and activists in electoral politics suggests, they get involved for mixed reasons ranging from the almost purely ideological to the most clearly interest-based.[16] Many of these elements have nothing in common but an abstract political affinity and the concrete project at hand. My focus here is not their separate electoral activities or their reasons for getting involved, but how the work they do with the campaign organization itself is organized.

A number of potential allies choose not to enroll in the assemblage but instead do nothing or perhaps pursue their own separate electoral programs. Staffers are highly critical of independent efforts, especially on the ground. One describes the efforts of the Internet-assisted progressive activist group MoveOn in terms parallel to those others used to describe independent efforts by labor unions or other sometimes allies:

EPISODE 4.7

"It is really annoying when people start building these parallel structures. During the [Ned] Lamont campaign MoveOn did their own thing, and people would go to their events, their phone banks, and be like, 'Hey, I'm helping Ned.' And I'm like, 'No, you are not.'" The campaign manager and I are on the highway on our way to the train station—I'm heading back to New York tonight.

"The problem was that the MoveOn effort was badly coordinated, poorly targeted, a bad use of people's time. They were getting the word out, but the word was already out, and all that Lamont needed was GOTV, which requires coordination of a kind that MoveOn didn't engage in. They, or these people, should have been working with us.

"Shit, I think we missed the exit," she says. We get off the highway at the next stop and start driving back. "Anyway, all this parallel stuff, it isn't helping. It just creates confusion, and people get fed up with getting all these calls. Of course, people are free to do what they like. But let's not kid ourselves. It doesn't work. If we want to win, we have to work together."

Independent efforts challenge the campaign organization's control over contacts, undermine their mobilizing work, and complicate organizing, without accomplishing very much that seems useful from the staffers' instrumental point of view. As far as they are concerned, other entities can do their own thing, but they should not be allowed to believe that it makes much of a difference. Orchestrating the field effort is particularly important to minimize duplication and maximize impact, to avoid a situation where every entity involved focuses its attention on the same limited number of identifiable swing voters and infrequently voting partisans—resulting in door knock after door knock, call after call to people who may not be all that keen on being bombarded, even as thousands of other voters are never contacted at all.

Each aspect of the network through which the campaign organization and its allies coordinate their work would be worth a detailed analysis in its own right (relations between the campaign and the unions, the campaign and progressive activists, etc.), but my focus here is on the parts of it where the political affinities and commonalities of interest appear strongest: between the campaign organizations and the various Democratic party organizations and elected officials that get involved. This particular facet of the wider network illustrates that even where campaigns and their allies seem most closely aligned and alike, involvement is open-ended and based on ongoing negotiations. While different in the details, this is even more the case for other allies', like unions or activists groups, and their involvement. Even among the party entities in a given district, some will choose not to get involved in the campaign assemblage. (A local candidate might worry that the congressional candidate's profile will hurt his chances in a district with a more or less partisan leaning; a particular town committee harbors a grudge or feels the candidate has nothing to offer them; and so on.) While attempts to orchestrate the efforts of most party entities are like campaign organizations in that they operate in the shadow of the party hierarchy, start anew every cycle, and are dominated by self-professed political professionals, they operate in very different ways. Even among party elements, where the network of allies looks most like the campaign organization, relations between the campaign organization and allies are akin to what Powell calls *network relations* and are characterized in particular by *ongoing negotiations*, their *recurrent nature*, and a *heterogeneous form of professionalism*.

All allies enrolled in the campaign assemblage recognize the shared project of the election, but everything else is subject to ongoing negotiations. Basically, the question is, what will they do? How many bodies will they bring, how often, when, where? Will they pay for their own gas, the phone bill, part of the rent? Every detail has to be hammered out. Even within the party itself, allies are looking to get something for their help, and this something is rarely quantifiable, often ill-defined, and always negotiable. The chair of the DCCC may want a new member of Congress to remember who helped from the outset—the state party, a grateful and potentially effective fund-raiser, a local mayor or state senator the ear of someone in D.C. Some allies have interests at stake, others ideological claims to make. Most have both. What they want and what is on offer are rarely clear and sometimes misunderstood.

Often the issue is not so much whether the candidate can *give* allies what they want as whether the candidate wants to *be* the candidate they want. Some unions and activists groups are particularly up front about this. "What we want is a pro-labor majority in Congress," says one. "Part of the project here is to change the Democratic Party," says another. But party officials and activists, too, have their priorities for what they want and who they want in office, and the two are rarely neatly aligned. Being the center of a network gives campaign organizations access to diverse resources but also subjects them to forces pulling in different directions. Consider the following two examples, one a machine regular and another a reform-minded volunteer who is part of his local Democratic Town Committee and active in Democracy for America (DFA).

EPISODE 4.8

On primary day in Connecticut, a political operative currently working for the city gives me the lay of the land. "Look, most of the Himes staffers don't know nothing about local politics," he says as we stand in front of a polling place, handing out flyers to voters. "The fundamental fact is that they need Bridgeport. The Farrell campaign in 2006 demonstrated that beyond reasonable doubt. And they lost it partly due to the high-handed way in which they dealt with us locals." (Diane Farrell was the Democratic candidate for Congress in the district in 2006.)

He smiles to a woman walking up the stairs and reminds her to vote for the machine candidate in the state assembly primary. He does not even mention Himes. Then he turns to me and resumes our conversation: "And they just won't take any advice. I've worked with everyone in this city, okay? I've worked with the chairman, I've worked with the Puerto Rican families, I've worked with the mayor. But they are more interested in listening to some stupid bloggers and the suburban DTCs [Democratic Town Committees] who treat politics as if it was a pastime. Look, it's our party, too, you know? If they want to win this, they have to come around and deal with the locals here."

I ask him for examples of what the 2006 campaign did wrong. "Well, for one, they didn't give us money, and two, they didn't ID for us. It was all Farrell, Farrell, Farrell. That's not going to do it, my friend. You need to cut some deals to make the locals care. Why would they care about a federal election? What's in it for them? Farrell and her people never made that clear to people, and nor has Himes. Politics is about power, money, and votes, and if you don't give something, you don't get something."

EPISODE 4.9

Brian has been at several of the DFA meetings I have attended in New Jersey. A quiet, unassuming man, he does not stand out at meetings, but people keep mentioning him in conversations about the group, so I have called him to get a chance to talk with him at length.

I ask him about his experience with politics. He says he has been involved as a volunteer in pretty much every Democratic presidential campaign since George McGovern's in 1972. Asked whether there is something new about DFA, Brian says, "In a regular campaign, it's like, 'Here is what we're going to do, now you go do it.' It was like that for Clinton in '92 and '96, and it was like that before. But then in '03, I got involved with the Howard Dean campaign, and the message from Vermont was different. It was like, 'What do you want to do?' And people just loved that. I've never seen so many people so involved. Of course, it was not like everyone took the lead, but some did. Some would come with ideas, some would gather to work on them, everybody would be working together."

I ask him if the campaign really did not give orders, and he says, "Well, [campaign headquarters in] Burlington would feed us information about the governor's policy on different issues, and they would help us with things, but Dean's message really was 'You are this campaign,' and people took that very seriously and took a lot of responsibility. The idea was 'You have the power,' and his people kept saying, 'We are just this little office, and we can't do everything. You have to do it.'" Asked if there were any drawbacks to this approach, Brian laughs and says, "Well, it's hard to have a clear message. Sometimes we were neither consistent nor coherent! I think that was part of the problem in Iowa [where Dean lost in the caucus]."

Later in the conversation I ask him how things have worked out for DFA after Dean stepped down and took over as chairman of the DNC. The New Jersey affiliate is considered one of the stronger and better-organized chapters, and they supported Linda Stender in 2006. Brian says he thinks they will again in 2008. But then he says, "I have to say, the campaign last time didn't give us the respect we deserve. They treated us as if we were volunteers, and we are, but we are also a group. We are organized now. We put together a field opera-tion for them in Hunterdon County; we organized a network of veterans to call through all the veterans in the district, and in general really beefed up their ground game. But they didn't treat us very well and didn't listen very much, and when you don't get much in return, you start to lose heart, you know? But we did well in Hunterdon, where we were most active, and people in the state party noticed that. High turnout, that's a language they understand."

I ask him if this changed anything in the relationship between the group and the party. "It sure did. For instance, the DNC hired these two young ladies [as part of the 50-state strategy], who worked out of Trenton, and they helped us with the nuts and bolts of campaigning the year after, in 2007. And we have really learned a lot from them, in terms of targeting, and all that stuff. So now when we move in and help with a local race, we know what we have, we know what we need, we know who the swing voters are, and it's just 'Go get them!'" He continues: "That was a good experience. Still, some in the party—and here I'm definitely not going to name any names—show no respect for DFA. Their attitude is that we are just this volunteer group here to work for them, to give them money. So it's complicated, but we are not going to give up. You know, the thing is, the party is so weak on the ground. We have organized this thing we call the county committee project, and we track all vacancies on the county committees and fill them with our people. We are going to take this party back from the machine and make it ours again."

The people in these two episodes are both active in Democratic Party politics, but they come from very different allied groups that help the campaign organizations for very different reasons and yet bring simi-lar resources—people willing to make calls and knock on doors—to the same kind of project. Each ally contributes something to the ground war project—not much, compared to the resources of the campaign orga-nization, but it is something distinct and something that adds up. Ten progressive volunteers here, twenty machine regulars there, a city coun-cilman with connections in the Puerto Rican community, a Democratic Town Committee that can spend twenty thousand dollars and make ten thousand calls on Election Day, a state senator who will spend thirty thousand dollars on getting out the vote for the congressional candidate in his district, though his own seat is safe, and so on.

Because allies want different things, the network around the campaign organization is full of tensions. An obvious example is the divergent interests and ideological differences that separate a machine regular from a progressive activist. A more interesting example—because in a sense it is more surprising—is the tension between two elements that have similar interests and claim no separate ideology: the campaign organization and the DCCC in Washington, two elements that both dearly want to win.

In competitive districts like those I look at here, the DCCC is involved early on, offering advice; providing data and connections to potential senior staffers, consultants, and donors; validating campaigns; and sometimes actually recruiting candidates to run in the first place. They are also involved in funneling money directly to the campaign organization through various channels and are involved in budgetary decisions, scripts, and the like. But though the DCCC might well be a more important and closer ally than the state party or anyone else, it never becomes part of the campaign organization itself; it is always outside of it. It operates as an ally, constantly negotiating the extent and character of its involvement with staffers, who always want more money and more autonomy.

"D.C.," as staffers call their interlocutors from national Democratic Party organizations, is primarily represented by a regional field director, who typically oversees half a dozen campaigns or more, and, by proxy, via consultants assigned to the race. (These are often seen by locals as more loyal to the DCCC—a steady source of jobs—than to the particular campaign organization—just one of many jobs.) Negotiations between the campaign organizations and the DCCC are not only about resources but also about control. "The D.C. people are very particular," says one senior staffer. "They want things done their way, and they want good numbers [in terms of contacts]. Otherwise they will start leaning on people and sometimes try to force them out." Staffers and their local allies detest this, complaining not only that the DCCC does not "know conditions on the ground" and thus sometimes gives bad advice, but also that it is trying to "take over" campaigns. This charge is serious in several ways. Not only is it a problem to be taken over if one is unsure of the outsiders' competence when it comes to winning (after all, the DCCC has so many races that it can lose one battle and still win the war, whereas an individual campaign organization cannot). It is also a problem because it can make other potential allies wary of getting involved in the assemblage; they may want to help the candidate but would not necessarily want to "do the dirty work for the people in D.C."

The DCCC is just one of many allies by whom the campaign might, to repeat an oft-used phrase, be "taken hostage." This is the balance, then, that the candidate and the senior staffers have to find in negotiations with allies: they want to be taken in, to tie another element to the assemblage, but they do not want to be taken over, which might distract them from their own goals and scare off other allies or voters. (Think of the standard charge that someone is the candidate of "big labor," "big business," or some such.) After all, the candidate is usually running to represent people in a district first, personal principles second, and perhaps a party third, and not a quilt of interest groups. While staffers sometimes appeal in public to abstract notions of "team spirit" or sentimental notions of the

"the Democratic Family" working together, in private they are usually cynical; "There is no 'Democratic Family'," one says. And of course, most allies agree that there is, and should be, no such thing (at least it would be a decidedly post-patriarchal, non-nuclear family). They, too, want their autonomy.

What there is, however, is the shadow of the future, the knowledge among potential allies that there will be another meeting, another negotiation, and another race, next year for another office, two years from now for the House seat, and so on. Even if the individual election is a one-off, the allies in the network are involved in a recurrent project. The allies were there before the campaign organization came to town, and they will be there long after it is gone. One local operative expressed it succinctly: "Politics didn't start yesterday." While an individual candidate may be a longtime player in local politics, the campaign organization itself is temporary and thus stands out from the network around it. The allies who get involved often have to face one another; labor unions meet at the District Council, party representatives in the state committee, the reverend and the city councilman at community board meetings, and so on. Many of the campaign staffers, on the other hand, go work somewhere else. Walter W. Powell's take on repeated interactions in networks is optimistic; he highlights how they can lead to the development of trust.[17] That is certainly true, but of course it can also ferment distrust and carry old grudges along. In each cycle, scores will be settled, favors returned, past slights revenged. One local town chair called in the chits in her area for Himes, and all the state-level elected officials she had helped over the years joined the campaign effort, even as some of them may have contemplated a run themselves. In another town, warring factions tried to harness the campaign for their own purposes in internal fights, punishing one local elected official for an imprudent primary challenge, wrestling over control of the Town Committee by proxy as money changed hands during the election. Local operatives and allies routinely criticize campaign organizations and staffers for ignoring their longer-term interests. One former elected official, now scheming to take over a local Democratic Town Committee together with his supporters, explains:

EPISODE 4.10

"I realize that they are just here for the election, but I am not, okay? So it's all well and good that they want help from us with fund-raisers, volunteer recruitment, and getting out the vote. Sure, I'd be happy to help. But how about them making some concessions to us? They are spending like there is no tomorrow when it comes to television, and then they turn around and say no when I want a little money and some names to try to build an organization here. How can they be surprised if I hold my horses?"

The sometimes incessant infighting among allies in the network is a source of endless frustration for the staffers in the campaign organization, who would very much like for people to put their differences aside and unite "even if just for this one election." As one staffer says, "Don't they realize how close this will be?" For local operatives and staffers in allied organizations, however, such pious hopes seem impossibly naïve. They know there will be another round after this one, and they have that and the one before it in mind, too, as they make their moves.

Many of the allies involved in the wider assemblage are at least partially professionally staffed organizations, most notably the party organizations and the labor unions. But what they introduce into the assemblage is a more heterogeneous form of professionalism than what is found in the campaign organizations, a dedication not to electoral work narrowly but to politics more broadly. Instead of starting from the need to win the election at hand, these professionals start from the fact that there are different interests and ideals at play, only partially united by the shared goal of winning the election.

This other kind of professionalism indicates an alternative career path open to staffers who want to stay in politics beyond the lifespan of the campaign. The electoral route is one that is dominated by de-territorialized specialists aimed at winning (and it is homogenized in campaign after campaign); another route is a more generalist one as a local operative (moving between elected officials, party organizations, and allied interest groups). Senior staffers are often de-territorialized specialists, each working almost exclusively on one side of campaigns, and they have to stay on good terms with the national party organizations and be willing to move to where the work is to get a job and get ahead. Some have previously lived in the states where they operate, but very few are locals. They come from jobs in Iowa, South Carolina, D.C., or wherever the last gig was and have no reason to expect that they will work in the same place again anytime soon—that is, in fact, rather unlikely.

But many of the professionals who work for allies—and some of those who take up jobs in campaign organizations—work more permanently in one area and take up many different roles in the course of their career, working on campaigns part of the year but also on policy, constituent outreach, and so on, depending on what opportunities present themselves. Local operatives, whether employed by allies or as parts of the campaign organization, are often viewed with considerable skepticism by the de-territorialized specialists, who worry if their colleagues' loyalty is to the campaign specifically or to people in and around the network of allies more generally (just as locals worry whether the de-territorialized staffers are more loyal to people in D.C.). One staffer put it like this: "[The campaign manager] is scared of the locals, and maneuvers to isolate them.

The problem is this: who are they really loyal to? And they have their own friends and connections, so they are not dependent on [the campaign manager] the way the rest of us are."[18]

It is precisely on the basis of the diversity and interdependence that these staffers deal with in their everyday life that cooperation is built. The campaign might have wished for a different union line, and the union might have wanted another candidate, but here we are, this is what we have to work with. "We may not agree on much," says one union staffer, "but we are all professionals." The same goes for various parts of the party effort. Those working for the DCCC, the state party, and various state- and local-level candidates and elected officials all consider themselves professionals too. But they are not part of *one* community the way the staffers in the campaign organization are. They represent diverse interests. "We can fight like hell one day and work together the next," says one. The contrast is clear: when staffers *within* the campaign organization fight like hell among themselves, someone often loses his or her job.

THE INTERFACE BETWEEN STAFFERS, VOLUNTEERS, AND PART-TIMERS

To say that staffers "fight like hell" with volunteers and part-timers would be to exaggerate, but there is still friction at the interface between the campaign organization and the individuals who are enrolled to help with the ground war. One problem is this: volunteers like those in episode 4.3 do not take orders from staffers like Rick the way he would have taken orders from his field director. When told by a field organizer that "making calls is really the most important thing to do right now," one volunteer asked out loud what many only talked about in private: "Why aren't *you* doing it then?" (A junior staffer would not ask such a question of a more senior staffer.) Part-timers like Donald (in episode 4.5) were often more vocal critics of the perceived shortcomings of the campaign organization than even the most disgruntled staffer or ally.

Whereas the staff community is relatively small, clearly demarcated at any given point, and turnover is moderate over time, both the volunteer and the part-time communities are larger and subject to more churn. The volunteer community is in constant flux. From early on, a few dedicated supporters come in to help with office work, identification calls, and anything at hand. Over the summer, people start to show in greater numbers. In the fall, thirty to forty people come in to offices across the districts to help out. Over the span of the campaign, hundreds and sometimes thousands of people will have volunteered at least once. Some will have been on board week in and week out for months; others will have helped a few times along the way, many just a couple of hours in the final days. (Thus, absolute numbers of volunteers tell one little—a dozen dedicated activists can put in more hours than a hundred casual drop-ins.) The part-time community is easier to identify simply as those doing paid casual work at any given point—in my two cases enough to fill thirty to forty shifts a day from early September to late October and about two hundred shifts every day of the GOTV weekend. (Some work every day; many work a couple of shifts per week.)

The relations between staffers and volunteers are treated as quite unproblematic in many books on campaigns (and the involvement of part-timers is often ignored), but close attention to their everyday interactions reveals important complications. Relations on the ground between staffers and the people who make most of the calls and knocks are *fundamentally ambivalent, individually established,* and embrace very *different communities*. Everyone involved continues to want to win—many different people had tears in their eyes when Linda Stender lost—and all recognize the project at hand. But they understand the project, their own involvement, and the other participants in very different ways, even as they work together.

First of all, the interface is characterized by *ambivalent relations*. Staffers, senior ones in particular, like to think of the volunteers and part-timers as parts of the campaign organization's hierarchy. From this point of view, those making the knocks and calls are only so many "bodies"—to use that particularly charming piece of staff jargon—interchangeable foot soldiers in the ground war. This is not how volunteers and part-timers see themselves. Volunteers think of the campaign as a joint project, more akin to Powell's networks of reciprocity and negotiation than to a hierarchy. Part-timers, on the other hand, see their involvement primarily in market terms. They have simply sold their time to the campaign, and they are no more dependent on it than they are on any other low-paying temporary job. Volunteers can leave any time to seek other outlets for their civic and political engagement. Part-timers can leave if they think they can find equally or more attractive work elsewhere, or if they can do without the money. Even if volunteers often recognize the ideological and communal incentives that motivate staffers, and part-timers, too, are remunerated for their work, neither community shares the staffers' professional investment in the campaign nor the constraints that come with the hierarchy of the campaign organization.[19]

On the one hand, staffers are reluctant to recognize the ambivalence and accept these differences. After all, they themselves generally identify strongly with their role as professionals in a control- and production-oriented hierarchy, and in a sense their work would be a lot easier if those they work with embraced this view of the assemblage too. It is easier to run the ground war as an assembly line producing knocks and calls by the thousands if you have subordinates than if you have vocal volunteer partners or sometimes rather particular part-time contract workers. Volunteers rarely come in and ask for calls or knocks to make, work that many people consider stressful, tedious, and ineffective. They simply come to "help," and the nature of this help is a subject of ongoing negotiations. Some ask to write speeches, or offer policy advice, to great staff consternation ("Policy work? Geez, that's like five minutes every week. Don't they realize that what we need is phone calls?" commented Jack, the volunteer coordinator in New Jersey, after one volunteer suggested she could write a background memo on education instead of making calls.) Part-timers are less self-motivated and more liable to simply sit around until someone puts them to use. But they will not do just anything; they have signed up for a specific job and are not subject to staff authority beyond the confines of their contract. (Typically they are hired to canvass and are reluctant when asked to phone bank instead.) On the one hand, it is difficult to extend the hierarchy to cover volunteers and part-timers, and attempts to do so ruffle feathers and make people leave. But on the other hand, not even trying to assert some authority seems to endanger the staffers' two key goals of control and productivity. Some sort of compromise has to be reached for the diversity to be an asset more than a liability.

The staffers who work at the interface—volunteer coordinators and field organizers most of all—cultivate ambivalent relations that help keep people involved, at least partially on their own terms. They thus cast their relations to volunteers as both hierarchical *and* network-based and their relations to part-timers as hierarchical *and* market-based. The organizing at the interface between the staffers, volunteers, and part-timers is not so much what Powell calls a "mixed form," with elements of both hierarchy and network in one case and hierarchy and market in the others, as it is continuously and deliberately kept ambiguous as to how exactly the work is organized—the balance is never clear and it constantly shifts. In their daily organizing work and interactions with those around them, adept field staffers work hard to keep it that way, positioning themselves to speak with everyone involved on their own terms, giving as many instructions as they can get away with, offering encouragement or other incentives as they seem necessary. Field staffers—junior ones in particular—are trying to make the most of limited resources while engaged in ongoing dealings with senior staffers in the hierarchy on the one hand and with outside partners who are not under their direct control on the other. With their superiors in the campaign organization, they talk the hard-nosed instrumental talk of control and productivity, bodies and numbers. With the volunteers and part-timers, they encourage people to think about their work in any terms they see fit, as long as they pay lip service to the script, make at least some calls and knocks, and bring the data back. These are the variables staffers are anxious to retain control over, because they are seen as the instrumental ones.

It is useful to return to episode 4.3 here, where the canvassing volunteers in Summit, New Jersey, treated Rick with something bordering on contempt and in all likelihood completely ignored the scripts he provided them with in favor of conversations about their friend Laura and her candidacy for city council. But they still took his walk sheets of targeted voters (defined by the campaign), knocked on about two hundred doors, and, according to Rick, returned most of the sheets with at least some response data. He was less than satisfied with the episode but highlighted the material outcome, saying, "at least we made some progress." In general, practical staffers are willing to make concessions in their dealings with volunteers in particular. "You can't just give people orders; it creates more trouble than it's worth," says one field organizer. "[The field director] has been leaning on me to give even the volunteers hourly quotas to meet—you know, target numbers of calls. I haven't done that. I prefer to create a friendlier work environment where people will keep coming back."

This approach keeps people involved, but it comes at a price. First, it takes time and skill to maintain the ambivalence and make diverse communities work together in face of their differences. Secondly, sometimes the divergent understandings do not simply coexist, but conflict—as when ideologically motivated volunteers stray too far from the campaign message and staffers step in and try to stop them, or when part-timers get too particular about not going out on rainy days, while insisting that they have not contracted to make calls, and staffers try to force them to either canvass or at least work the phones. Here is how one staffer narrates a run-in with volunteers:

EPISODE 4.11

"There was a bit of a clusterfuck in Summit this weekend. I don't know if Rick told you," Jack says. "He had organized a volunteer phone bank out of a private home, and the guy hosting it turns out to be a Republican for Obama. So when he realized that Stender and [Democratic senator Frank] Lautenberg were also on the script, he gave Rick a hard time. But Rick stood up to him and basically told him, 'At least some of you will be making calls with these scripts, off my lists, or I'm outta here. Then you can make calls off the Obama website or whatever.'" I ask what happened then, and Jack says, "Well, at least some of them made calls off those lists. That's good; the kid has a scrappy fighter in him. You can only tell with organizers when they've had to face a situation like that."

In these situations, staffers have to choose if they want to maintain the ambivalence and spend time talking their way to a compromise that leaves at least parts of the messaging, targeting, and data in their hands; try to impose hierarchical control by giving orders—at the risk of people leaving—or find some other way. This work is what makes staffers talk of volunteers in particular as "high maintenance." "In that sense," one adds, "the paid canvassers are easier." Incidents like episode 4.11 are provoked by volunteers and even part-timers' resistance to staffers' pushing their hierarchical view of the situation too far, by challenges to staffers' professional identity, and sometimes by something as prosaic as the wear and tear of months of long days spent working under pressure. Toward the end of the campaign, most organizers were worn down, prone to lapses like one incident where an organizer told anyone in the campaign office who cared to listen, "I've had enough of volunteers who just come to argue with me. Can't people just shut up and do some work?" and another where a team leader snapped at his part-timers, "Enough stupid questions—just do as I say." These are the kinds of little incidents that bring the tensions to the forefront during ordinary workdays. The staffers may think they are giving orders in a hierarchy, but from a volunteer point of view, it is a twenty-something acting up, and for a part-timer, a temporary employer who is out of line. "I don't have to listen to your bullshit," one paid canvasser told a field organizer during an argument. Here, the ambivalence is threatened as an unambiguously hierarchical view is asserted, and individual volunteers and part-timers have to choose if they can live with this. And some choose not to—as Jack explains as we continued the conversation reported in episode 4.11:

EPISODE 4.12

I ask if things always pan out so well when staffers have run-ins with volunteers. Jack says, "Well, most of them are just here to help, right? But there are some who are really opinionated and just won't listen. So we have all these discussions of what to put in the script and who to call and whatnot. Everybody thinks they are experts on this. But the real problem is when they start insisting and try to boss *us* around.

"Some of the Obama activists are the worst. They are smart, self-confident, and new to this and think that every Democrat is here to help Obama. So they organize phone banks in the campaign office without clearing it with us, they steal volunteers out of this district—though the Obama campaign and the state party are telling them not to—and they are making calls out of this district, which will be really close, and into Pennsylvania, where he [Obama] will win by fucking ten percent."

I ask him for a concrete example of confrontations between staffers and volunteers in this district, and he says, "One of the field organizers had a volunteer canvass that he had to call off because people wouldn't do it. They didn't like the script, that we don't use the Democratic Party brand, and they don't like the fact that Obama isn't in it at all. So they argued back and forth, and in the end the volunteers decided to go to New Brunswick and register voters, and he had to give up. That kind of stuff happens all the time."

Such open conflicts cast a shadow over the organizing at the interface, and they are not isolated to relations between staff and volunteers. Part-timers, too, sometimes balk at staff orders. Those who know what lengths campaigns have to go to in their efforts to recruit and keep part-timers are especially not above challenging staffers who they think try to micromanage things or push them too hard. On an everyday basis, staffers try to maintain control over the instrumentally most important parts of the situation—scripts, targets, response data—without explicitly challenging alternative understandings of what is going on. From a staff point of view, volunteers and part-timers do not need to think they are "bodies" in a larger machinery as long as they act that way. (Just as from other points of view, staffers are free to think they have authority as long as they do not try to exercise it.) "To each his own" seems to be the principle at work when the interface works most smoothly, where a kind of constructive ambiguity is cultivated.

The main ways that staffers try to control volunteers without exercising authority they do not really have are through scripts, lists, and by creating a setting where there is little to do but work. Although the scripts are largely useless in terms of controlling interactions with voters, as explained in chapter 3, the call lists and walk lists made available to people who want to phone bank and knock on doors are much more effective and are entirely defined by the staffers' instrumental perspective. (I deal with the targeting behind them in chapter 5.) Even if a volunteer ignores the script and chafes at the idea that staffers have any control over her, using these lists aligns her efforts at least partially with those of the rest of the assemblage. (I only once saw a volunteer reject the lists and call people of his own choosing, and though canvassers sometimes talk to people they meet while on the streets, I never saw anyone knock on a stranger's door without having the address on the staff-issued list.) This is an important first step for staffers. But to make sure that people not only accept the lists but also make some calls, staffers try to construct a setting conducive for work and little else. When someone enters a campaign office to volunteer, they are usually led to a separate "volunteer room" that contains scripts with the campaign message, daily printouts of call lists with the target universe, deposit boxes for filled-out sheets, and phones ready for people to sit down at—and, ideally, little else. Felipe, a field organizer in one of the campaigns, called it "an attempt to define the ways in which they can participate." His phrasing recognizes the point of intersection between the staffers' need to get people to do something instrumentally useful and most volunteers' desire to be part of something. Staffers try to ease volunteers into a controlled, productive environment where they do not have to try to order them around. And once they are in, talented field staffs will take the time to "work the floor," stopping by to check in on volunteers once in a while, encourage them, ask them to call through just one more sheet tonight, and in general "keep an eye on them." Jack, for one, was in the habit of cooking up tasks for people to do that he could use as a pretext to break up small clusters of volunteers if some spent what he saw as too much time chatting and too little time on the phones, asking the most talkative ones to help him with a mailing, with taking inventory, with data entry—anything at hand that might get the others back on the phones.[20]

Staffers also try to control part-timers through scripts and lists, in much the same way as they do volunteers, but since part-timers work mostly on their own on the streets, knocking on doors, staffers cannot really control them by shaping the setting. Instead, they rely on something they cannot really bring to bear on volunteers—surveillance. Staffers know full well that part-timers can, and do, cut corners. As long as they knock on doors in at least most of their turf and do not consistently average fewer than ten doors and three contacts an hour when canvassing, staffers can live with that. But contacts have to be actual conversations with voters. To combat the tendency for some part-timers to fabricate data about nonexistent contacts, staffers select some households from the data collected by canvassing teams during the day and call them to check whether the part-timers actually did talk to these voters and if the information recorded is accurate. If the voter reports that an encounter never took place (whether because it did not or because they do not remember it), the particular part-timer's contacts are checked more systematically, and if there is too much "bad data," the person will most likely be fired—often in front of all their colleagues the next day before the work begins. This happens occasionally. One staffer says, "I hate doing it. It's so embarrassing to have to confront grown people like that, but on the other hand it has a wonderfully disciplining effect on the rest." Though in principle staffers could subject volunteers to the same surveillance—check the contacts they report, or, depending on the phone system used, sometimes even listen in on conversations with voters—they generally do not. One staffer offers the official explanation: "The volunteers come here of their own accord, so the assumption is that they will do the work." Luis was less circumspect: "What are we expected to do if they make things up? Fire them? At best, I can pull their data from the file and try to get them off the phones to do something else."

The staffers' focus on productivity—understood solely in quantitative terms of numbers of calls and knocks—explains why, after all the work that has gone into generating the contact with a voter (all the mobilizing, organizing, targeting), *as soon as it is made* the canvasser or phone banker will start to wonder if he or she should cut it off and move on. The rule of thumb suggested to both volunteers and part-timers is "two minutes, max." Volunteers wonder about the logic. One says, "I don't understand why they are so eager for us to move on. I mean, come on, I talk to maybe three people in an hour [on the phones]. Can't I at least have a conversation with them when there is someone at the other end?" A part-timer says, "If they just want us to say hi and rattle off that script, that's fine with me. I don't think people care that much, frankly, but, hey, that's their [the staffers'] problem." On the one hand, staffers are understandably eager to ensure high contact numbers—they do, after all, have very large target universes, thousands of voters they aim to contact. On the other hand, there is a danger of goal displacement here, a slide from the supposed goal—influencing people's voting behavior—to a preoccupation with metrics—quantitative goals for so and so many knocks or calls. Knocks and calls do not win elections. Votes do. And, ironically, experimental research suggests that more leisurely conversations are more likely to have an effect on whether people change their minds or turn out to vote than are shorter and more scripted conversations.[21]

The relations that keep volunteers and part-timers involved in campaigns are individually established in two senses. First, they are established as *individual relations*, the terms of which are established anew each time, even as people enter organized settings and have certain expectations, partly based on previous experience. A common saying among staffers about volunteers is that "they come for the candidate; they stay for you." Secondly, the work of dealing with them is *individualized* on the staff side—that is, one organizer is responsible for all volunteers or part-timers in a given office or area. In campaign offices there is usually one designated go-to person, the official or de facto volunteer coordinator. Part-timers are assigned to regionally organized canvassing teams, each headed by a field organizer, and are usually kept out of the office and out of touch with volunteers. Other staffers generally speak to volunteers only when spoken to, even when working for hours in close proximity. It is not their job to talk to these people, and it is not something they seek out. (Working with them is, after all, low status and takes one outside the peer group of aspiring professionals.)

Thus, individual staffers become the face of the campaign for people who often do not know anyone else in the organization and frequently do not recognize staffers or even distinguish them as a group from other people involved. Among the more comical illustrations of this latter fact were two scenes in particular toward the end of the campaign in Connecticut. In one case the wound-up campaign manager took time between two meetings to profusely thank a volunteer working on the phones for her help, clasping her hands between his and repeating several times, "We are really grateful for all your help," while she sat stunned and looked at him. After he left, she turned to me and asked, "Who *was* that?" The other scene was a pizza and beer shindig in Stamford after a long Saturday of canvassing, where a couple of part-timers failed to recognize Jim Himes himself when the candidate stopped by to thank them for their work. The operational and symbolic hierarchy of the campaign organization is neither visible nor particularly meaningful for these people, who are mostly outside it. Both volunteers and part-timers accept the individualization of their dealings with the campaign and quickly come to expect it. In my experience, people asked for the person they were used to dealing with, and especially volunteers were often impatient with substitutes and openly critical of what they perceived as their shortcomings: "I already talked this over with Jack. Why don't you just listen to me and give me that damn list?" "Why don't you have Felipe call me back?" (Some local operatives leverage this individualization into their own jealously guarded lists of "good volunteers," maintained and updated from campaign to campaign.)

The tone of these remarks illustrates how volunteers and part-timers are consistently freer and more vocal in their criticism of the campaign than staffers are, less beholden to the hierarchy. It is one thing that volunteers (like Lucia, in episode 4.4) compare the organization unfavorably to their own daytime job or previous work experience. They are, after all, often relatively privileged, and a temporary campaign organization spending $3 million is unlikely to be as professionalized as a medical center with a $30 million turnover or a corporation with $300 million in revenue. What is perhaps more surprising, and definitely more revealing, is that part-timers, too, are harsh in their assessments. One compared her experience to a previous job, making fund-raising calls for a nonprofit, saying, "We had much better scripts, scripts that you could actually use, that actually worked in conversations. And we got much more feedback on our work. I think that was much more well-organized." Another, a high school dropout, compared it to his last job, working at Burger King, and says, "When I worked there, we got all this training. I ain't seen none of that here. This is just kinda 'Read this and go talk to people.' And I'm like, 'Sure, dude, whatever you say.'" Such criticism rarely makes it beyond the staffer who hears it first. The critique is partly rooted in a limited understanding of the work that volunteers and part-timers are doing. As made clear in previous chapters, it is stressful, tedious, and often seen as futile by people who regularly ask, "Why are we doing this?" Staffers at the bottom rungs of the campaign organization's hierarchy may not know how to answer this question. Indeed, many of the field organizers asked *me* to explain the mechanics of field to them—why are the scripts like this; why do we have all Republican women one day, all Democrats in Woodbridge the next; what is the information we gather used for—apologizing for their self-professed ignorance along the way: "That kind of information doesn't filter down to me." Working in a low-information environment, they themselves simply did not know. And having their hands full, they rarely had or took the time to try to find out. Their instructions to volunteers and part-timers reflected this lack of understanding. People involved in campaigns are generally told *what* to do but not *why*. This works with staffers, who follow orders and are invested in performing well. It is harder with volunteers, who do not necessarily follow orders, and part-timers, who are often less conscientious about "doing well." Consider this episode from Connecticut:

EPISODE 4.14

Dwane sits down for a brief meeting with his team of part-timers every day before they go out to canvass. Today is an unusually hot, cloudless October day, and nobody seems to be too eager to get out and knock on doors. Monica, one of the regular paid canvassers, who has been working for about a month now, asks him—as she has done before—"Does it make any difference? The stuff that we're doing?" She complains that the work is hard, that she is wearing herself down, and that it would be "nice to know if this all matters." She asks Dwane, "Does it show up in the polls?" He is evasive and says, "It does matter, but I don't have numbers." Monica insists, "How do you know?"

One of the other canvassers changes the subject: "The people we meet ask all these questions about Himes. Can't you give us some more information? People don't care about all this stuff in here [he waves a piece of paper with the talking points]. 'Wants to improve health care.' What the fuck does that mean for someone in Bridgeport? I don't even know what that means. And what about his background? People ask about that, what kind of man is he? Some people have told me he ran his own business, someone else that he worked some job on Wall Street." One of the others interrupts: "That's not going down so well right now, that Wall Street stuff." Dwane looks around and says, "We can do the role-playing again if people want to train more." Monica laughs at him and says, "Shit, Dwane, we ain't asking for more role-playing. We play these roles every day. We want to know what the hell is going on."

Field organizers like Dwane find themselves in a delicate position. On the one hand, their superiors hold them accountable for the number of knocks their teams make. On the other hand, their volunteers and teams of part-timers pressure them for more information, training, substance and attention than the campaign organization will invest in them. Senior staffers might splurge on a training session or two at the beginning of September for the first teams of part-timers taken on board, but from then on, with a constant trickle of new hires and a consistently high turnover, on-the-job training will have to do. (Volunteers come and go, and many part-timers leave after a few shifts.) And as mentioned before, this is training by people who are not necessarily well equipped to do it. Dwane himself recognized as much when I talked to him after the scene in episode 4.14, saying, "Normally I find myself making shit up to answer half their questions and get them out to knock on some doors. I don't know what else to tell them. What do I know about what Himes's position would be on some roadwork being done outside Trumbull? How am I to find out? Do they expect me to waste [the campaign manager's] time with that? If it doesn't sound crazy, then we are for whatever the voter is for, and then we'll just hope for the best."

Finally, the relations at the interface continue to encompass *very different communities*. For field staffers, this is a bit of a challenge, because they have to move beyond the comfort zone of their own occupational community and engage with people who problematize their professional identity and often come from a different background. Especially junior staffers have this problem. Within the campaign organization and the community of staffers, a graduate from a top university may be praised profusely for his ability to make two hundred phone calls a day to strangers and may embrace the camaraderie and sense of purpose and accomplishment shared with others who have chosen a life they openly describe as one of "long hours, low pay, and no life." It all becomes more complicated when volunteers and part-timers do not play along. Volunteers, for instance, often refer to junior staffers as "the kids." They may do as they are asked to do but rarely defer to staffers' claims to authority and expertise, instead demanding reasons, explanations, and suggesting other ways of doing things. Some volunteers, like Lucia, quoted in episode 4.4, see staffers more as facilitators or even service personnel meant to enable their involvement rather than professionals above them in a hierarchy. Although the organization chart from the Himes campaign (figure 4.2) included part-timers at the bottom of the hierarchy, I never once heard any one of them refer to a staffer as their boss, the way junior staffers often referred to their superiors in the campaign organization. Part-timers sometimes wonder openly why the staffers have made the career choices they have ("I don't get it. Who would want to work so hard for nothing?"), which is no doubt uncomfortable for the staffers.

As with the network of allies, the most important thing to note here is not simply that people join the assemblage with different backgrounds and motivations. It is that, unlike in the campaign organization, this diversity is recognized, maintained, and coexists at the interface. Attempts to impose hierarchy drive people away, and insistence on autonomy leads to detachment. Junior staffers are consistent when asked about relations with volunteers and part-timers—"You can't treat everyone as if they were on staff." The campaign organization cannot be extended to encompass the entire assemblage. Even when they lapse from this stance in practice—from cross-pressures that become too hard to handle, from challenges to their balancing acts, or from exhaustion when they slip back into a staff-centered perspective on what is going on—they are reminded by volunteers and part-timers who, just like allies, will push back against purely hierarchical definitions of their involvement.

* * *

Contemporary competitive ground wars are waged by complex campaign assemblages anchored around campaign organizations populated by staffers but that also include networks of allies and communities of volunteers and paid part-timers who contribute tens of thousands of hours of work, making calls and knocking on doors. Whereas some particularly technical kinds of campaign work are contracted to outside consultants (like direct mail, polling, and media buys), and others are mostly the domain of staffers (fund-raising in particular), field operations rely on a diverse range of elements, organized in different ways, with different motivations and modes of operation. Campaigns cannot be reduced to simply the hierarchical campaign organizations at the heart of most campaign assemblages. They do not operate in a command-and-control fashion. Allies, volunteers, and part-timers are not incidental, but are integral, to the field efforts—all the way from the presidential to the local level. "Because I say so" works within the hierarchical campaign organizations but not in the wider campaign assemblage involved in the ground war. When staffers occasionally forget this and start trying to boss allies, volunteers, and part-timers around, or when senior field people talk too loudly about how campaign organizing is like "industrial engineering" or "logistics," they run the risk of alienating people whose help they need to pursue personalized political communication on a large scale. The division of labor varies from campaign to campaign, but in the two I studied, allies channeled a limited number of people for calls and knocks along the way and a substantial number for GOTV work, volunteers made most of the phone calls, and paid part-timers knocked on most of the doors. It would have been impossible for the campaign staffers to reach their contact goals without all of these people.

Though staffers cannot rely on authority alone to orchestrate these extra elements, they still have to try to coordinate the work done, lest diversity becomes more of a liability than an asset. People do not come together spontaneously and do not work together without friction and occasional infighting. In this chapter I have dealt with how these diverse actors collaborate on the shared ground war project. I have made a distinction between the campaign organizations (characterized by their hierarchical form, temporary duration, and the cultivation of a homogenous professional identity), the network of allies (characterized by ongoing negotiations, the regular recurrence of collaboration among parts of the network, and a more heterogeneous kind of professionalism), and the interface between staffers and the volunteers and part-timers they work with (characterized by ambivalent relations that are established on an individual basis and that tie together very different communities).

Analysis of all these three facets show how field operations in competitive districts are neither a form of "grassroots politics" nor as thoroughly professionalized as some other parts of politics. Ground wars are waged by self-styled professionals working with often ideologically driven and community-oriented "amateur" activists and with casual workers who are usually less interested in the campaign or the cause than their take-home pay. They involve highly professional specialists but also generalist political operatives, a wide variety of allied organizations, and hundreds of individual volunteers and part-timers with no professional commitment to electioneering. They deploy a set of institutionalized and routinized campaign practices developed and passed on by a de-territorialized population of ambitious staffers who move from campaign to campaign and maintain constant ties to national party and political organizations, but they also rely on local partners, both organized and less so, and have to contend with their customs and cares. All of these elements are parts of often sprawling campaign assemblages held together partly by overlapping interests and ideologies but also by the ongoing and intricate work of organizing examined here.

CHAPTER 5

Targeting Voters for Personal Contacts

EPISODE 5.1

Charlene and I are heading out for another canvass in the Bridgeport area. As we walk from the campaign office toward her car, we pass by a man wearing a janitor's uniform. He is smoking a cigarette outside a downtown office building. She approaches him and asks, "Have you heard of Jim Himes?" He has not.

They have a brief and friendly conversation—it turns out that he is a union member and "always" votes for Democrats. Charlene takes down his name and contact information, scribbling it on the back of one of her walk sheets, identifying him as a solid Democrat and a Himes supporter. The two of them talk a bit about health care—he is insured and she is not—and about the risk of unemployment. We bid our farewells and continue to the car. Charlene says, "It feels kinda wrong to walk by people without talking to them." I steal a glance at her notes while we drive. The man's address suggests that he lives outside the district.

EPISODE 5.2

Denise is a field organizer working her first full-time job in politics. She has organized a volunteer phone bank out of a local law office because some of the suburban white volunteers from her area are reluctant to go into the poor urban area where the campaign office is. Tonight five people, including a mom and her somewhat reticent teenage son, have showed up to make calls. As is often the case, the volunteers start by discussing the most recent developments in the campaign and complaining about the scripts. Then they start asking Denise about the call lists. A man named Matthew, who is active in the local Democratic Town Committee, leads the charge. He asks, "Who are these people?"

First Denise says, "They are solid Democrats." Matthew asks, "Then why are we calling them?" and she backtracks: "No, wait, I think they are lazy Democrats." Someone points to a "U" next to one of the names on the list and says, "Doesn't this mean he is unaffiliated?" Denise picks up some call sheets and leafs through them, and I look at mine. Some of the voters are registered Democrats, some of them are unaffiliated. She says, "Yeah, you're right; there are also some unaffiliated here. So it's lazy Democrats and unaffiliated. The script should reflect that, so you can just stick to it. These people shouldn't be too hostile."

Later she says to me, "I actually don't care. It makes no difference to me whether we are calling Democrats or unaffiliated, but it would be nice to know so I had something to say when they start asking questions."

EPISODE 5.3

"In targeting, you get what you are given." That's how Luis tries to put an end to the conversation at a local Democracy for America meeting where he is presenting the neighbor-to-neighbor online interface that the Democratic National Committee has developed to facilitate distributed canvassing and phone banking. "There will be opportunities to tweak it if there happens to be someone on your list that you don't like personally, but fundamentally, you get what you're given. If you want to change it, you have to call the state party or the coordinated campaign and get them to tweak it for you." The man who has been pushing Luis on the targeting issue shakes his head and says, "So you give us the scripts and the lists, and we do the work? That's neat."

Canvassing and phone banking is hard and often stressful work, comes with numerous organizing headaches, and requires time and money that could be put to other use. No wonder, then, that political operatives try to make the most of it by paying particular attention to how personalized political communication is targeted. Voters are not approached at random—though it sometimes seems so to volunteers and part-timers—but are carefully selected for contacts. The daily work of canvassing and calling people is structured around walk sheets and call sheets with names, contact information, and a few basic details about those targeted. (See figures 5.1 and 5.2 for examples of a walk sheet from Connecticut and a call sheet from New Jersey. Similar information can be made available on PDAs.) These sheets are the products of a new targeting scheme that has come to dominate Democratic ground war efforts over the last few years. Before 2008 even well-funded efforts that were engaged in competitive elections would often cobble together their own more or less improvised targeting schemes, relying on a mix of information provided by political action committees, lists acquired from state parties and commercial vendors, and local organizations who claimed to know the area at hand and who to talk to. Especially in down-ballot races, such a mix remains widespread, but federal and statewide races today rely on the increasingly dominant and increasingly standardized targeting scheme that I analyze in this chapter.

This scheme, which some call "the new political targeting," is not after voters. It is after *these particular voters*. It is not after everyone in the precinct, it is not after everyone on Lakeside Drive (the street on the walk sheet reproduced as figure 5.1) or every woman or African American on Lakeside Drive, or even after all the Democrats or all those registered

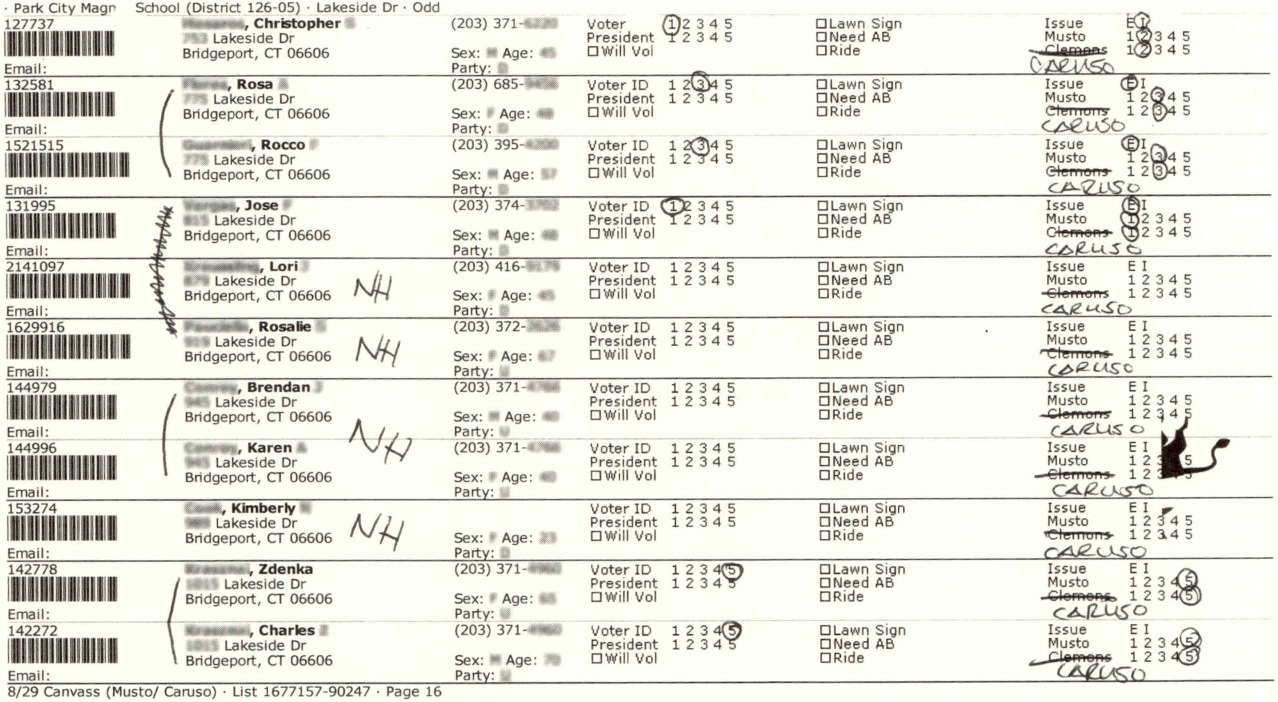

· Park City Magn School (District 126-05) · Lakeside Dr · Odd

127737 Email:	, Christopher Lakeside Dr Bridgeport, CT 06606	(203) 371- Sex: Age: Party:	Voter 1 2 3 4 5 President 1 2 3 4 5 ☐Will Vol	☐Lawn Sign ☐Need AB ☐Ride	Issue E I Musto 1 2 3 4 5 Clemons 1 2 3 4 5 CARUSO
132581 Email:	, Rosa Lakeside Dr Bridgeport, CT 06606	(203) 685- Sex: Age: Party:	Voter ID 1 2 3 4 5 President 1 2 3 4 5 ☐Will Vol	☐Lawn Sign ☐Need AB ☐Ride	Issue E I Musto 1 2 3 4 5 Clemons 1 2 3 4 5 CARUSO
1521515 Email:	, Rocco Lakeside Dr Bridgeport, CT 06606	(203) 395- Sex: Age: Party:	Voter ID 1 2 3 4 5 President 1 2 3 4 5 ☐Will Vol	☐Lawn Sign ☐Need AB ☐Ride	Issue E I Musto 1 2 3 4 5 Clemons 1 2 3 4 5 CARUSO
131995 Email:	, Jose Lakeside Dr Bridgeport, CT 06606	(203) 374- Sex: Age: Party:	Voter ID 1 2 3 4 5 President 1 2 3 4 5 ☐Will Vol	☐Lawn Sign ☐Need AB ☐Ride	Issue E I Musto 1 2 3 4 5 Clemons 1 2 3 4 5 CARUSO
2141097 Email:	, Lori Lakeside Dr Bridgeport, CT 06606 NH	(203) 416- Sex: Age: Party:	Voter ID 1 2 3 4 5 President 1 2 3 4 5 ☐Will Vol	☐Lawn Sign ☐Need AB ☐Ride	Issue E I Musto 1 2 3 4 5 Clemons 1 2 3 4 5 CARUSO
1629916 Email:	, Rosalie Lakeside Dr Bridgeport, CT 06606 NH	(203) 372- Sex: Age: Party:	Voter ID 1 2 3 4 5 President 1 2 3 4 5 ☐Will Vol	☐Lawn Sign ☐Need AB ☐Ride	Issue E I Musto 1 2 3 4 5 Clemons 1 2 3 4 5 CARUSO
144979 Email:	, Brendan Lakeside Dr Bridgeport, CT 06606	(203) 371- Sex: Age: Party:	Voter ID 1 2 3 4 5 President 1 2 3 4 5 ☐Will Vol	☐Lawn Sign ☐Need AB ☐Ride	Issue E I Musto 1 2 3 4 5 Clemons 1 2 3 4 5 CARUSO
144996 Email:	, Karen Lakeside Dr Bridgeport, CT 06606 NH	(203) 371- Sex: Age: Party:	Voter ID 1 2 3 4 5 President 1 2 3 4 5 ☐Will Vol	☐Lawn Sign ☐Need AB ☐Ride	Issue E I Musto 1 2 5 Clemons 1 2 CARUSO
153274 Email:	, Kimberly Lakeside Dr Bridgeport, CT 06606 NH	Sex: Age: Party:	Voter ID 1 2 3 4 5 President 1 2 3 4 5 ☐Will Vol	☐Lawn Sign ☐Need AB ☐Ride	Issue E I Musto 1 2 3 4 5 Clemons 1 2 3 4 5 CARUSO
142778 Email:	, Zdenka Lakeside Dr Bridgeport, CT 06606	(203) 371- Sex: Age: Party:	Voter ID 1 2 3 4 5 President 1 2 3 4 5 ☐Will Vol	☐Lawn Sign ☐Need AB ☐Ride	Issue E I Musto 1 2 3 4 5 Clemons 1 2 3 4 5 CARUSO
142272 Email:	, Charles Lakeside Dr Bridgeport, CT 06606	(203) 371- Sex: Age: Party:	Voter ID 1 2 3 4 5 President 1 2 3 4 5 ☐Will Vol	☐Lawn Sign ☐Need AB ☐Ride	Issue E I Musto 1 2 3 4 5 Clemons 1 2 3 4 5 CARUSO

8/29 Canvass (Musto/ Caruso) · List 1677157-90247 · Page 16

Figure 5.1. **Walk sheet with individual target voters.**
Street numbers, phone numbers, last names, sex, age, and party registration have been blurred to protect the people on the list. (Part-timers typically have this information on a PalmPilot or other type of PDA rather than on paper.) Notice how the canvasser has circled answers depending on each voters' response to ID questions about who they support ("1" is a solid Himes supporter, "3" someone undecided, and "5" a solid Shays supporter), what they care about ("E" is the economy, "I" the war in Iraq) and marked down who is not home ("NH"). Apparently the voter file provided the wrong name on who was running for state senate here, hence the hand-written name "Caruso" on each line. The bar code facilitates data entry.

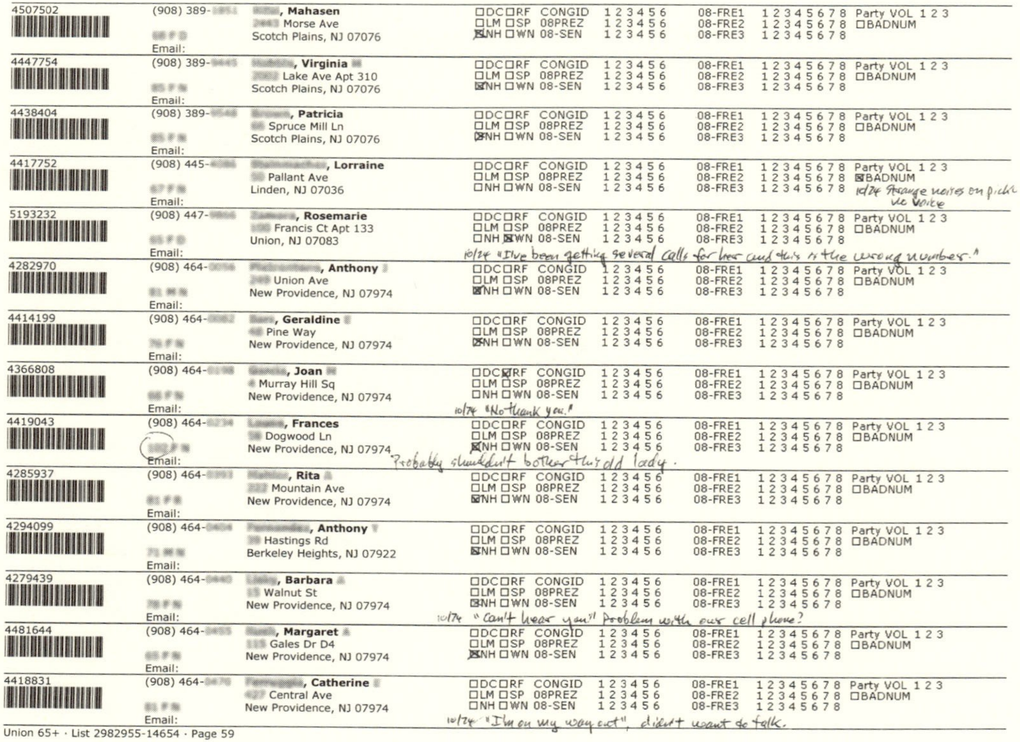

Figure 5.2. Call sheet with individual target voters.

Street numbers, phone numbers, last names, sex, age, and party registration have been blurred to protect the people on the list. Note the handwritten comments made by the volunteer who called through this list, information that will not fit into the VAN system. The name of the list, Union 65+ (in the bottom left corner), indicates the county and the age demographic covered. Older voters are typically called during the day, younger voters after 6 P.M. One voter on the list is 102 years old, several are in their eighties. Not a single one of these fourteen people answered any of the ID questions. Again, the bar code is for data entry.

without party affiliation on Lakeside Drive. It is after Christopher, Rosa, and everyone else on that list, because they have been individually identified as high-value persuasion or get-out-the-vote targets. Whereas some forms of political communication, like television advertisements, are based on a broadcasting model aimed at relatively large and undifferentiated audiences, the dominant targeting scheme aims at so-called narrowcasting, at communicating with select individuals instead.[1]

Consultants claim that new forms of political targeting can identify voters as undecided or infrequently voting partisans—the two key target universes for personalized political communication—with 80 percent accuracy. It is not hard to see why senior staffers are enthusiastic about this. In the past, it was difficult to identify which individual voters might be "persuadable" and thus worth a time-consuming personal contact. Previous forms of targeting for GOTV efforts were based on knocking through entire "base" precincts, where many would have voted in any case and some intended to vote for the opposition. Thus, many undecideds were never contacted, and many contacts were made in vain to people who already supported the candidate and intended to vote or who were firmly committed to the other side.

To illustrate the potential of the new political targeting, take the case of get-out-the-vote contacts. One staffer suggested that previous forms of targeting could identify worthwhile targets (so-called lazy Democrats, reliably partisan voters with low and irregular turnout) with about 65 percent precision. An improvement to 80 percent then effectively *doubles* the net impact of a given campaign's GOTV work.[2] A seemingly marginal improvement in precision makes each labor-intensive and logistically demanding person-to-person contact dramatically more efficient. This is obviously quite an attractive prospect for campaigns spending hundreds of thousands of dollars and thousands of hours of paid and volunteer work on the ground war.

THE DOMINANT TARGETING SCHEME

The most visible artifacts of the new and increasingly dominant targeting scheme are the ubiquitous call and walk sheets that volunteers and part-timers are handed whenever they begin their work. Sheets like these may seem rather prosaic—just a list of people to talk to and a few boxes for recording their responses—but they play an important part in processes of personalized political communication. The sheets are produced on the basis of the dominant targeting scheme's particular combination of (1) predictive modeling done by outside specialists, (2) certain everyday work routines that staffers try to enforce on the ground to generate response data, and (3) vast amounts of individual-level data drawn from a detailed digital national voter file called "VoteBuilder" and accessed through an online interface called the "VAN." (These specialized tools have been developed by a partisan political consultancy company called "Voter Activation Network" [hence the acronym] for the Democratic National Committee, which controls access together with the state parties.) The sheets list targets and serve to feed further data back into the targeting effort, based on how callers and canvassers record voters' responses to the questions about candidate leanings, party identification, and about issues they care about. (As chapter 3 has shown, voters rarely answer many of the questions included in the scripts.)

The dominant targeting scheme is often referred to more generically as "microtargeting," but the practices involved have evolved in important ways since this term was first introduced in the political vocabulary in the late 1990s. As long as they work together effectively, the elements involved represent an instrumentally effective and continually self-improving tool with potentially profound consequences not only for the impact of personalized political communication but also for how campaign assemblages and party organizations operate and who are in a position to steer electoral activities. It is thus important to note here that although most contacts made by the campaign assemblages are made under the aegis of the dominant targeting scheme, a significant minority are not. Though senior staffers, who believe in its instrumental value, push and promote the dominant scheme, some of the allies enrolled in the assemblage choose to opt out of it altogether and maintain alternative targeting schemes of their own—even when they recognize that their own schemes may be less instrumentally effective in terms of winning the election. They opt out because they recognize that targeting is not only about who is targeted but also about who does the targeting, and ultimately about how the capacity to target is distributed and maintained among those involved. The new political targeting not only makes personalized political communication more effective (from a partisan point of view). It also gives party organizations and political operatives more control over field activities than they have had in the past, because they are the ones who control access to the new digital tools integral to the dominant scheme, and because they are the ones who know how to use them.

Targeting is an obscure and rather technical side of campaigns, an infrastructural substrate of contemporary politics that is rarely studied in detail. Scholars have raised important concerns about the potential violation of privacy norms involved in using detailed individual information for political purposes, arguing that the wider information architecture of consumer-profiling algorithms, routinized feedback practices, and detailed databases that underpin much of this work represents a new and pernicious form of social control that has recast America less and less as a society and more and more as a series of distinct "segments," "niche audiences," and "lifestyle clusters."[3] Everyone writing about the political use of these techniques recognizes that the main motivation between the development and deployment of these specialized tools is instrumental—that campaign staffers, political operatives, and outside consultants are primarily using them because they think they help them win. But scholars disagree over what the likely implications are. Some argue that tailored messages to finely targeted segments of voters will exacerbate existing political inequalities by further narrowing and polarizing the electorate.[4] Others claim that these new practices make it cost-effective for well-funded competitive campaigns to actually expand the universe of targets for their get-out-the-vote programs, thereby mitigating, in however limited a fashion, the clear age, class, and race biases of the American electorate.[5]

I return to these broader issues at the end of the chapter, but the main question I address is how the dominant targeting scheme shapes processes of personalized political communication, how it makes phone calls and door knocks more cost-effective in terms of influencing people's voting behavior—and therefore more attractive from an instrumental point of view—but also how it gives staffers greater control over the field effort. Targeting is certainly tied in with the questions of privacy, surveillance, and audience construction that many have written about. But it also has important consequences for the instrumental efficacy of personalized political communication and helps structure how campaign assemblages pursue it. Targeting ultimately influences the relative position of the elements involved in it by strengthening the party organizations that have privileged access to the underlying data and control the infrastructure that stores the information and makes it available and actionable in the field. The new dominant targeting scheme leaves the point of contact—the interactions between callers and canvassers analyzed in chapter 3—largely untouched, but it introduces to campaigns elements of the back-end information and communication technology revolution that has transformed much of the corporate world over the last thirty years.[6] Just as supply chain management and customer relations management tools have transformed large swaths of the retail sector without perceptibly changing our shopping experience, the new political targeting is transforming the ground war without fundamentally altering the interactive dynamics analyzed in chapter 3. To demonstrate how this is being done, I first outline the logics of predictive modeling as it is used in politics. Secondly, I look at everyday work routines involved in targeting, both of those who work with the dominant scheme and of those who reject it and use alternative schemes. Thirdly, I deal with the development of the national voter file that the new dominant targeting scheme relies on. In the concluding part of the chapter, I return to the broader implications of the adoption of these new tools for campaign purposes.

THE USE OF PREDICTIVE MODELING IN POLITICAL TARGETING

Predictive modeling brings sophisticated statistical techniques to bear on large amounts of quantitative data to try to divine the probability of people's future behavior.[7] It is a key element of the new dominant targeting scheme. Whereas previous forms of targeting were primarily concerned with identifying demographic groups (soccer moms, NASCAR dads) or geographic areas (highly partisan low-turnout precincts), the new political targeting is oriented toward identifying and clustering individuals together on the basis of statistical predictions of their probable electoral behavior, and then matching them with contact information so that they can be contacted at home, one at a time, by callers and canvassers (or via direct mail). Whereas polls are aimed at finding out how the overall *electorate* will behave, predictive modeling is about finding out how *a specific individual* will behave. Such techniques have been used to create credit scores since the mid-1970s and have been adopted for direct marketing purposes since the early 1980s to identify profitable potential customers on the basis of analysis of the large amounts of consumer data that is being collected by companies like Acxiom, Epsilon, and InfoUSA. By continuously gathering response data and tracking results over time, marketers have improved the precision and performance of their communications to ever more carefully defined segments of particularly valuable customers. Similar techniques have been adopted for political use since the mid-1980s, initially for fund-raising purposes, but increasingly also for voter contact through direct mail programs.[8]

The adoption of predictive modeling for ground war purposes was hampered until recently by the still relatively high costs and slow pace of large-scale quantitative analysis, and by the fact that the politically relevant information available and amenable to such number crunching was limited at best. But as the price of data storage and the turnaround time for quantitative analysis have fallen in recent years, and as the digitized information readily available about most of the population has grown and become easier to access—all due in part to the development of computing technology and the concurrent growth of the consumer information industry—predictive modeling became a practical tool for voter contact programs too.

The breakthrough at the national level came in 2001 and 2002 when the Republican consultant Alex Gage and his company TargetPoint Consulting introduced what he called "supersegmentation" in Mitt Romney's lavishly funded campaign for governor of Massachusetts. According to Gage, those of Romney's advisers who came from the business world were flabbergasted when they learned that such techniques, mainstays in many parts of corporate America, were not already widespread in politics. They became so over the following cycles. The Republican National Committee tested Gage's approach in low-profile state- and federal-level elections in 2002 and 2003 as part of Karl Rove's attempt to close the ground gap vis-à-vis the Democrats. Now known as "microtargeting," predictive modeling became the subject of much journalistic speculation when it was pursued on a large scale by the Bush campaign in the 2004 presidential election.[9] Comparable efforts were made on the liberal/progressive side by America Coming Together and others, but were hampered by various problems, including uneven data, problems with the technical interfaces, and the absence of a standardized way of using these tools.[10]

Predictive modeling is generally done by specialized outside consultants, and not campaign organizations themselves. Strategic Telemetry, which did targeting work for the Obama campaign in 2008, is the best-known Democratic company, but today there is a small industry of often partisan political consultants providing these services. Each of these companies has their own proprietary way of working with the data and returning to the campaigns only their predictions, not their models (these are in turn taken and used largely on faith by staffers). However they are branded, all of these targeting models share some basic similarities. The point is to go from what is known with certainty or near-certainty about *most* voters (from various sources of historical data) and a *sample* of voters (from campaign-generated identification calls and from large polls) to statistical inferences about the individual-level probable behavior of *all* voters, who can then be sliced and diced for various forms of contacts depending on their estimated "value" for a given campaign. In politics, predictive models are primarily used to score voters on a scale from 0 to 100 in terms of their propensity to vote and who they are likely to support. In contrast to scientists working with statistical methods, targeting consultants are not looking for associations to establish causation. Correlations will do, as long as they hold until the election is over. From a campaign point of view, it does not matter *why* there is a strong relationship between a certain set of characteristics and a tendency to cross party lines or an inclination not to vote, as long as the models can identify relatively precisely who might be swing voters in this election and which of a candidate's likely supporters are infrequent voters.

Like every other kind of analysis, predictive modeling is subject to the principle of "garbage in, garbage out." No matter how you treat it, inaccurate data will provide invalid results. What is available varies in quality depending on its source. There are three main kinds of data fed into these models: data from voter files, consumer data, and "response data" gathered by various political organizations. Voter files (and other public records) are maintained by government authorities and vary in quality and format from state to state and sometimes county to county. Even after the Help America Vote Act was passed in the wake of the 2000 election debacle, some areas continue to have at best uneven records of registered voters. Though many states restrict commercial access to voter lists, all currently allow candidates and campaigns access to them. These records provide the backbone of most targeting efforts because they provide individual-level contact information (address in all cases and phone number in many states) and important basic demographic information (date of birth, gender, and in a few states race too). Both major parties now compile this data in national voter files and enhance it through various forms of data cleaning and by supplementing it with the rich, detailed, and continuously updated and verified data sold by consumer information companies. Finally, predictive modeling relies on response data gathered by canvassers and callers contacting voters on behalf of political organizations and campaign assemblages. This latter data plays a central role in targeting efforts, because it is the most recent information available on people's partisan leanings and candidate sympathies, and thus provides information on two of the critical dependent variables that modeling specialists are trying to predict: the voter's propensity to cross party lines for *this* candidate and the likelihood they will stay home *this* election.

Journalistic coverage of predictive modeling in politics has often focused on the inclusion of esoteric data points—like who owns a snowmobile or what brand of liquor people prefer. While this makes for good copy, targeting consultants themselves agree unanimously that accurate data on socioeconomic status (age, gender, income, race); past voting habits (frequent or infrequent); and up-to-date response data on people's partisan leanings, candidate sympathies, and issues of interest (gathered by campaigns themselves) is more important than almost any kind of consumer information or personal exotica when it comes to predicting electoral behavior. This makes the quality of the data taken from public records and the data gathered and maintained by political entities themselves of preeminent importance. As mentioned earlier, consultants estimate that when based on solid data, contemporary models can predict voter behavior with about 80 percent accuracy.[11] In the remaining 20 percent of cases, the results on the ground are sometimes absurdly off.

EPISODE 5.4

"Hey, Rasmus, come here, I've got something you can put in your paper!" Luis shouts. I walk over, and he points on the VAN interface on his laptop and says,

"This is an eighty-two-year-old woman, probably senile or something. We have contacted her five times so far, and she keeps saying she is undecided. We have even contacted her twice the same day, called her and knocked her door on the same day. Since she's undecided, she keeps going back on the list. I'll check her once in a while to see how often we hit her."

A week later, he asks me, "You remember that old woman we talked about?" I nod, and he says, "We contacted her again, and now she's leaning toward us!" He turns to John, the field director, and says, "Then she's out of the universe, right? We take leaners out of the persuasion universe too?" John says, "Yeah." Luis pauses for a second, then says, "Maybe we should hit her six more times to move her to 'solid.'" They both laugh.

The walk and call sheets do not allow canvassers and callers to distinguish between voters who are genuinely on the fence and those who either do not care that much (like Daniel Vieira, the ex-marine in episode 3.8) or those who are not in a position to care (as the potentially senile woman above may have been). All of these are taken down as either "undecided" or "not home." The former identifies them as high-priority targets (potentially persuadable); the latter keeps them in whatever target universe they were already in. They may well receive another knock or call the very next day, especially toward the end of a race, when campaigns are generating thousands of contacts every day.

Ideally, campaigns can test the modeled scores by drawing samples of voters with a certain predicted likelihood of supporting their candidate, calling through a number of them, and comparing the identification results with the score provided by consultants. This happens in early states in presidential primaries and in battleground states for the general election and similar crucial contests, but, as one senior staffer in one of the campaigns I followed frankly admitted, "We rarely have time to do that." Even senior staffers treat predictive modeling as what sociologist Bruno Latour calls a "black box," a naturalized procedure where internal complexities are invisible and all people care about is input and output.[12] Staffers focus on securing access to the relevant data sources, gather additional information through the field program, and then simply trust that the targeting will work as intended. As I show below, volunteers, part-timers, and many allies are less inclined to let the consultants work their magic without asking impertinent questions or offering other ways things could be done.

To appreciate the importance of predictive modeling and the development it is part of, it is worthwhile to compare the new dominant targeting scheme with what preceded it. On the Democratic side, a kind of targeting bricolage mixing and matching three different and sometimes overlapping schemes was the default for much of the 1980s and 1990s.

The first and most widespread scheme was precinct-based targeting, conducted on the basis of data provided by the National Committee for an Effective Congress (NCEC). This Washington-based political action committee works closely with Democratic campaigns across the country, providing them with information about past party performance, voter turnout, and estimates of the number of swing voters at a precinct level. On this basis, campaigns can identify all of those parts of a given district where Democratic candidates typically capture two or more votes out of every three cast (precincts that have what is called a Democratic Performance Index, or DPI, of 65 or more). These are then ranked by turnout among registered voters and targeted wholesale for get-out-the-vote efforts, starting with the lowest-turnout precincts—campaigns try to knock on every door and call every phone in these areas.[13]

The second scheme was list-based targeting, relying either simply on the voter files maintained by public officials or, where available, on voter lists maintained by state parties, incumbent elected officials, or local consultants. Only in the late 1980s did the DNC begin to systematically encourage state parties to build such files, and as late as 2002 only thirty state parties had centralized digital lists available.[14] In areas with many competitive elections, independent voter list companies maintained their own data and leased it to candidates, but in much of the country there was no market to sustain the costly hard work it takes to gather and maintain a comprehensive file.[15] A typical form of list-based targeting would be to acquire lists of all registered voters in a district and then simply target registered independents or "unaffiliated" voters (the categories differ from state to state) for persuasion and target registered Democrats for get-out-the-vote efforts. In contrast to precinct-based targeting hitting entire areas for GOTV, this gives campaigns the ability to target individual voters rather than several hundred voters at a time, and makes it possible to target for persuasion.

The third scheme was based solely on response data, on campaigns' own identification contacts, the contemporary heir to old-school "counting the votes," pursued by individual campaigns or local party organizations keeping track of the leanings of the constituency. Campaigns themselves would try to identify potential swing voters, and likely supporters in the electorate, by contacting people directly through their field program in the months leading up to an election. In a few areas, machines—whether urban in the classic Chicago style or rural akin to courthouse circles of the old Harry Byrd organization in Virginia—would sustain a durable and fine-grained network of local regulars who would keep tabs on their precincts by making regular "rounds" to talk with people and work to deliver the vote on Election Day.[16] John C. Green and Daniel M. Shea suggest that at least remnants of such forms of informal and qualitative targeting were in use into the 1990s, and they undoubtedly still are at the local level in some places.[17] But in most of the country this option has been effectively off the table for many years, given the state of local party organizations, leaving it to time- and cash-strapped campaigns to do their own identification work at the last minute.

Seen from a staff perspective, each of these schemes suffers from different weaknesses. Precinct-based targeting is useful because the National Committee for an Effective Congress effectively does the targeting job for the campaign, leaving to them only the tasks of operationalizing the ranking provided and generating enough contacts. But the problem with this method is that it omits all potential targets in precincts with mediocre or poor partisan performance. (Only a minority of all precincts have a consistent enough partisan leaning to qualify as targets under this scheme, leaving out all the swing voters and partisan infrequent voters who live in precincts with a DPI under 65.) Precinct-based targeting provides a comprehensive targeting scheme but no individual-level information and is most effective for getting out the vote in base areas.

Lists, in contrast, afford individual-level targeting. But the problem with this method is that the quality of the data is unknown and hard to verify, and there is no practical way that campaigns can ascertain in advance whether those on the lists—registered partisans, supposed supporters, and so forth—are actually going to come out and vote for their candidate or are actually susceptible to persuasion. A substantial number of registered Democrats, for instance, regularly vote for Republicans, and a raw list will not tell a campaign who these people are. List-based targeting in some cases provides a comprehensive and individual-level scheme, but often it hardly amounts to targeting at all, just a mere selection on the basis of party registration or some demographic variable like gender or race. One experienced Democratic operative calls this "barely an improvement" over using the phone book.[18]

Counting the votes, finally, is problematic because it is costly, either because it necessitates campaigns spending valuable time, money, and manpower identifying people one-by-one, or because it requires striking a deal with potentially awkward partners in the form of entrenched, sometimes corrupt, and always self-interested political organizations. Even where local party organizations are available to help, or where resourceful campaigns take the time to try to count their votes, this scheme is rarely comprehensive, even if it may provide good individual-level targeting. (It is mostly used in high-stakes, low-turnout contests like the Iowa caucus.)

Until the 2008 election many Democratic ground war efforts relied mostly on precinct-level targeting oriented toward getting out the vote on Election Day, combined with rudimentary microtargeting in areas where state parties or commercial list vendors maintained decent voter files. They therefore ended up focusing almost exclusively on traditional base areas that often make up only a small proportion of a given district, mixed with a bit of list-based targeting of potential swing voters and sporadic counting of the votes here and there. Predictive modeling was mainly used in fund-raising, direct mail, and a few exceptionally well funded voter contact programs. Today, however, predictive modeling is integrated into the new, dominant targeting scheme, based on data from the national voter file (made available for a nominal fee by the DNC and the state parties). It offers targeting that is both comprehensive and individual-level, improving the accuracy and expanding the reach of personalized political communication, and it only requires campaigns to gather up-to-date response data and pay for the modeling work itself.

EVERYDAY WORK AND TARGETING

Even as sophisticated predictive modeling done by consultants, who are often far away from the districts and the din on the ground, guides more and more targeting decisions, these decisions are still deeply dependent on the everyday work of those directly involved in the campaign assemblages on the ground. Targeting relies on the ongoing work of campaigns themselves, because only the so-called response data generated by field programs is current—everything else is historical data.

Response data is important for two reasons. First, it serves to verify existing information, most importantly addresses and phone numbers. It does not matter how precisely a potential swing voter or infrequently voting partisan's behavior has been modeled if the campaign cannot contact that person. If an early contact suggests a voter is not to be found at the expected address, the campaign has a chance to remove that person from the target universe until new information on his or her whereabouts arrive, thereby minimizing the number of contacts made in vain. This may sound like a trivial matter, but the Census Bureau estimated that close to 12 percent of the population changed their addresses in 2007–2008 alone. Among those under the federal poverty line, the figure is over 20 percent. The rate of data attrition on contact information is high for many key Democratic constituencies, including African Americans, Latinos, and younger voters. Over time, this adds up if the voter files are not constantly updated and cleaned. Secondly, response data is important because it provides the only up-to-date information on the current candidate leanings of individual voters. It is useful for the consultant scoring voters to know that someone has voted for Democratic candidates in the past. But it is even more useful to know that this time a particular person is leaning toward supporting Jim Himes or Linda Stender. This eventual choice, after all, is what the predictive model is meant to predict. Hence, up until the very end of the election, all contacts made under the aegis of the dominant scheme are not supposed to simply influence voters but are also intended to gather information about them for targeting purposes. As one field director put it, "Everything we do in effect doubles as one giant poll." This is what all the questions included in the scripts discussed in chapter 3 are for. As made clear, canvassers and callers rarely get a chance to ask many of these questions. Quantitative data confirms this. The progressive data vendor Catalist reports that the 127 million individual contacts their client organizations made during the 2008 elections resulted in only about 60 million pieces of response data—less than one answer per every two contacts.[19] But response data still identifies many wrong addresses and phone numbers well in advance of the get-out-the-vote effort and adds crucial current information to the data sets available for targeting purposes.

The development of online-integrated interfaces allows staffers to quickly operationalize the target universes defined by predictive models, and the VoteBuilder database maintained by the DNC and the state parties allows them to return data on how those contacted respond to consultants on a daily basis. This continuous feedback loop depends on callers and canvassers actually using the lists provided and converting their experiences on the phone or at the door into the categories that the interface and the rest of the system recognize (which does not always correspond to the caller's or canvasser's experience of the encounter). Even recognizing that some volunteers and part-timers will always stray from the scripts the staffers use to structure the field program, the point at which one can tell whether an actor in the assemblage operates under the dominant targeting scheme is therefore whether or not they use the call and walk sheets. (As a local party regular in Bridgeport told me, "We keep our own lists.") Below, I deal first with the relations between everyday campaign work and the dominant targeting scheme and then discuss an example of an allied organization from within the Democratic Party itself that opted out of the dominant scheme in favor of its own alternative targeting scheme.

The interface: The interface between the VoteBuilder database and the campaigns that use it is called the VAN. It is a piece of online-integrated software that allows anyone with the appropriate clearance to access varying levels of data and functionality from any computer with an Internet connection. It gives campaigns access to parts of the information already in VoteBuilder and lets them add the data they produce through their identification contacts. It is integral to the design of the VAN that it has to be many things to many people. The software is designed for users with varying (and generally low) levels of familiarity with the system and allows for carefully calibrated levels of access, in accordance with state party regulations and campaign decisions that differ from case to case. Different parts of different communities use it in different ways.

For senior staffers in the campaign and party organizations, the VAN is a tool for accessing and sharing data, for strategic planning, and for managing junior staffers. It gives them high-level and instant access to VoteBuilder and allows them to share data quickly and easily among themselves and with outside consultants. Information that as recently as twenty years ago was primarily stored on paper, punch cards, and magnetic tapes today has been not only digitized but also made sharable via secure online connections. The data can then be used to plan everyday work, monitor progress toward quantitative contact goals, and manage subordinate staffers on the basis of how many knocks and calls they and their teams of volunteers and part-timers generate.

For junior staffers, the VAN is a very different tool, primarily important for day-to-day planning and for surveilling part-timers. They can access only some of VoteBuilder's data and use a limited number of functions. The most time-consuming part of their everyday work is to translate the canvassing targets of the day into "turfs" of fifty or so relatively adjacent doors. The VAN combines the data in VoteBuilder with Geographic Information System (GIS) software to literally map where a given target universe of voters live (see the turf map reproduced as figure 5.3). Since the system does not yet include the functions that companies like FedEx use to predetermine delivery routes, junior staffers themselves cut each individual turf on the screen, trying to make it as compact and "walkable" as possible. Although this system is much faster than the scissors-and-glue approach that was the standard well into the 2000s, it still takes something like five minutes to prepare each walk packet for a canvasser, complete with walk sheets and a map printed from the VAN plus directions and various canvassing tips. After Labor Day, when each field organizer leads a team of ten to fifteen part-timers, many staffers end up spending a couple of hours getting things ready every morning. Meanwhile, call sheets are printed for volunteer calls. In both cases the work has to be carefully done, or the rest of the day will be plagued by "list confusion"—the problems that arise when several people are making calls or knocks with the same targets, a situation that neither part-timers, volunteers, nor voters enjoy in particular.

Sheets like figure 5.1 and figure 5.2 are the main point of contact between the VAN and the volunteers and part-timers, lists meant to identify voters for personalized political communication and to ensure that response data is coded in terms amenable to further predictive modeling. Some volunteers and part-timers also encounter permutations of the VAN in its software form. The VAN they use has an even lower level of

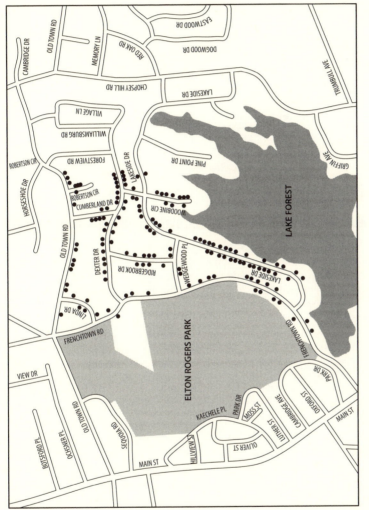

Figure 5.3. **Turf map with target voters located.**
Each dot marks a target voter. Several overlapping dots suggests several targets at the same address. Often, canvassers are supposed to talk to only one or two out of several members of a household.

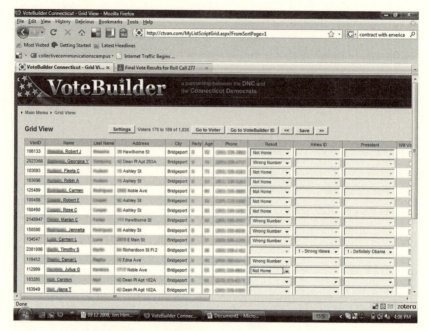

Figure 5.4. **Screenshot from VAN interface used for data entry.**
Street numbers, phone numbers, last names, sex, age, and party registration have been blurred to protect the people on the list. Notice the frequency of wrong numbers and the entry of basic response data on candidate leanings, in this case a strong Himes supporter (a "1") who also expressed an intention to vote for Barack Obama. This person—Timothy on Richardson Street—will be added to the GOTV universe and canvasser and will be called in the final days of the campaign if his past voting record suggests he does not always vote.

data access and functionality than the one used by junior staffers (underlining their place in the staffers' conception of campaigns as hierarchies). Volunteers primarily use the VAN if they are helping with data entry in the campaign offices, typically logged on to a special user account that does not allow them to do anything but enter data. Part-timers, who rarely work in the offices, encounter a separate piece of software called the "MiniVAN," loaded onto the PalmPilots/PDAs they carry as they go canvassing. This software allows them to enter data on contacts while they are on the street and can then be automatically synchronized with VoteBuilder, cutting out the usual work of first entering information by annotating walk or call sheets and then subsequently entering this information manually into VoteBuilder using the VAN interface (see the screenshot reproduced as figure 5.4).

In principle the combination of predictive modeling, the VAN interface, detailed data on the electorate, and an intimate knowledge of the human resources at each assemblage's disposal should allow staffers to carefully tailor the field program and match messages to the voters they are trying to reach. This is how targeting is used in direct mail and online advertising.[20] Early in the cycle, senior staffers in both campaigns in which I did my fieldwork were talking about how they would use these tools to match canvassers to the areas they canvassed, relying on locals, preferably having volunteers and part-timers contact co-ethnics, have veterans call veterans, women call women, and so on, and talking about tailoring the scripts and issue appeals to reflect local concerns. In practice these aspirations quickly receded into the background as quantitative goals took priority and as staffers became concerned primarily with recruiting enough people to meet their numeric benchmarks in the first place. In both Connecticut and New Jersey, the field programs had too few people, too little time, and not enough organizational capacity to engage in even the most rudimentary tailoring of their field contacts to the targeted voters. Personalized political communication is narrowcasting in the sense that it is oriented to individuals and mediated by individuals, and the individual encounters play out in different ways, but deliberate customization of contacts, pursued in high-end direct marketing and by some civic associations (see chapter 3), is well beyond the resources of even well-funded and competitive campaigns like the two I followed.

The VAN on the Ground—Using Sheets and Generating Data

The VAN walk and call sheets are ubiquitous in Democratic campaigns. Their simple rows of names and numbers do not betray the complex calculations, sophisticated software, and detailed databases behind them. The ability to define and produce these lists gives staffers a powerful tool for coordination and control that allows them to sidestep some of the organizing problems discussed in chapter 4. As Luis put it in episode 5.3 above, "In targeting, you get what you are given," and few volunteers or part-timers know enough or care enough to question the matter-of-fact sheets they are provided with—lists are taken at face value. The main challenge staffers face in their everyday work of enforcing the dominant scheme is thus not so much to make people *use* the lists (though there are occasional disputes over that too) as it is to make them use them in what the staffers consider the *right way*, a problem originating in a lack of understanding of the purposes that the lists are meant to serve. The problem is grounded partly in junior staffers' own relative lack of understanding of how targeting works and what role their own work plays in it, and partly in the virtual absence of any concerted effort to educate people on the targeting purposes that the walk and call sheets serve. As in many other situations, staffers may tell people *what* to do but rarely *why*.

"Oh, I see, so this is targeted?" is one volunteer's reaction when told by a staffer to "stick to the list." What she had done is what many are inclined to do: speak to whoever picks up the phone or opens the door—spouses, teenage children, whoever happens to be there—and take down their reactions. Both volunteers and part-timers tend to see their work in terms of influencing people in general, not in terms of high- and low-value targets and the various cost-effectiveness calculations that figure prominently for senior staffers and consultants. Callers and canvassers generally see those they talk to more as *voters* than as *targeted voters*. "I don't understand it, don't we have to talk to everyone eventually anyway?" one volunteer asks after being told (again, in that oft-repeated phrase) to "stick to the list." But they do not have to talk to everyone eventually. Even in the most lavishly funded and intensely competitive race, attention is focused on the persuasion universe of voters identified as undecided and the GOTV universe of people identified as partisans who may need a reminder to go vote. While staffers have little control over what callers and canvassers actually say to voters (as demonstrated in chapter 3), they have a great deal of control over which voters they talk to, at least down to the household level.

Unaware of their full purpose, most volunteers and part-timers see call and walk sheets not as a specific number of targets that are to be identified and classified in accordance with the categories included on each sheet, but as a handy list of recommended people to contact. Because of the low level of training and volunteers' and part-timers' consequent limited understanding of the purpose of the sheets, plus the frequent absence of staff supervision, volunteers in particular routinely fail to return sheets, fill them out without adhering to the standards held by staffers, or richly annotate them with data that VoteBuilder has no place for. This becomes clear when staffers or volunteers sit down to enter the data via the VAN interface.

EPISODE 5.5

"These calls have been made by first-time volunteers," Christian, a junior staffer doing data entry, complains. "They are totally messed up. Some of these people just don't get it. Why write 'OK' on the sheet? What's the use? What does that even mean? That it was okay that we called them? That the call went okay? Why don't these guys follow the protocol?" People have hand-annotated many of the call sheets he is about to enter into VoteBuilder, some with "OK" or check marks and some with little comments ranging from "Nice guy" and "Thanked us for calling" to crude remarks presumably provoked by unsatisfying encounters with voters.

The source of mild amusement as Christian provides running commentary on what he calls people's "inane" comments, unorthodox annotations are also a practical problem for him. "I'm only going to enter data when I'm sure what it means, like when they write 'Not home' and 'Wrong number,'" he says. But even this presents problems. After entering half a page, he pauses—"As much as I would like to, I find it hard to believe that all these people have signed up to volunteer." He holds up a sheet where the box marked "VOL" is checked for every single voter. Christian muses, "What does this mean?" Jagdish, working next to him, suggests, "That they will vote?" Christian says, "Even that would be an amazing run, thirteen people in a row?"

The various boxes to the right of each voter's personal information on walk and call sheets (see figures 5.1 and 5.2) are used to translate the qualitative experience of each interaction into quantitative data that can be entered into VoteBuilder via the VAN interface (see figure 5.4) and used for further modeling and targeting. Canvassers and callers are asked to score people they talk to on a scale from 1 to 5 in terms of whether they are "solid Democrats," "leans Democrat," are "undecided," "leans Republican," or are "solid Republicans," and to repeat the different ID questions for each candidate on their script and ask what issues—from a predetermined list—people care about the most (see the script reproduced as figure 3.1 in chapter 3).

I do not have data to accurately estimate how often people use sheets in their own ways, but the hundreds of unorthodoxly annotated call and walk sheets I have seen in campaign offices, the frequent staff complaints about people "doing it all wrong," and the stacks of sheets I have seen shredded or thrown out after they had been deemed useless suggest these problems are not uncommon. Even when done in accordance with instructions and under staff supervision, classification is not uncomplicated. As the chapter on contacting has made clear, interactions with voters rarely play out in a straightforward manner, and volunteers and part-timers often have to improvise a great deal when it comes to filling out these identification questions. Does a slammed door signify a Republican? For some it does. If someone says, "Yeah, I'll vote for him," and hangs up, is that a solid Democrat across the board or simply a Himes supporter? People make these judgment calls all the time and are not always told that they are supposed to leave unanswered questions blank rather than trying to infer what the answer might have been. One constant problem is determining when exactly a phone call or door knock should count as "Refused." In one campaign, junior staffers were under instructions from their superiors to minimize the use of this category, since voters thus marked are automatically removed from the target universe and left out of the voter contact program for the rest of the election, a technical response that senior staffers regard as too drastic in all but the most acute cases. "Only use 'Refused' when you have had an experience with a voter that you under no circumstances want anyone else to have" is how Jack, the volunteer coordinator in New Jersey, explains it to a volunteer. The practical problem here is that there is no middle road between "Refused," which takes people out of the universe, and "Not Home," which retains them, often resulting in another call or knock, sometimes as soon as the next day. Volunteers and part-timers often have particularly bad experiences with voters who have (or pretend to, or believe they have) already announced that they do not want to be contacted.

EPISODE 5.6

I've made a call to an eighty-eight-year-old woman and had a couple of minutes of extremely confusing conversation with her when I'm interrupted by her caregiver, who scolds me for "pestering a senile old lady" and hangs up on me. Afterward, I ask Jonathan, one of the field organizers, if it's okay that I put her down as "Refused" so that the campaign does not call her again. He says, "You probably shouldn't do that, but you can write a note about it. Then the person entering it into the VAN can make a note that we shouldn't contact her until right before the election. That way, I think, we won't print her tomorrow." A minute later, while Jonathan is out, Karen, a volunteer making calls next to me, and who overheard the conversation, says, "I would put that down as 'Refused.'"

So while volunteers and part-timers generally accept the lists they are given at face value, they do not always stick to them or use them in what staffers consider the right way.[21] And when contacts are made but not recorded; or recorded on sheets that are not returned or returned but not entered; or recorded in unorthodox ways that staffers dismiss as "data overflow," the feedback loop between target lists and further fresh response data on which the dominant targeting scheme thrives is broken or contorted. As one common staff saying has it: "If it isn't recorded, it didn't happen." (This is very much a staff perspective, as from the point of view of the volunteer or part-timer who did the work, and those they talked to, of course it happened.) And if the voter in question has been modeled as an attractive target, he may be contacted again the very next day when lists are printed anew, often to his consternation.

Opting Out of the Dominant Scheme

The problem of multiple contacts is aggravated by the fact that a considerable number of contacts happen outside the dominant scheme—not only because volunteers and part-timers stray from their lists, or because of parallel efforts by outside interest groups that are not involved in the campaign assemblage, but also because some allies involved in the assemblage deliberately eschew the dominant scheme, even as they work with the campaign organization on the ground war project and the election more broadly. Even if coordinated targeting along the lines of the dominant scheme is evidently more effective from an instrumental point of view, it also entails ceding control to those doing the targeting and effectively reducing—however momentarily—an ally to an appendage to the campaign organization and the party organizations that control the national voter file. Instead, various unions and other powerful interest groups have their own targeting schemes for member-to-member efforts, and groups like MoveOn have particular demographics that they focus on (younger voters, newly registered voters, etc.). Well-endowed organizations may adopt schemes that are analogous to the dominant one—that is, they are based on predictive modeling and detailed individual-level data and even coordinated among several distinct organizations. (Two examples are the umbrella organization America Votes, which brings together most of the largest progressive interest groups in many battleground states, and the partisan data vendor Catalist, which only does business with a select set of liberal interest groups.) But they typically operate with their own target universes, irrespective of campaign and staff priorities, and many of them can rely on old-style list-based targeting, because their main efforts are directed toward their own members. They take part in the shared electoral project that defines the assemblage but opt out of the dominant targeting scheme.

It is more remarkable that even actors *within* the Democratic Party also opt out. Some candidate campaigns and party organizations eschew predictive modeling and the national voter file and rely exclusively on targeting practices and data that they control themselves, even in some cases where they recognize that this may reduce their impact on a race. They reject the implicit trade-off between autonomy and the impact involved in using the walk and call sheets that are produced by consultants and distributed by staffers (the logic behind the "you give us the scripts and the lists, and we do the work" remark quoted in episode 5.3). I discuss just one of several examples of this here: the case of a well-organized local Democratic Town Committee in one of my districts that worked closely with the campaign organization throughout the fall but nonetheless stuck to its own targeting scheme as it generated thousands of contacts over the get-out-the-vote weekend, even in the face of considerable pressure from other elements of the assemblage to take part in the joint effort. I call the town Hillsville here. It was one of the larger towns in the district, an area where the candidate in question needed to do well to win.

The Hillsville Democratic Town Committee's alternative targeting scheme was list-based and relied on the voter file maintained by the town's registrar of voters. After the final deadline for registration some weeks before the election, the town party chair's assistant acquired the public record of all registered voters in the city. In addition to party registration, this included basic information: name, address, sometimes a phone number, and a unique voter identification number. The raw list was enhanced and verified with some additional information purchased from commercial vendors. (All of this data is also in VoteBuilder.) From this locally compiled list, party regulars manually removed all households made up of only unaffiliated voters or containing one or more Republican voters. (This is a form of nonstatistical data analysis implemented for the same purposes as predictive modeling—to define the target universe more precisely.) The remaining voters—all of them Democrats living either alone or in households with other registered Democrats or unaffiliated voters—made up the local GOTV universe. This was markedly different from the universe the dominant targeting scheme would have produced, because it included even Democrats who always turned out to vote and Democrats who predictive modeling suggested would support the Republican candidate, and because it left out many unaffiliated and even Republican voters who had been identified or modeled as likely supporters. From a campaign staff point of view, it thus had too many low-value targets, included people who should not be targeted at all, and excluded many high-value targets.

The alternative scheme came with instrumental advantages, too, however. With each voter's unique identification number at hand, the local party regulars could prune their target universe throughout Election Day itself, removing people as they voted and focusing only on getting out those who had yet to vote. This setup required a level of local organization and experience unmatched anywhere else in the district (and one that is probably rarely found). On November 4 local party activists were stationed at all polling locations, and every hour from ten in the morning onward, they would check the ledgers and provide their own headquarters with the identification numbers of those who had already voted at each location. Those voters were then removed from the target universe in real time, even as volunteers were calling through the lists. Every time callers reached someone who had not yet voted, that person's name was marked and the person was not called again for three hours. If at the end of that time the person had still not voted, he or she received another call. Thus, the target universe was winnowed down during the day as information about turnout streamed into the office and as calls focused on an ever-narrower group of people.[22] In contrast, in the rest of the district the campaign used a single master list defined by the dominant scheme and printed from the VAN the night before the election, with no running updates of who had or had not voted, resulting in thousands of supposed get-out-the-vote calls to people who had already voted.

Turnout among Democrats in the town in question has historically been consistently higher than in comparable towns across the state—90 percent or more—a point of considerable pride for the Hillsville Democratic Town Committee and its chair, and something that has helped ensure virtually total Democratic dominance of local and state-level offices in the area. But while staffers working on state- and district-wide campaigns acknowledge these accomplishments, they still complain that the city could deliver a bigger margin if the Hillsville Democratic Town Committee embraced the dominant targeting scheme. I had one late-night conversation with an experienced staffer who had worked in the area several times in different functions and who had this to say about the local setup:

EPISODE 5.7

"[The chair] lays down the law here. Of course, we [staffers from the campaign organization] and the folks in D.C. [the Democratic Congressional Campaign Committee] would like them to use our lists [from the VAN], but from their perspective, what's the point? There's a little bit of an 'If it ain't broke, don't fix it' mentality."

I ask what the problem is if it "ain't broke." "Well, the thing is, we win [Hillsville], but we don't perform. We could get a bigger margin. And that's a problem, because this is going to be really close." "But wouldn't the local Democrats want to improve performance too?" I ask. The staffer says, "Their model works really well at the local and the state level. I mean, look around; this is a Democratic town, through and through. They don't need the voters that we need further up the ballot." "But what do they have to lose by using your lists?" I ask, and get the response: "It's also about control. We need them more than they need us, frankly."

The alternative scheme may reduce the Hillsville Democratic Town Committee's overall impact on the district-wide result (and even this is at least debatable, as the chair pointed out to me, given the turnout they produce). But it allows the local organization to retain control and maintain some autonomy from the state and national party.

In this case a local party organization opted out of the dominant targeting scheme from a position of strength (as the line "We need them more than they need us" suggests), whereas in other areas, candidates and their local networks of supporters sometimes opt out from a position of weakness. In areas where the party organizations are either entirely absent or notoriously dysfunctional and riddled with fractions and internal conflict, individual incumbents all the way down to the local level often rely on their own decisions about whom to target and maintain their own voter files.[23] In this way, they increase their autonomy vis-à-vis a party that they do not always trust or believe they have a stake in—and sometimes rightfully so. I heard several stories about how party officials or senior staffers had used their high-level access to VoteBuilder to influence party-internal politics in primaries and elsewhere. In one particularly egregious case, a state party chair allegedly not only leaked voter identification data gathered by one primary campaign to the competing establishment-backed candidate but also personally called many of the individual registered Democrats who had been identified as supporters of the insurgent and encouraged them to reconsider. That is not supposed to happen, but if it does, and a candidate or organization has handed over their data to the state party, there is little the local organization can do to prevent or counter it other than to opt out (belatedly) of the dominant scheme and the shared system. (I have been unable to ascertain how widespread such use of the national voter file is. Representatives from the Voter Activation Network whom I spoke to acknowledge that what they call "misuse" is possible but insist that such misuse is virtually nonexistent.)

This danger, which looms large for local candidates and organizations making decisions about what targeting scheme to adopt and whom to trust with what data, is of little concern for most of the staffers, who have no long-term commitments in a given district. They are interested mainly in ensuring that what is, from their perspective, the instrumentally superior dominant targeting scheme is adopted as widely as possible—and, if need be, imposed. This is a source of much friction between local and D.C.-based operatives, but it is also a logic that helps a plethora of local list vendors and decentralized candidate and party voter files survive in the face of the more sophisticated, instrumentally effective, and often cheaper dominant targeting scheme pushed by the national party.

CONSTRUCTING A NATIONAL VOTER FILE

From a staff point of view, the problem with previous precinct-, list-, and identification-based targeting schemes; with people straying from their lists and instructions; with allies opting out; and with the general balkanization of voter files that reigned for much of the twentieth century is that it all undermines the overall instrumental effectiveness of personalized political communication. The dominant targeting scheme, from the staffers' perspective, is evidently superior, and praise for it is profuse. However, its usefulness alone cannot account for its emergence. The basic predictive models and database technologies it relies on have been available for years, and yet on the Democratic side, the current scheme only started to coalesce in the run-up to the 2008 election. While the new political targeting is clearly useful, attempts to introduce it faced a set of formidable technological and political obstacles that have begun to be overcome only in the last few years. Given that modeling expertise was available from consultants, and that campaigns already had many routines for gathering various sorts of response data, the central remaining challenge was to construct a shared and continuously maintained national voter file and an interface that made it possible to not only use it for fund-raising and direct mail but also to integrate it into the everyday hustle and bustle of field campaigns. Without a national voter file to start from, predictive modeling would be an option only for extraordinarily well funded campaigns with the resources to construct their own detailed voter files well in advance of an election. Without an interface to return response data and match it to other sources, even extensive voter identification pursued by campaigns amounts to little more than old-fashioned counting of the votes. In combination, the development of VoteBuilder at the back end and the VAN interface at the front end is the third and final element (after predictive modeling and the everyday work that goes into targeting) in the new dominant targeting scheme that is now spreading quickly throughout the Democratic Party and is increasingly commonplace in competitive races.

The idea of building a national voter file is thus evidently attractive from an instrumental point of view—and hardly new. People have dreamed of a "perfect list" since the days of Abraham Lincoln, and probably before, and many have worked hard to compile such a list. In 1892 Grover Cleveland's campaign manager, James Clarkson, boasted that he had "with two years of hard work secured a list of the names of all the voters in all the important States of the North, in 20 or more States, and lists with the age, occupation, nativity, residence and all other facts of each voters' life, and had them arranged alphabetically, so that literature could be sent constantly to each voter directly, dealing with every public question and issue from the standpoint of his personal interest."[24] Even if Clarkson did not enjoy the advantages that new information and communications technologies afford political operatives today, he had a crucial advantage over them when he put together his list: he operated at a time when a strong party organization was considered an essential asset by political elites. Even as predictive modeling evolved, online interfaces became available, database technology developed, and the mountains of publicly and commercially available information grew, it would be well into the twenty-first century before the two major parties had voter files that could match Clarkson's nineteenth-century list.

The absence of a good voter list was a source of intense frustration for Democratic campaign staffers and political operatives throughout the

1990s. Not only could they see how direct marketing and political fund-raising were exploiting predictive modeling and the increasing amounts of data gathered and maintained by private data vendors. They also had to witness the Republican Party's launch of their so-called Voter Vault in 1995, exactly the kind of shared and continuously updated national voter file that would eventually make it possible for them to capitalize on the new targeting models across a whole range of voter contact programs, starting with direct mail, but gradually spreading to personalized political communication.[25] With the adoption of predictive modeling for voter contact purposes in the early 2000s, this laid the targeting groundwork for the Republicans' successful field campaigns in 2002 and 2004 (discussed in chapter 2). Not only did the Democrats not have anything like this list. They could not even buy it. While there is a market for data in politics, it is far smaller and more seasonal than the constant and massive demand that has fueled the growth of the various giants of the consumer information industry, who do most of their business with corporate America. Even before the consolidation brought about by the construction of the two major parties' national voter files, commercial vendors of specifically political data had a hard time making a living in many parts of the country.[26] In the absence of a shared voter file, every new campaign would have to start largely from scratch, building their own voter files by collecting public records on registered voters, buying commercial data to enhance it, and making identification calls. Once the elections were over, the entire painstakingly constructed database would typically simply disappear, be retained in-house by incumbents, or be carted away by entrepreneurial consultants who understood its lasting value.[27] Well into the 1990s, it was not uncommon for the voter files available to Democratic campaigns to be stored on 3-by-5 index cards or magnetic tapes at the county level and formatted in different ways from place to place—hardly the handiest of media for ongoing modeling work, flexible planning on the fly, and the accumulation of large and detailed data sets. In a few areas industrious consultants or exceptionally well organized state parties did build statewide, comprehensive, and relatively up-to-date files, but in most areas neither the market nor the party could provide Democratic campaigns with a solid national voter file to start from. So this is what centrally located senior party players set out to create.

The Rise and Fall of "Demzilla"

When Terry McAuliffe took over as chair of the DNC in 2001, he complained that although 50 million people had voted for Al Gore in the 2000 election, the party had not retained a record on any one of them—and he vowed to change this by providing the party with an up-to-date technological infrastructure.[28] At a point when people were already considering personal computing and Internet access increasingly mundane, the national party had only an off-line list of about seventy thousand donors, hosted on in-house servers and accessed through a green monochrome display evoking the early days of desktop computing some twenty years before. The Democratic Party did not make a particularly convincing case for the existence of high-tech politics or effective "parties in service." The Republican Party, in contrast, had the Voter Vault, with about 175 million names in it—more than two hundred times the Democratic count—and it was put to good use in elections at all levels in 2000. Internal reviews after that election identified data and targeting as among the areas where the Democratic Party was falling behind the Republican Party. In 2002 McAuliffe made an initial investment of $3.7 million to rectify this situation, creating a new IT infrastructure developed by QRS Newsmedia and Plus Three, and subsequently spent additional millions on data from InfoUSA. All of this was part of what was called "Project 5104"—the name signaling the purpose of building the Democratic Party's capacity to capture 51 percent or more of the vote in the 2004 presidential election.

Compared to the sums spent each election cycle by campaigns, the DNC's investment seems modest, but the money spent on technology alone represented almost 10 percent of total expenditures during McAuliffe's two first years as chairman. A national voter file seemed within reach, and the data and targeting gap between the parties looked like it might be closed. The new setup was often referred to as "Demzilla." (Technically, this referred to only the donor and activist part of the database and the interface, whereas the voter file at the core of the system was called the "DataMart.") The basic design was similar to that used in the Republican Voter Vault (and indeed in the later VoteBuilder). A central database would maintain a comprehensive voter file combining data from a variety of sources. State parties were supposed to provide the foundations by handing over their state-level voter files. The DNC would then enhance these by appending census data, consumer information from outside vendors, and various additional public records, and campaigns using the system would continually verify and update the available information and add their own response data to the file. Each entry in the database would have its own unique personal identifier so that detailed profiles could be built and maintained over time, even as people moved around the country, married, changed names, and so on.[29] In early 2004 the system contained 168 million individual files with up to three hundred data points appended, supposedly one file on every single registered voter in the country (thus leaving out tens of millions of people who were not registered to vote, just as the Republican Voter Vault did).

McAuliffe was bullish as always when he marketed the new system. In the summer of 2004, he proclaimed:

> You could ask me about any city block in America, and I could tell you how many on that block are likely to be health care voters, or who's most concerned about education or job creation . . . And I could press a button and six seconds later you'd have a name, an address and a phone number for each of them. We can then begin a conversation with these people that is much more sophisticated and personal than we ever could before.[30]

There were only two problems with the Demzilla system: the data was not quite as good as McAuliffe claimed it was, nor was the technology supposed to give campaigns access to the data.[31] The database was web-enabled, and interfaces existed for the various state parties and the presidential campaign to access what they had input and what had been subsequently added, but no interface for use in individual campaign offices had been developed yet, so field campaigns across the country had no ability to enter into a feedback loop with consultants by tweaking their work along the way and sharing response data with the people doing the targeting. Furthermore, on the data side, many state parties did not buy into Demzilla. Three years after Project 5104 started, on the cusp of the presidential election, only thirty state parties had agreed to share their data, and many had yet to actually hand it over. Several contested states, including New Hampshire, did not take part, nor did large states like California and Massachusetts (important for fund-raising, though not exactly battleground states). There are no indications that the system was put to use in any of the state or local elections in 2003 that could have served to test it. (This is in contrast to the way Gage and the Republican National Committee tested their predictive modeling during that off-year cycle.) Many state parties and campaigns continued to use their own systems, seemingly unimpressed with the data and functionality of the DNC's effort and distrustful of its guarantees that their data would be safe in the DNC's hands. It turned out to be fairly difficult to sell to state parties and down-ballot campaigns a project explicitly designed to help future Democratic presidential candidates—even for a master salesman like McAuliffe.

But without these partners the system could not work, because the basic data on which everything else was supposed to be built was not there. In the summer of 2003, more than a year before the election, the D.C.-based insider publication *Roll Call* published an article harshly critical of the progress so far. One Democratic consultant (anonymous, of course) complained that "the quality of the data is far from a level that would make it immediately useful," adding that "the system architecture is overly cumbersome and the result is that the data is not easily retrieved."[32] The article goes on to report that some searches involving several variables could "take weeks to complete," a situation that would make the system basically useless in the intense final months of a hard-fought election. The article did not register beyond the trade press, however, and the news media continued to quote McAuliffe on the wonders of Demzilla up until the election. Into 2004 even experienced reporters continued to write as if the two parties were racing neck and neck in the data race.[33]

Unfortunately for the Democratic Party, the critics turned out to have been prescient. In reality, they had been well behind their Republican opponents. After John Kerry's defeat, staffers and consultants involved complained that the information in Demzilla's database was "so bad as to be useless," and the interface giving campaigns access to it was dismissed as "[not] designed for real-world use."[34] In August 2004 it had turned out that the Demzilla data on Florida was so riddled with errors that it had to be rebuilt from scratch at the last minute. More than a million out of about 12 million registered voters had been missing from the voter file in this epitome of a battleground state. In September 2004 the interface giving staffers access to the data crashed in both Ohio and Pennsylvania, leaving the field campaigns in these crucial states with very limited access to the information they needed to plan their get-out-the-vote efforts. After the election the American Association of Political Consultants' magazine, *Campaigns and Elections*, reported that Demzilla had been "effectively abandoned."[35] Thus, while it had certainly improved the party's fund-raising operation, McAuliffe's investment did little to push Democratic field campaigns beyond the usual bricolage of different schemes.

Demzilla failed for two reasons. One the one hand, the problem was technological. Consultants who were closely involved in the process complained that many of the solutions chosen were substandard, even as they were careful to point out that this was not clear to the principals at the time. One says, "It is hard to explain in five minutes what a big difference it makes whether you use one kind of matching software or another, whether you chose the database solution with six fields for each address or the one with nine, but these decisions matter, and [under McAullife] they were rushed. We relied on a hodgepodge of vendors with little experience, and little experience with politics in particular." On the other hand, the problem was political. In the words of one Democratic operative quoted in the 2003 *Roll Call* article: "Demzilla is an idea that on paper makes a lot of sense . . . the problem is that [the DNC] took the idea and let the technology run ahead of their relationships with the people who had to participate in it."[36] Another consultant quoted in the same article explained, "[There is] an inherent distrust between the state parties and the [DNC]," a point summed up in a blunt statement by a third operative: "No one trusts the DNC to not steal stuff from their lists." The two problems were exacerbated by how the Demzilla project was pushed as a part of a solution to a national problem—winning the presidential election—with little concern for the particular problems of the state parties and various campaigns that would have had to buy into the project to make it work. With a flawed technical setup and a lack of participation from the necessary partners, the DNC found itself with a large database of basically useless data, and everything but the donor side of the database was abandoned after 2004 as the party tried again to build that elusive national voter file.

The Coming of VoteBuilder and the VAN

When Howard Dean assumed the chairmanship of the Democratic National Committee in February 2005, he basically reiterated the vows McAullife had made four years earlier. A new national voter file was to be built, largely from scratch both in terms of data and technology. The basic principles in the new $8 million effort were the same as before, a relational database hosted by the national party but built on data from the state parties and campaigns. The vendors and technologies employed were different, however, and so was the political process. Again, each individual entry in the relational database was equipped with a unique personal identifier, and up to nine hundred data points were appended from a wide variety of sources, including public records, consumer data, and campaign-generated response data. The most important partners in the project were Intelligent Integration System, who built the database, and the previously mentioned Voter Activation Network, who built the interface. (The latter company, now merged with another to form NGP-VAN, continues to do most of the back-end tech and database work for the party.)

Politically, Dean framed the database investment in a way that was very different from how McAuliffe had done it. Whereas Demzilla was part of the latter's Project 5104 and aimed at the presidential election, VoteBuilder was launched from the start as an integral part of Dean's 50-state strategy and was coupled with a promise to bankroll training and staff on the ground to help all state parties make use of the new tool for elections at all levels. In addition, Dean worked hard to convince the principals at the state parties and in campaign organizations around the country that the DNC could be trusted with their data, and the technologists involved in designing the system all stress that data can be kept entirely compartmentalized according to user specifications. Thus, even as almost all state parties have today bought into the VoteBuilder project and share their data, they continue to control the terms of access.

This means parties can charge campaigns for access or stipulate what data can be used for. Importantly, such data-sharing agreements almost always include the specification that campaigns will share all of their user-generated data with the state and national parties once a given election is over. With this system in place, VoteBuilder grew quickly, and by 2006 thirty state parties and hundreds of campaigns used the new database (achieving in little over a year the penetration rate Demzilla had after more than three years).

The database and the information in it were widely praised after the midterm elections, but there were still problems with the interfaces that give campaigns decentralized access to it. In 2006 the DNC had contracted with three different companies—Sage Systems, Blaemire Communications, and the Voter Activation Network—to develop tools to make the data available and useful for campaigns on the ground. In addition, many state parties had themselves contracted with these or other developers to provide online-integrated interfaces for VoteBuilder or the relevant state party file. Many of these tools, however, turned out to be as fragile as those used in 2004. In many states the interfaces crashed; in other areas local staffers and party regulars, frustrated with the limitations of the tools at hand, resorted to ad-hoc combinations of commercially available off-the-shelf tools like Microsoft Access—good for their immediate needs but fundamentally undermining the feedback loop between campaigns, state parties, and the national database that Vote-Builder was supposed to feed off. After this experience the DNC issued a request for proposals for one standardized national tool, and in February 2007 the Voter Activation Network, the company deemed to have had the best performance in 2006, and which already had contracts in hand with twenty-five state parties, won a contract to provide it. The company was also paid to expand the database to cover even those states where the local state party had decided against taking part. (By 2008 only California and Massachusetts remained formally outside the system, largely for reasons having to do with the political economy of state politics.)

In a sense the prolonged 2008 presidential primary offered a perfect test for the new and truly national VoteBuilder/VAN combination. While both the Clinton and the Obama campaigns also drew on other providers, such as Catalist and Blue State Digital, they eventually made the party-provided tools the backbone of their targeting and field efforts. Not only did doing so provide a trial by fire for the database and interface technologies themselves in the run-up to the 2008 election. It also generated enormous amounts of new response data, verified or corrected much of what was in the system, and provided a litmus test of the DNC and their technologists' promises that state parties and campaigns' data would be safe in VoteBuilder. As far as I have been able to ascertain, there were no instances where either of the two presidential primary campaigns considered their data compromised, and Dean's effort thus proved to the far-flung field of actual and potential users that the new national voter file was not only useful but perhaps trustworthy as well (though, as mentioned above, there seem to have been some problems at the state and local level).

VoteBuilder today is considered a success. When former Virginia governor Tim Kaine took over as chair of the DNC in 2009, he was the first new chairman in ten years *not* to make a new technological infrastructure for data and targeting one of his main priorities. Why did VoteBuilder succeed where Demzilla failed? How did the Republican National Committee manage to establish their Voter Vault years ahead of the Democratic Party? All of these three initiatives were motivated by the same desire to leverage demonstrably effective modeling techniques and database technologies that were long common in commercial marketing and use them for electoral purposes. And yet the Democratic Party consistently lagged behind. Republican efforts were initially based on the party's existing lead in the area of direct mail. But there are both technological and political reasons why the Republican National Committee managed to turn this into a three- to four-year head start in the adoption of predictive modeling and for the construction of a national voter file, reasons that also help account for the failure of Demzilla and the success of VoteBuilder.

On the technological side, building an online-integrated database containing hundreds of data points on hundreds of millions of individuals is not like installing off-the-shelf software. (Both the corporate world and the public sector have their own long histories of ambitious technological initiatives gone awry.) It is a complicated challenge, one that developers will only truly know they have solved when the system has been tested in practice. While the Republican National Committee has maintained the Voter Vault since 1995 (and some of the data comes from older, less comprehensive systems for fund-raising and direct mail), it is only in 2002 that they unrolled their first online-integrated user interface for the system (after a torturous development process involving controversial off-shore programming work done in India[37]). During their trial runs in 2002 and 2003 they continued to experience significant technical problems when using the interface. But because the RNC took the time to test the system in practice during these cycles, they went into the 2004 presidential election with a battle-tested and improved interface to go with their superior national voter file. Demzilla, in contrast, was developed by vendors with limited political experience and had not been battle-tested when it was put to use in 2005. VoteBuilder and VAN, on the other hand, followed the example set by the Republican National Committee. They were built by experienced vendors selected through a competitive request for proposals and were subject to repeated field testing in 2006, 2007, and the 2008 presidential primary before they faced the ultimate test during the general election of 2008. That year, many of my interviewees argue, the Democratic Party for the first time went one better than the Republican Party in the targeting and data arms race.

On the political side, the Republican effort in the early twenty-first century was eased by the fact that the party had a clear center of gravity with considerable clout with state- and local-level partners in the figure of President Bush. In the early stages of the development, Ken Mehlman and Karl Rove had an authority that Terry McAuliffe could only dream about. With the 2004 nominee in place well in advance, and a prodigious fundraiser to boot, the Republican National Committee could invest early, test along the way, and count on the collaboration of local partners who stood to benefit both from the improved Voter Vault and potentially the largesse of a reelected president. The DNC had none of these advantages and structured their investments in Demzilla around the abstract Project 5104 rather than a concrete candidate who could reward and punish potential partners. The later VoteBuilder, on the other hand, was built not around the upcoming 2008 presidential election (though surely with an eye toward it), but as an integral part of Howard Dean's 50-state strategy. It was thus much more clearly aligned with the needs and self-interest of the state parties and down-ballot candidates who needed to buy into the project to make the national voter file work and make it possible to maintain the data over time. The new infrastructure not only provided state parties with hosting, tech support, development work, and, eventually in the VAN, the state-of-the-art interface that Demzilla had also promised (but never delivered). It also allowed both state parties and candidates to retain a great deal of control over their own data. This recast the balance within the party from being the DNC versus everyone else, in the struggles over data leading up to 2004, to being the DNC and the state parties against the scattered group of local organizations, incumbent officeholders, and most importantly outside list vendors in 2008. VoteBuilder is a tremendous asset for Democratic field campaigns at all levels—its humming servers in Somerset, Massachusetts, are as important for Democratic field campaigns today as any local partner—and it has arguably brought the party to parity with (and perhaps ahead of) the Republican Party. It is also a shift of power from local data sources to national and state-level ones, and from outside providers to party-affiliated ones.

* * *

The targeting of voters for personalized contacts by callers and canvassers is increasingly based on a new scheme combining sophisticated predictive modeling, campaign assemblages' own everyday work of gathering response data, and vast national voter files built and maintained by the political parties over the last ten years. This new dominant targeting scheme is motivated by the search for instrumental efficiency and is premised upon a larger information architecture that raises question of privacy violations, the dangers of pervasive surveillance, and an ongoing segmentation of the American population. It is also tied in with issues of how campaign organizations and campaign assemblages operate, who controls what within them, and ultimately how they pursue personalized political communication.

Parties and campaigns have always targeted who they talked to, but the ways they do it are changing rapidly and continually today as new predictive models and database technologies are adopted from commercial marketing and elsewhere. The general direction of these efforts is clear: away from the qualitative "local knowledge" of old-school ward bosses, away from the crude precinct- and list-based targeting of the last decades of the twentieth century, and toward a new form of political targeting based on (1) analysis of quantitative data to identify individual voters for persuasion and GOTV contacts, (2) response data collected by campaigns themselves, and (3) technological infrastructures largely controlled by the national party organizations and partisan vendors working closely with them. Targeting of voters based on "microtargeting" by external consultants and the VoteBuilder/VAN combination offered by the DNC makes personalized political communication more cost-effective and vastly expands the universe of potentially valuable targets. It also helps campaign managers and field directors monitor their subordinates and measure progress in quantitative terms of knocks and calls generated, contacts made, and response data gathered. It helps junior staffers organize their teams of canvassers and helps volunteer coordinators run their phone banks. It directs who volunteers and part-timers end up talking to on the street, and, when used in line with staff instructions, it makes their efforts more effective and allows them to translate their highly variable and qualitative experiences of encounters with voters into quantitative data useful for further targeting and planning.

Even though the dominant targeting scheme is accompanied by many practical challenges and is not always equally well understood by those who rely on it, its instrumental usefulness is undisputed by those involved in campaigns. Nevertheless, some allies, even within the Democratic Party itself, choose to opt out and pursue older, alternative forms of targeting. They refuse to trade their autonomy for the increased impact that comes with using the call and walk sheets provided by staffers. They do this because they realize that not only is the new political targeting about efficiency and an expanded target universe. It also gives the national and state-level party organizations—who have privileged access to the voter file, and who ultimately determine who can use it—greater control over the wider campaign assemblages. This is especially clear since the establishment of new and cheap party-run interfaces and voter files have led to a dramatic consolidation of the market for political data, putting many previous vendors out of business. The "parties in service" are partially reconstituting themselves through data and technologies that campaigns need to win elections, but conflicts between different organizations within the party, between parties and campaign organizations, and between campaigns and their allies continue to complicate and shape the adoption of these new tools.

No matter what targeting scheme they rely on, no partisan political organization engages in undifferentiated or blanket personalized political communication. Despite the beliefs of some civic-minded volunteers and part-timers involved, campaign assemblages do not intend to "talk to everyone eventually anyway" (as the volunteer quoted earlier suggested). From a partisan point of view, blanket canvassing and phone banking are self-defeating, because valuable time is wasted talking to committed supporters of either party, and an increase in turnout across the board offers no tactical advantage. Take get-out-the-vote efforts as an example. Campaign staffers are not principally committed to low turnout among people voting for the other side. But they know that every additional voter for the other candidate raises their own bar by one more vote, thus they never knowingly contact anyone but likely partisans for get-out-the-vote purposes. Those who remain genuine swing voters until the last minute may break for one side by a few percent but will have to come out in droves for their final decisions to make much of a difference. So they are off the lists for GOTV purposes. And as one staffer put it, "We leave it to the Republicans to get out their voters. They are doing just fine, thank you very much. We will focus on getting out our own voters." This is the sentiment behind partisan targeting of personalized political communication. Persuasion contacts are made until the final weekend; thereafter get-out-the-vote focuses exclusively on likely supporters. Whereas some volunteers and part-timers may think they are simply being sent out to talk to voters, in reality campaigns operate with a clearly defined set of universes of specific voters targeted for personalized contacts.

Does the increasingly precise and individualized targeting possible today, then, expand the electorate, as some have suggested, or does it in fact narrow it, as others have argued?[38] On closer inspection it turns out it does both, depending on the strategic situation. On the one hand, the new dominant targeting scheme identifies numerous new high-value persuasion and get-out-the-vote targets that were entirely invisible under the demographic and geographic targeting schemes that preceded it. The swing voter with an unusual demographic profile can suddenly be identified. The infrequently voting partisan who happens to live among supporters of the other party can be ferreted out. In this sense, the dominant targeting scheme clearly expands the universe of targets and thus enables much more ambitious persuasion and GOTV programs. But on the other hand, campaign assemblages typically only bother to contact such targets if they face strong opposition. Thus, as Marshall Ganz has warned since the early 1990s, in the vast majority of districts where elections are not effectively contested, the new political targeting may in fact narrow the electorate by helping campaigns focus on an ever more clearly defined plurality of highly motivated and highly partisan supporters who turn out on a regular basis to return the incumbent to office. But in competitive districts the new targeting scheme makes it possible for campaign assemblages to leverage their considerable resources to actually *expand* the electorate in significant ways, both in terms of persuasion efforts and get-out-the-vote efforts—and when the stakes are high enough, even through voter registration efforts. These have long been left for well-meaning civic associations and nonpartisan groups, but were taken up again and pursued with considerable energy and finesse by the Bush campaign among conservative Christians in 2000 and 2004, and by the Obama campaign among African Americans, Latinos, and college students in 2008 on the basis of new forms of political targeting.

CHAPTER 6

Always Fighting the Same Ground War?

EPISODE 6.1

Bill, Glenn, and I are in the basement of the Mount Aery Baptist Church, setting up tables with snacks for people to enjoy as they mingle a bit after a last-minute rally. Jim Himes is about to appear before the congregation of this important African American church alongside several prominent local and national Democrats. His chances pretty much hinge on turnout here in Bridgeport.

Bill is in his seventies and retired after a successful career in public relations. He has been volunteering countless hours on the campaign. Glenn is in his late twenties, works for a local elected official, and has been helping out the last weeks too. He is a little frustrated that the other volunteers who were supposed to help us prepare the event aren't here. They are upstairs instead, hobnobbing with various local elected officials in the lobby.

Glenn says to Bill, "I really like you, man. You don't give us no trouble, you don't talk all the time." He continues: "That's the problem with all the volunteers, and many of those college kids. They don't want to work. They are like, 'I don't want to make calls. I don't want to knock on doors.'" Glenn shakes his head and says, "If you don't want to work, I don't know what to tell you."

EPISODE 6.2

"I have volunteered on pretty much every Democratic campaign since McGovern in '72," Brian says, and continues: "They are almost always like, 'Here is what we're going to do; now you go do it.'" Later in our conversation, he returns to the issue: "Look, I really don't mind helping out. But sometimes they just don't care what you think, what you would like to do, and what you have to say. And it can be somewhat off-putting, especially since sometimes the kids who run these things just have no fucking clue." He laughs.

Then he says, "Some of them are good—I don't mean to suggest anything else—and I have learned a lot from them, but . . ." He pauses for a moment. I don't say anything. Then he continues: "That's probably why the Dean campaign felt so special. They really took us seriously. Of course, that didn't work very well. Maybe that's why they don't run these things like that. I don't know. There must be a different way."

EPISODE 6.3

Alvin came half an hour late for the training session for new paid canvassers and spent most of it yawning demonstratively and drawing doodles on the notepad in front of him. He didn't want to do the role-playing at the end and went out to smoke a cigarette instead. He got the part-time job anyway.

I talk to him afterward outside the Holiday Inn conference room. "I did this for Kerry in '04 and have done it for a couple of other guys in between. I saw the flyers for this campaign and decided to do it again. I work in a bar and play in a band, you know? So it's kind of a good supplement." I ask him if it has changed much. He says, "No, man, it's pretty much the same."

The unusually energizing candidacy of Barack Obama and the strategy pursued by his campaign brought the ground war out of the shadows during the 2008 elections. Journalists began to complement the usual commentary on the horserace, the advertisements, and the media spin with sometimes breathless accounts of previously often ignored phenomena like personalized voter contacts, field organizing, and political targeting—sometimes as if field operations had just been invented from scratch or at least only recently rediscovered. In the 2008 elections, about 100 million people were contacted at home, millions of volunteers and tens of thousands of part-timers were involved in talking to them, and thousands of staffers were employed by candidate campaigns, party organizations, and various interest groups that used both old techniques and new technologies to contact people, organize their efforts, and target voters. More than $100 million was spent on the ground war.

But all that had been true in 2004 too. The victorious Democratic presidential campaign in 2008 was special in the scale and sophistication of its field campaign and the degree of volunteer involvement but not in its emphasis on it. As made clear in chapter 2, the Obama campaign was just the most recent and visible example of a decade-old resurgence of interest in—and institutional and infrastructural investment in—personalized political communication. Even if the Democratic presidential primary had ended differently, there are few reasons to think a Hillary Clinton campaign would have paid less attention to the ground war (even though it might have fought it in a way more reminiscent of those analyzed here). The main reason the McCain campaign did not try to emulate the Republican efforts of 2000 and 2004 was arguably not that it did not want to but that it could not—it commanded neither the money nor the manpower that had propelled George W. Bush to office twice.[1]

Personalized political communication happens, and it works. Those facts were the starting points for this book, in which I have asked the question of *how* it works—and by extension *why* it works in those ways, and *what that means* for our understanding of political communication in particular and of political organizations, political participation, and democracy more broadly. To answer the question, I have traced the recent history of the ground war and analyzed two relatively similar competitive, well-funded, and important—but ultimately ordinary—Democratic congressional campaigns, and not the extraordinary presidential juggernaut. There is no doubt that Barack Obama's campaign will go down in history, not simply as victorious, but as outstanding. It will assume its place alongside Nixon's campaign in 1968 and Reagan's campaigns in the 1980s as one that has left a mark on American politics, partly because it successfully combined a competently staffed multimillion-dollar campaign organization with a whole slew of new technologies and a large-scale and energetic volunteer movement for change. Its architects, among them David Axelrod and David Plouffe, will be remembered by political connoisseurs alongside Republican operatives like Kevin Philips, Lee Atwater, and Karl Rove—controversial, perhaps, but undeniably accomplished.

Jim Himes's and Linda Stender's campaigns, on the other hand, will be forgotten. No one will remember who worked on them, what allies they mobilized, who volunteered, and who took a part-time job with them. It is precisely because in the larger scheme of things they were so unremarkable that they can tell us so much. The 2008 Democratic presidential campaign involved more staffers and volunteers than probably any other since the 1960s. It broke all fund-raising records and integrated old organizing strategies from community, labor, and religious organizing with new social media practices and recent targeting innovations adopted from corporate marketing. It seized the moment, embraced a movement, and made the most of it. But most campaigns do not have such a moment, movement, or even the means or motives to make the most of it. And that is unlikely to change. Barack Obama has announced he will run for reelection in 2012, and his candidacy will attract the top Democratic political operatives, a core of energized supporters, and countless eager donors. His campaign may repeat some of the innovative gambles that paid off during his first run for the presidency. They may also make new ones. A movement for a second term might even crystallize around the campaign if his first term has not disappointed too many people too much. But hundreds of other candidates will be running for the Senate, for the House, for governorships and state- and local-level offices across the country. Most of them will have field campaigns that have more in common with the rather more prosaic ones analyzed here than with the sometimes exhilarating "machinery of hope."[2] When asked whether the more generously staffed, volunteer-involving, high-tech, and collaborative aspects of the 2008 Obama effort would spread to other campaigns, one of its senior staffers said to me:

> "The premise [is a] pretty motivated base, right? The question is then how do you take this motivation which is a pretty value-based motivation and turn it into structured activity that can actually produce votes and build upon itself.

If you are trying to elect some jerk who nobody really cares about and there is nothing at stake, you have a different situation. . . .

"I think a lot of conventional field campaigns are a function of having candidates that aren't all that interesting. I don't mean they got to be Barack Obama, but still. [His campaign's] kind of organizing really comes out of social movements. And they involve charismatic leadership at multiple levels. You don't see that in most campaigns. . . .

"The premise [for social movements and campaigns like Obama's] is a desire to change the world, a desire to change oneself, and you have a moral perspective there that is a big motivator. The conservative movement had this going for them for a long time. And I think that's one of the reasons they related so well to their base. The Democrats just didn't even know how to talk the talk, I think. And it's a lot harder to do it successfully when nobody cares."

This staffer is not a romantic advocate of "grassroots politics" speaking but an experienced political operative who wants to win and knows what it takes—votes. In his view, leveraging volunteer energies and the mobilizing potential of social media to create the kind of highly effective campaign assemblage that formed around the Obama campaign requires a motivated base, a resourceful campaign that embraces a form of organizing with multiple levels of leadership and invests in it, the cultivation of charismatic leadership, and a common desire to change the world. These preconditions are as clear and convincing as they are routinely absent from electoral politics. That is why it is so important to understand how ordinary campaigns operate without them.

The senior staffers on the Himes and Stender campaigns clearly recognized how exceptionally different the Obama phenomenon was from their own situation and from the campaigns they had worked on before. It is not that they did not *want* to accommodate volunteers or embrace a movement. It is that they craved control, feared that nobody cared, felt the time pressure, and knew that no national institution or permanent campaign could give them what they needed for their field operations. Few organizations are there on the ground to help local campaigns, and staffers recognize the often deep conflicts of interest and ideals between the various entrenched groups that might join the assemblages they build to wage ground wars. Despite the occasional bout of rhetoric about how volunteer engagement is what wins elections and about how "Team Democrat" is "the party of the people" working together, it is difficult to overstate just how much campaign staffers feel they are on their own and must positively *extract* everything they need from unwilling surroundings. While it is undoubtedly true that many Americans avoid politics and remain largely indifferent to campaigns, the staffers' attitude also seems like it is part of a self-fulfilling prophecy.[3] At least their fears are not conducive for movement-type organizing in electoral politics.

Instead, most campaigns pursue politics as usual, relying on the slowly developing occupational consensus of top political operatives, inherited routines, and at-hand resources analyzed throughout this book. Candidates hire senior staffers with an instrumental perspective and a few cycles of experience; some junior staffers who are eager to work in politics and to network with the usual allies in their districts and beyond; and enroll as many volunteers and part-timers as they can find. Nothing *forces* campaigns to operate this way. But a powerful and persistent set of tendencies, dispositions, and constraints make them *likely* to do so, and the results are endorsed by a shared professional common sense. "That is how we do it," says one campaign manager, and adds, "though I guess it could be done differently." The basic playbook followed by the staffers in the core campaign organization—oriented toward mass production of knocks and calls by volunteers, part-timers, and the people channeled by allies—is passed on in oral tradition and everyday routines, inscribed in the institutional and technological infrastructure maintained by the national party organizations, and taken for granted by most of the consultants working with campaigns.

These standard operating procedures put more emphasis on popular participation than they have for years, because political operatives again have come to believe that labor-intensive practices of personalized political communication can serve their instrumental interests. But they are only partially institutionalized, because ground wars remain fundamentally dependent on the ability of staffers to expand their campaign beyond the campaign organization and its party allies in D.C. and reach out to a recurrently renegotiated network of allies and to the hundreds (and sometimes thousands) of individual volunteers and part-timers involved in each election. Campaign organizations have a fairly standardized and institutionalized form, the wider campaign assemblages formed around them less so, built as they are in a much more contingent, modular, and ad-hoc fashion. It is at the multiple intersections between the campaign organizations, the allies around them, and the volunteers and part-timers enrolled that campaign assemblages build the capacity to wage ground wars and that contemporary forms of campaign engagement are constituted.

PERSONALIZED POLITICAL COMMUNICATION AND MASS POLITICAL COMMUNICATION

From the outset of this book, I have argued that personalized political communication should be understood as a distinct kind of political communication, one arm in the arsenal available to campaigns. It is distinguished by the fact that it is mediated by people rather than by traditional mass media like television, radio, or newspapers. However, the reliance on people and live interaction should not lead us to romanticize it. It is not necessarily morally superior to the alternatives. As I have shown, a knock on the door can be as unwelcome as a thirty-second spot on television or a pop-up advertisement on the Internet, and a conversation over the phone can be as prejudiced as a piece of direct mail. Staffers think such campaign tactics are undisciplined, and most of those who engage in them find them at least occasionally unpleasant. But we should appreciate the distinct qualities of person-to-person encounters, the peculiar challenges of generating them in large numbers, and the implications their resurgence has for political organizations, political participation, and for the practice of electoral democracy more broadly. Personalized political communication involves the unrehearsed dramaturgical dimensions of everyday life highlighted by Erving Goffman, the emotional labor discussed by Arlie Hochschild and Robin Leidner, and it invokes an entire spectrum of nonverbal cues and social norms that are absent from most technologically mediated communication.[4] These factors may help us one day explain the consistent finding that a knock on the door or a call from a live human being has greater immediate impact on people's electoral behavior per contact than mass political communication or political pamphlets arriving by mail.[5] Personalized political communication works—it is instrumentally effective.

This is something that sales representatives, religious proselytizers, and movement organizers have long known and acted upon and that American political operatives rediscovered during the 2000s. That realization—and the concomitant investments in the institutional and technological infrastructure underpinning field efforts—reenergized the pursuit of personalized political communication and has led to record numbers of contacts. That realization is why the prediction that personal contact would decline as a tool for political campaigns has turned out to be wrong. This resurgence challenges both the idea that canvassing and the like are "old-fashioned" and the idea that electoral politics has become so thoroughly "mediatized" that the traditional mass media have a monopoly on the means of communicating with voters. There are other kinds of political communication available to campaigns, and in their "layered" approach they mix and match among all of them as they see fit, with different consequences.

The scholarly literature from the 1990s deemed political communication "out of order" for depressing turnout through negative advertising, for being obsessed with personality and process over substance and fostering cynicism among citizens through horse-race-oriented news coverage, and for spreading disinformation through devious direct mail schemes.[6] It arguably got all these important kinds of political communication right. But the picture painted of political communication *as such* remained incomplete, because it left out the ground wars waged under the cover of the air war to sway the undecided and bring out partisan voters. In the same way, in the literature on political communication in the changing communications environment of today, the absence of attention to deliberately orchestrated and large-scale person-to-person campaigns is problematic. It is undoubtedly true that the massive increase in media content and audience choice among it will increase the relative importance of "pull" media that people choose to attend to based on their own preferences.[7] But the same development only increases the attractions of the remaining available "push" media, media that can cut through the din and the dizzying amount of stuff "out there"—in the way an intrusive canvasser knocking on your door or a phone call interrupting you at dinner might.

Serious attention to personalized political communication enriches our understanding of campaign practices and highlights how different kinds of political communication are pursued at the same time, with varying and sometimes conflicting effects, and by distinct entities. Mass political communication relies not only on campaigns and their activities but also on what we have come to refer to perhaps too glibly as "the media," the commercial news institution and the adjoining market for advertisements. Direct mail depends on the postal system and the extensive range of commercial vendors specializing in political communication that use it. Computer-mediated communication depends on the technical infrastructure maintained by telecommunications companies and by the platforms offered by a few large corporations. In contrast, resources for personalized political communication are not thoroughly institutionalized in the political parties or by their interest group allies, and few businesses offer full-scale field operations for hire. Instead, campaign organizations build assemblages around themselves to pursue it, assemblages like those analyzed here.

CAMPAIGNS TODAY AND TOMORROW

The two campaign assemblages I have focused on were built around Democratic candidates and involved in competitive races for the House of Representatives. Most contemporary Democratic field campaigns in contested elections in districts like these or larger—whether for Congress, governorships, or even presidential campaigns in battleground states—will have much in common with them. Even as national institutions change their priorities and start to invest more in field, as targeting schemes and database technologies are developed, as the organizational landscape of party organizations and their regular allies change from locale to locale, and as the relative enthusiasm of the diverse base of the Democratic Party waxes and wanes, variations of the logics identified here have played out across the country throughout the first decade of the twenty-first century and will again in coming cycles. (Because campaign assemblages are shaped by the interests, ideas, and resources of those involved, I suggest that the party affiliation, population of potential allies, and relative competitiveness of any given race will probably mean more for *how* personalized political communication is pursued than whether the campaign is in the Northeast or the South, whether a given district is rich or poor, urban or rural.)

Whether a district is competitive or not is probably the best predictor of whether it will be pursued at all. Candidates in effectively uncontested races are likely to limit themselves to a minimum of mass media and a few mailings, services that can be bought from outside consultants. Their staffers may not bother to build a more complex operation on the ground to increase what under all circumstances will be a comfortable margin of victory. Their campaigns can be built with impunity "in the air," just as the Philadelphia machine that muckraking journalist Lincoln Steffens wrote about.[8] Faced with no effective opposition, they need no field operations to fight for the last few percentage points to take them over the top. This is probably why a prominent political consultant like Hal Malchow has mischievously suggested that though field was underrated in the 1990s, it may be overrated today, as even high-turnout areas and solidly partisan districts are sometimes targeted for get-out-the-vote efforts. As one staffer on the Himes campaign said, "When something like ninety percent of the registered voters in Greenwich turn out to vote anyway, it probably means that the rest do not *want* to vote, no matter how often we contact them." And when elected officials in entirely safe seats—like state senator Ed Gomes or state representative Andres Ayala of Bridgeport in the same district—engage in field, it is not to win their own races, but because they have joined a larger assemblage for other reasons.

The many commonalities between the Himes campaign and the Stender campaign, corroborated by interviews with numerous senior staffers and political operatives about other campaigns, suggest a relatively uniform paradigm for contemporary competitive Democratic field campaigns with comparable resources and a shared repertoire of practices. This paradigm is deeply shaped by the staffers' conceptions of how ground wars should be waged and puts emphasis on standardized scripted messages meant to guide contacting; on mobilizing heterogeneous assemblages of allies, volunteers, and part-timers to talk with voters; and on the establishment of a hierarchical and mass-production-oriented campaign organization populated by staffers. It deploys highly rationalized, quantified, and abstract targeting of individual voters with the help of external consultants, campaign-generated data, and party-maintained voter files. As made clear throughout this book, the paradigm is never realized in a pure form. Reality spoils even the best-laid plans as callers and canvassers stray from scripts, people or allies refuse to let themselves be mobilized or imprint their own aims and aspirations on the wider assemblage, and as the predictive models and data used for targeting rarely match the hype surrounding it. But in the meeting between staffers and those around them they depend on, compromises are worked out, a common project is established, and campaign assemblages are built—human, imperfect endeavors that are shaped by the divergent interests, ideas, and resources of those involved. They are neither quite the professionalized "Astroturf campaigns" that many warn against, nor the "grassroots movements" some pine for. Instead they are complex combinations of fundamentally and never fully integrated mutually dependent actors who then go their separate ways once the election is over.

Campaign assemblages do not *have* to take this form, but the form is tied in with the professional self-conception of senior staffers, and the routinized ways in which it operates is spread through personal networks and taught to junior staffers. It is what regular volunteers and returning part-timers have encountered again and again (and again), and what new ones will have to confront. It is what allies and party organizations have come to expect. It defines the metrics used to measure performance and progress before Election Day, and it is inscribed in the technologies and databases available. It matches the art of the possible with the inherited and continuously evolving occupational common sense of Democratic political operatives, and staffers will try to reproduce it on-site as far as local conditions allow. Allies, volunteers, and part-timers then have to decide how they want to engage with these fairly standardized campaign organizations, and they do so for their own different reasons. Their involvement not only empowers campaign assemblages through the resources and manpower they bring, but it also complicates attempts to command and control ground war efforts. The complications arise partially from the sheer complexity of heterogeneous, loosely connected, and highly networked contentious collaborations and also from the different aims and aspirations of those involved. Just as voluntary associations and individual good government reformers in the past have tried to change parties both from the outside and the inside, so too today allies and activists affiliated with old players like the labor movement and new ones like the Internet-assisted "netroots" actively try to transform their party partners.[9] From the point of view of party insiders like Rahm Emanuel, occasional infighting and differences over practical priorities and political principles may suggest that outside allies and ideologically motivated party activists are, to use the then White House chief of staff's own colorful language, "'fucking retarded.'"[10] An alternative interpretation is that such conflicts represent legitimate disagreements between diverse partners with different interests and ideals.

Campaigns are not always fighting the same ground war, but change is piecemeal, often driven by external forces, and it faces considerable internal resistance. As each new campaign deals with the merciless time pressure of the ever-approaching election deadline, the expectations of allies around it, and the staffers' desire for control and candidates' risk-averseness, campaign workers tend to embrace the political common sense at hand and on offer. Like much common sense, it is not as much optimal or ideal as it is what Herbert Simon has called "satisficing." It gets the job done for most of the people, most of the time.[11]

BEYOND POLITICS AS USUAL

A few campaigns are different, of course. The large-scale outsourcing of the Democratic field effort in many battleground states to America Coming Together in 2004 has already been discussed in chapter 2, and despite the best intentions of many of its architects, this outsourcing ultimately came close to being the kind of electoral strip mining that some critics lament. Others come closer to grassroots ideals—for example, Paul Wellstone's Senate campaigns in Minnesota in the 1990s, Howard Dean's 2004 campaign in the Democratic presidential primary, and in some ways the Barack Obama campaign in 2008. But these are outliers and have to be recognized as such. Their exceptional qualities are part of the reason they have attracted so much attention compared to the scores of campaigns that have more in common with those analyzed here.

Broadly speaking, change often seems to come from above, outside, or below—and very rarely from the majority of campaigns "in between." Advances in targeting and technology, normally based on long-term investments, have often come from strategists planning the next presidential election or nationwide efforts (both Demzilla and VoteBuilder are examples of this). New vehicles for mobilizing and organizing have come from above too (think of the coordinated campaigns instituted in the 1980s, America Coming Together in 2004, and today Organizing for America). Outsiders, whether engaged in politics or entirely different pursuits, have provided important innovations too—in the form of organizing practices imported from community organizing by, for example, Jesse Jackson, Paul Wellstone, and people around them, and in the form of social media introduced to politics by techies working for Howard Dean and other such examples of people outside the common sense of politics bucking the trend wittingly or unwittingly. Finally, insurgents (and Jackson, Wellstone, and Dean count among them) also have been innovators. Unlike front-runners and establishment candidates, insurgents have incentives to take risks and experiment, knowing that politics as usual will usually leave them the losers. Barack Obama's primary campaign in 2008 is probably the most powerful recent illustration of this point. A politician with no previous record of campaign innovation set out to challenge the presumptive nominee, recruited some of the people behind Deval Patrick's upset victory in the 2006 Massachusetts gubernatorial primary to manage his operation, and in turn embraced both the activist movement and outside entrepreneurs from the tech world and elsewhere that flocked to Obama's campaign as it built momentum. All of this took place well before the general election, where Obama ran as a favorite and primarily seemed to innovate "from above," being so clearly ahead of and better endowed financially and in terms of volunteer support than his rival.

All of these examples of innovation are recombinant practices—not de novo acts of creativity, but combinations of the tried and true common sense and elements from elsewhere adopted under competitive and circumstantial pressure.[12] Changes in campaign practices are motivated by the desire to win, but they are also spurred by changes beyond the control of those involved. As outlined in chapters 1 and 2, the current emphasis on field is at least partially driven by potentially profound changes in the communications environment in which the mass-media-oriented campaigns of the latter half of the twentieth century were designed to operate. But just as larger developments well beyond the control of political elites and operatives undermined previous party systems, political organizations, and forms of campaigning without determining the reaction, nothing in the forces nibbling away at the power of the press and the centrality of traditional television today determines how campaigns will adapt to a post-broadcast environment. That is a challenge for innovators, who rarely come out of local campaigns (that do not have the resources), uncontested races (that do not have the incentives), or even competitive campaigns for close seats (that dare not, and are often accountable to a lot of others who do not want to take risks). Ironically, there seems to be too much at stake for campaigns to innovate in close elections when they are within striking distance pursuing politics as usual, working with the usual suspects, and thinking in the usual terms—unless they are forced to do otherwise by outsiders.

PERSONALIZED POLITICAL COMMUNICATION AND POLITICAL ORGANIZATIONS

The practices of personalized political communication analyzed here provide new material for understanding campaigns and their allies as political organizations. Over the last thirty years, the idea that politics is becoming increasingly professionalized has become something of a truism in the social sciences.[13] Officeholders, their policy advisers, their interlocutors from interest groups and industry lobbies, and their campaign staffs are all held to be professionals today, as opposed to the supposed "amateurs" of yesterday.[14] The idea of professionalization captures the fact that in the past fifty years we have seen a substantial growth in the number of people who have full-time, paid, and increasingly specialized jobs in politics. What this idea tends to obscure is both how recent the supposed alternative of "grassroots" campaigns is and especially how uneven the current professionalization of politics really is.

As has been pointed out by authors like James Q. Wilson and Alan Ware, the idea of volunteering in politics is a relatively new phenomenon, something that became widespread only after World War II.[15] Before that, campaigns were the province of party regulars, who were not formally employed like the staffers of today but certainly not civically motivated citizens like most contemporary volunteers either. Coming from a variety of backgrounds, almost all party regulars were involved in one way or another in the system of spoils that animated much of American politics, and they were rarely political dilettantes. The idealistic reformer was not only a rarity but also an object of ridicule and frequently unwanted, as captured in the old machine axiom "We don't want nobody nobody sent." As many analysts have shown, the party organizations of the late nineteenth and early twentieth centuries marshaled tens of thousands of hardworking party loyalists and frequently turned out voters by the millions when it served their interests, but they were not open to everyone who wanted to take part or indiscriminate in who they turned out to vote, when, or where.[16]

Some contemporary campaign practices require technical competences that the ward heelers and precinct bosses of yore did not possess. In that sense, areas like polling, fund-raising, and many kinds of political communication (advertisements, public relations, and direct mail) have become areas of specialized expertise. No competitive campaign for federal or statewide office will leave it to a volunteer to conduct a survey, do the data mining, or design a thirty-second television spot. Few would be able to do it if they got the chance. These areas of campaigns have become professionalized, and they consume much of the campaign budget. But when it comes to the field efforts that continue to involve the majority of the staffers hired and consume hundreds of thousands of dollars at the congressional level and tens of millions at the national level, the professionalization turns out to have some limitations. Personalized political communication is labor-intensive, pursued in concert with allies, volunteers, and part-timers who are not political professionals (or at least not campaign professionals), and even the professionalism of the staffers involved is questionable. Here it would be more precise to talk of uneven professionalization.

Take the staffers first. While junior staffers quickly come to regard and present themselves as political professionals, they hardly approximate what we usually mean by "professionals."[17] In contrast to volunteers and part-timers, junior staffers are full-time employees, usually salaried, and often orient themselves toward a career in politics. But as an occupational group, they have more in common with the millions of white-collar workers around the country than with paradigmatic professionals like lawyers or doctors. The majority of campaign staffers are young, inexperienced, and possess no distinct technical competencies beyond some college education. They are uncertified. They belong to no professional associations, read no trade magazines, and receive little training beyond a kind of informal apprenticeship. They work as generalists, often in fairly menial positions in a precarious and highly cyclical labor market. While their incentives and self-conceptions are different in terms of what they do, campaign staffers are the political equivalents of door-to-door salesmen, telemarketers, customer service representatives, and low-level shop floor supervisors in the service industry. Senior staffers are different, but most are still young. To have worked ten years on campaigns makes someone a real veteran. Out of the fifty-some people on the staff of the two campaign organizations I studied, only four were over forty and a handful were in their thirties. Half of the staffers were working their first full-time job. Some had never even been interns or volunteers on a political campaign before. This is hardly the profile that comes to mind when one talks about professionals or a professionalized organization.

This complication is corroborated by how volunteers and part-timers talk about the assemblages they are involved in. Many volunteers are serial activists with several campaigns under their belt. Most are older, very often college-educated, and sometimes indeed themselves professionals (though not political professionals). Apart from the high school and college students hired, a considerable proportion of the part-timers, too, have work experience outside of politics. Both volunteers and part-timers are often harsh, even unforgiving, when they judge the staffers and their work. A volunteer who has fund-raised over the phone for his college complains that phone bankers in the campaigns receive almost no training and that the scripts are "stilted" and "impossible to use." A part-timer who has worked at a fast-food franchise calls the canvassing "disorganized" and the role-playing that constitutes most of the training "useless" compared to what he experienced in his previous job. An older volunteer who runs her own company was scathing in her criticism of the campaign, saying that "the kids" (an oft-repeated phrase) who run it do not know what they want to do, let alone how to do it. "I feel like they are throwing away my money!" she, a significant donor, added indignantly. These cross-sectoral comparisons beyond politics illustrate how comparatively low the level of professionalization is, how partial the adoption of new technologies that are common in corporate America (or indeed parts of everyday life more broadly) is. Your local supermarket is very likely to be more organizationally and technologically sophisticated than your local congressional campaign. Staffers themselves admit privately that much of the criticism hits the mark. Contacting is indeed poorly structured and rarely supervised, mobilizing is haphazard, organizing is old-fashioned and top-down, and even targeting—one of the most specialized areas they are involved in—is deeply dependent on campaign-generated response data that one staffer complains is often "total crap."

Campaigns are a billion-dollar industry in the United States, and they continue to grow. The Federal Election Commission reports that candidates for the presidency, Senate, and the House of Representatives spent a total of $2.8 billion in 2007–2008. That is, to put it mildly, a lot of money ($22 per vote cast in the 2008 general elections). Additional billions were spent by party organizations, political action committees, interest groups, and on state and local elections. Campaign watchdog groups are surely right to worry about what donors expect in return for their dollars. It is nonetheless important to maintain a sense of perspective. If we imagined that the $2.8 billion reported to the FEC went to one single vendor of campaign services, this conglomerate would only squeak in at the bottom of the 2008 Fortune 1000, between the fast-food chain Jack in the Box and the manufacturing company Carlisle. And there is a long way to the top. A congressional campaign organization like Linda Stender's, which spent $2.6 million, is an operation about the size of a typical McDonald's "family restaurant" ($2.2 million in annual revenue on average in 2008). At the core of ground war efforts there is a campaign organization staffed by full-time employees, some of whom are experienced professionals and who rely on specialized expertise from outside partners. But that is only one element of a larger campaign assemblage, and it is deeply dependent upon allies, volunteers, and part-timers in its pursuit of personalized political communication.

PERSONALIZED POLITICAL COMMUNICATION AND POLITICAL PARTICIPATION

The combination of this dependence and the increased elite interest in field operations raises the question of what kind of political participation it is that the rekindled interest in personalized political communication may foster. Precisely because ground wars are so labor-intensive, no entrenched institutions or market vendors can provide campaigns with the manpower they need, and all professionals agree that volunteers are instrumentally more effective than part-timers, recent election cycles have seen a new interest in mobilizing people to serve as media for political communication. This is dramatically different from the 1990s scenario described by Margaret Weir and Marshall Ganz, where volunteers were turned away by campaign staffers who did not know what to do with them.[18] It is probably no accident that this decade also marked a historical low point in campaign activism as the presidential election between Bob Dole and Bill Clinton saw just 2 percent of those surveyed volunteering for parties or campaigns—the lowest number since the American National Election Survey began almost fifty years before. That figure has been inching upward ever since, to 3 percent in 2000 and 2004, and to 4 percent in 2008. Today everyone who is willing to work is welcome in a competitive campaign—even a researcher.

We know from the vast literature on political participation, civic engagement, and social movement activism that many different factors propel some people to take part in campaigns and make others decide not to. Persistent inequalities in social and economic status matter; individual-level variations in sociopsychological motivation matter; interpersonal networks, associational membership, different understandings of politics, and perceptions of the stakes involved—all this and more matter; and all are largely beyond the control of individual campaigns. But we also know that the actions of political actors *themselves* matter, whether and how they try to recruit people, who, when, and under what conditions.[19] This is what makes the "civic transformation" that Theda Skocpol and her collaborators have identified so important in this context.[20] Since the mid-twentieth century, the large trans-local voluntary cross-class membership associations that dominated American civic life and politics for decades of popular politics and played a central role well into the twentieth century have been displaced or transformed. In their place we have seen the rise of increasingly bureaucratized, centralized advocacy organizations based on direct-mail fund-raising, Washington- or state-capital-based lobbying, and mass political communication. Skocpol characterizes the overall change as one from "membership to management," and Alan Ware describes the development of local Democratic parties as a gradual "breakdown" from the 1950s onward.[21] Like previous historical transformations of the organizational interface between individual citizens and the complex realities of electoral politics, these trends are of crucial importance if we want to understand not only levels of political participation but also what political participation is. Millions of Americans experience the look and feel of electoral politics through campaign work every year. Such involvement is not an ahistorical phenomenon but entails concrete practices that change over time as political organizations and assemblages develop. One does not simply "work for a candidate campaign or a party"—to use a standard survey question—but for a *particular* campaign, and each person gets involved in particular forms of organizing that afford particular kinds of civic engagement.

Close analysis of contemporary campaigns and their practices of personalized political communication thus not only helps us to better understand political communication as such, and political organizations themselves;

it also demonstrates what political participation as a volunteer is like today, and this speaks to the role of people in political—and democratic—processes. If you want to do more to influence an election than simply cast your vote or donate what money you can spare, campaigns are where you go, and personalized political communication is what you will be asked to engage in. You will be enrolled in a campaign assemblage trying to reach people in person, and you will be sent out to knock on doors or asked to sit down and make phone calls. Throughout this book, I have described and analyzed what you will be asked to do and what kind of machinery it is that you become part of when you make yourself one of the 3–4 percent of adult Americans who in the early twenty-first century chose to work or volunteer during an election. Campaigns constitute one of the places where people encounter democracy in action. What they meet matters—for electoral outcomes, and for what electoral democracy *is*.

DEMOCRACY IN ACTION

The kind of machinery analyzed in this book is not an exercise in "deliberative," "direct," or "strong" democracy but is premised upon a certain degree of popular participation and partially oriented toward expanding the electorate.[22] It is not the kind of late-twentieth-century campaign described by some as "thoroughly professionalized" and open "by invitation only," the types of campaigns where staffers sent away potential volunteers because they saw no use for them.[23] Throughout the first decade of the twenty-first century, campaign assemblages like those analyzed here have offered millions of Americans an opportunity to play an active part in electoral politics and have turned out millions more who would not have voted without that one extra phone call or knock on their door. The rediscovery and reinvention of ground war practices offer a more inclusive form of electoral politics than do campaigns based only on mass media, mail, and money. The increased importance of field operations gives political elites renewed incentives to invest in and prioritize volunteer involvement. It leads to more popular participation and higher turnout. These are good things for American democracy.

This does not mean that present ground war practices are perfect—far from it. Campaigns are highly instrumental in who they talk to, there are remnants of institutionalized racism and other inequalities in who they mobilize, and they offer no ways for those involved to influence the overall direction and operation itself. In this respect, contemporary campaign assemblages and many of the party organizations and infrastructures that support them are different from the nineteenth-century cross-class member-based associations and mass parties that Skocpol and others have analyzed. The forms of political participation afforded today are different. Even though the political parties and civic associations of the nineteenth century were often oligarchic, exclusionary in terms of gender and race, and dominated by self-interested elites, it is important to recognize that most of them had formal structures of internal democracy that were institutionalized down to the local level, where most maintained a permanent presence on the ground.[24] The political parties today retain elements of these structures; so do important allies like unions and even some recently established activist groups like Democracy for America. But campaign organizations and the wider campaign assemblages built anew every cycle do not. Getting involved in one of these will not give you any influence over its policies, position, or strategies. Neither the candidate nor the campaign manager is directly accountable to those involved. Even if campaign assemblages and new organizational forms like Organizing for America, the 2008 Obama campaign's spin-off, are increasingly oriented toward mobilizing volunteers, it is a highly circumscribed and instrumentally oriented form of activism that volunteers are invited to. In a sense campaign assemblages are trying to have it both ways: to mobilize the masses associated with membership-based associations while retaining the centralized control characteristic of management-dominated advocacy groups. Political operatives want membership *and* management (even as they find it hard to mobilize and control people). Campaign assemblages are not in themselves democratic institutions, and they are not meant to be.[25] What they are is ground war machines, designed to influence the outcome of the election at hand.

There is a certain honesty to this aggressive single-mindedness, something I have tried to retain in the title of this book, adopting the metaphors of strife and struggle that are endemic in campaigns (you "beat" your rival, etc.). These metaphors highlight how the American political system and electoral climate remain confrontational, consequential, and sometimes competitive beneath the occasional impression of identical suits running for remote offices, professing indistinguishable positions on interchangeable talk shows. Campaign assemblages today do not offer ideal, equal, or evenly distributed opportunities for civic engagement. But where campaigns are engaged in competitive elections—where ambition is still made to counteract ambition—it is in their own interest to offer citizens a chance to translate their time and effort into a little bit of power to influence the outcome. And, as previously noted, we have reason to believe that they sometimes can. Personalized political communication is unlikely to produce wild swings, but political operatives believe a good field campaign can swing a outcomes by a couple of percentage points, and social scientists estimate that each fourteen contacts at the door will bring out one more voter.[26]

188 • Chapter 6

For the sake of argument, let us assume that you are volunteering for a campaign partly because you want a particular candidate to win. Let us further assume that the campaign's field effort is impeccably organized and targeted, so the moment you enter the door to help, you are whiskered away to a suitable turf and asked to talk to carefully selected infrequently voting partisans. These are strong assumptions, and we will make two more. Let us say that those you talk to are all going to vote for your candidate if they vote at all, and we accept the estimate that fourteen contacts at the door turn out one more voter. Then you can spend five hours working hard, interrupting people in the middle of dinner, having doors shut in your face with nothing but a mumbled apology, getting yelled at by a few strangers, talking to a dozen indifferent voters and to an occasional friendly person—to do what? To effectively double your impact on an election. You go vote for the candidate of your choice, and now, after this long afternoon of sometimes stressful work, someone else, who would not otherwise have done so, will go and vote too. And if you work more, more voters are to come. This is tedious, perhaps, but futile it is not.

I opened this book with two quotations. The first I often heard on the campaign trail, usually attributed to the fictional president Jed Bartlet in Aaron Sorkin's television series *The West Wing* (though it is originally attributed to the anthropologist Margaret Mead). It goes like this: "Never doubt that a small group of thoughtful, committed citizens can change the world," and it claims that such groups are the only thing that has ever brought about change. Strictly speaking, this is utter nonsense. Very often, committed citizens have no chance at all of changing the world, and frequently forces beyond our control change the world more than we can ever hope to. But the quotation captures very well, I believe, how many staffers and volunteers think about what they are doing. The other quotation I opened with I never heard in the field, though it often resonated in my own mind while I was on the campaign trail. It comes from Samuel Beckett's play *Happy Days*, where Winnie says, "There is so little one can do." She adds, after a pause, "One does it all." Another pause. "All one can." This captures better my own sense of the strange practicality, power, and potential pointlessness of personalized political communication—and politics more broadly—especially in its tentative, hesitating, doubtful claim that one does all one can. Does one? In a sense that is true. Staffers, volunteers, and part-timers certainly give it a shot, and many work harder than they ever have before. Sometimes it is in vain, and sometimes it meets with success, not at all unlike life itself. I have analyzed here what campaign assemblages, small groups of thoughtful, committed staffers, volunteers, and part-timers, *actually* do when they engage in personalized political communication. When and where that is enough to change the world, I cannot say.

Research Appendix

Political ethnography is a risky business, at once intensely sociable and
deeply isolating. On one side, its effective pursuit requires close involvement with political actors, and therefore [implies] the danger of becoming
their dupes, their representatives, their brokers, or their accomplices. On
the other, bringing out the news so others can understand depends on
multiple translations: from the stories that political participants tell into
stories that audiences will understand, from local circumstances to issues
that will be recognizable outside the locality, from concrete explanations
for particular actions to accounts in which outsiders will at least recognize analogies to classes of actions with which they are familiar.
            —Charles Tilly, quoted in Auyero, *The Political*
                                        Ethnographer's Compagnon

Participant-observation is the only method I know that enables the researcher to get close to the realities of social life.
                        —Herbert J. Gans, *The Urban Villagers*

This book was motivated by an interest in how people come to serve as
media for forms of political communication that are analyzed neither by
the extensive research on interpersonal or social communication about
politics nor by the even larger literature dealing with mass mediation and
computer mediation of political communication. My intention has been
to supplement the growing literature on the impact of canvassing and the
like with a qualitative assessment of the implications that contemporary
ground war practices have for political communication, political organizations, political participation, and ultimately for American democracy
more broadly. I write about the origins of the project here to lay out the
reasoning behind the research design, the methods employed, and the
writing of the book as it developed over three years. Throughout my
fieldwork I kept a research diary, and I share some of these thoughts and
further reflections here not because they are particularly original—they
are not—but because the decisions they informed were consequential for
the data gathered and hence the findings. They should therefore be shared
with those who want to critically evaluate the arguments I make along
with their validity. Though participant-observation gets one close, it does

not offer unmediated access to reality. It is a method for producing data about realities, a way to systematically transcribe processes as they are pursued and narrated by research subjects and observed and experienced by the researcher.[1] As with any other method, participant-observation is accompanied by real dilemmas and enduring tensions. There is no one "best way" of doing fieldwork, only a succession of choices, a plural set of conventionalized guidelines, and the obligation to be transparent about how the choices were made.[2] In this appendix I lay out the practical challenges I faced and the reflections that guided my decisions.

RESEARCH DESIGN

Confronted with the dearth of research on the day-to-day working of contemporary American campaigns on the ground, and with the clear shortcomings of relying only on interviews or the available secondary sources (news coverage, trade magazines, and books by campaign staffers or consultants), I quickly decided to make ethnographic fieldwork in the districts themselves the centerpiece of my research. I do use other sources, including various conference transcripts, journalistic coverage, and the writings of political operatives themselves, especially in chapters 2 and 5, but the bulk of my data comes from ten months of participant-observation carried out from February to November 2008.[3]

After my on-site research was over, I encountered a formulation by Mitchell Duneier, one of the most prominent ethnographers active in sociology today, which I think captures well what I hoped to accomplish all along. In his contribution to a review symposium in the *American Journal of Sociology*, Duneier writes, "Sociology is constantly criticized for documenting the 'obvious' when, in fact, there is more than one obvious. More important, such documentation can show just how the 'obvious' works."[4] (The argument that "the how is the why," or at least a large part of the why, has been developed by several notable social scientists in different fields.[5]) In other words, analysis must start by producing and validating data that captures the multiplicity of actors and perspectives involved in a situation that is not always well understood or broadly known in advance (whether it is an indigenous community, the urban ghetto, or political campaigns).[6] This work alone, as is often pointed out, almost always brings to light previously unavailable information, debunks prevailing myths, and changes the researcher's own understanding of the site.[7] I had initially thought that only staffers and volunteers would be involved in personalized political communication and was surprised to discover that the campaign assemblages built substantial paid part-timer operations of their own too. I also had not anticipated that targeting would turn out to be such an important and integral part of the processes that I would eventually come to dedicate an entire chapter to it. Both would have been fairly obvious had I worked on or researched American campaigns before.

As a researcher, one comes to sites and their combination of obviousness (there is an election and a campaign trying to win it) and plurality (it is different things to different people) with a more or less clearly defined analytical interest that is refined and revised over time and has to find a way to both document and respect the integrity of the situations(s) encountered and retain and develop a scholarly focus. This is the research tactic that Charles Ragin calls "casing."[8] Cases do not represent themselves but have to be identified and defined as such. Contrary to how some would have it, it is a question of seeing *worlds*, not "the world," in each grain of sand and then connecting them with wider processes. In my own work, *I* was the one who imposed the notion of personalized political communication on the two campaigns I was trying to fashion as cases precisely as a way to make this connection and strike the balance between my analytical interest and my empirical cases, between the situations and their obviousness(es). For staffers this is "field," an integral part of a larger instrumental enterprise. For volunteers it is a form of civic engagement, a way to make a difference. For part-timers it is a temporary job that many of them have only a halfhearted interest in. On the one hand, this imposition pushes the participants' voices in the background, because it is not their term. On the other hand, it comes to serve as the point of translation between their different stories and one about broader issues I can tell my outside audience.

The starting premise for my search for material to "case" was the idea that there are no elections in the United States that can in any meaningful way be considered "representative" of the entire universe of cases. There is no microcosm available that can provide a safe bedrock for generalizations like those proffered by statistical researchers; there are too many dimensions involved, too many differences, too many variables that are not known in advance or where averages and medians are meaningless. And yet one has to choose, and choose carefully; speak, and speak broadly. The two districts I ultimately ended up working in (Connecticut's 4th congressional district and New Jersey's 7th) were chosen as minimal variation cases because they shared a number of traits with each other (and with a limited number of other districts around the country). Several of these traits are important enough to mention: they are both competitive districts; they are both in an expensive media market; neither were in battleground states or bit parts in any other election further up the ballot; both are in the Northeast, where, comparatively speaking, the parties have been well-organized historically; both have high average household incomes; both are geographically small and predominantly suburban; both are a little less ethnically diverse than the nation as a whole; in both, the Democratic Congressional Campaign Committee got involved early on and in force; both Democratic candidates were proven fund-raisers; and neither of them were incumbents. There are also notable differences between the two, of course: Connecticut's state Democratic Party is generally considered weaker than New Jersey's; Jim Himes was a political neophyte running against a twenty-three-year incumbent, Linda Stender an experienced state legislator running for an open seat; the two states have different electoral calendars, with state-level elections in Connecticut in 2008 but only a few local elections in New Jersey; and Connecticut's 4th district contains more urban areas and fewer suburbs than New Jersey's 7th district.

Other congressional districts across the country share only a few of these traits. Most notably, of course, only a minority of these districts are competitive. For reasons that have to do with the electoral system, demographic developments, and periodic and highly politicized redistricting efforts, only about 50 to 100 of the 435 House Districts in the United States are likely to be in play in any given election cycle, and often as few as 10 actually change from one party to the other. This presents researchers with one fundamental choice when campaigns and elections are cased: are they to be taken from the entire universe, among noncompetitive races (both the mean and the median), or only among competitive races? I decided to look at competitive races because my interest was in campaign practices, not their predictable absence in the many districts where incumbents run practically or entirely unopposed.[9]

I chose to focus on congressional elections for three reasons: (1) because the districts are large enough that the classical local and state-level "retail" strategy of having the candidate knock on every potentially friendly door in the district is practically impossible; (2) because substantial amounts of resources are involved, making congressional elections a good critical test of the hypothesis that personalized political communication was on the decline generally and mostly used by resource-poor campaigns; and (3) because I thought each of these campaigns would offer more manageable research objects than larger assemblages involved in presidential or Senate elections. With these criteria in mind, the list of potentially interesting districts near New York City (where I lived at the time) came down to the following six: Connecticut's 4th district; New Jersey's 3rd, 5th, and 7th district; and New York's 13th and 19th districts. Of these, only the ones I eventually decided to research, plus New Jersey's 3rd, actually turned out to be anything like close races. The others were shaped by the kind of cast that sometimes makes American politics look like a made-for-TV movie, populated by blind rabbis, drunk drivers, out-of-wedlock children, and marine corporals turned lawyers turned long-shot candidates, and all.

I studied two districts simultaneously because I wanted to have at least two independent and potentially different cases to look at, both to be able to examine differences and similarities and to minimize the risk that I would be saddled with a single and for some reason unusable case. Initially I had hoped to follow three districts, but early on I came to the conclusion that splitting my time between three districts would make each case study too superficial. While two is not a crowd, this design still offers an opportunity for "controlled comparison," an oft-expressed if rarely realized ambition in ethnographic research.[10] With minimal variation between the two districts I explored, the processes identified here as common to them are likely to be analogous to what takes place under similar circumstances elsewhere.

In both districts I made the campaign assemblage built around the Democratic candidate for Congress my research object. I chose to study only one side of the partisan divide for the following three reasons. First, it quickly became clear that there would in all likelihood be important differences between how the parties campaigned. Secondly, I felt more comfortable doing participant-observation among Democrats. Thirdly, I thought it would be necessary to choose only one party to maintain the minimum level of trust that all fieldwork requires. In terms of my own dispositions, my general sympathies are more progressive than conservative, and given my early decision to focus on only one party, I saw no need to complicate matters by doing research within the Republican Party and its environs. While I would love to analyze or see analysis of conservative campaigns, I think now that the decision to do fieldwork on only one side of the electoral divide was not only the best for me but also strictly *necessary* to gain and maintain access to the campaigns.[11]

In both campaigns, staffers later told me that, despite my protestations to the contrary, they initially believed I was a spy sent by Republicans and, for some time after they had abandoned this notion, at least believed I was working on both sides. "That's why we never let you near any of the data [in the summer]," one later explained. They did not trust me fully—and I cannot say that I blame them. Why would they? To take just a few quotes from my field notes: "What are you writing in your little notebook?" "What have you found about us so far?" "Now, you're not going to make us look bad, are you?" (I mostly tried to answer such questions with a combination of unobjectionable generalities and incomprehensible academic jargon.) But I did not trust *them* fully either. Even months into my fieldwork, I double-checked factual statements and anecdotes about past elections when possible and nearly panicked on one occasion when I lost one of my notebooks and in my paranoia imagined the staffers poring over it. (I spent hours that night literally retracing my steps trying to find it.)

> Losing my notebook illustrates the importance of getting those notes written down. But I also fear that they will read it and find something offensive or the like. Or information about others, and start wondering more about what they can tell me and what not. What will they make of some of the more pedestrian things I take notes on? Some of it must look ridiculous.
> —Research diary, October 7, 2008

GETTING IN

Getting in is a crucial step in any ethnographic study, and the campaign staffers' fear of spies and double-dealers illustrates why this is not always a simple one. When I did my first interviews in December 2007, I quickly realized that what would later become my main sites—the core campaign organizations—were not yet amenable to fieldwork. Until April these were basically full-time fund-raising machines involving only the candidates and a few finance staffers. Instead I focused my early research on getting to know the districts in general and in particular the population of past and potential allies. I visited local Democratic Party organizations, activist groups, and labor unions and spoke to various community leaders with a record of political involvement. I introduced myself simply as a graduate student interested in doing research on political campaigns, and most people took time to talk with me. A few found it peculiar that someone from Denmark would study American politics. To those who asked why, I explained that though I am not American myself, I care about American democracy, about political communications, and about campaign practices in democracies more broadly and that these interests motivated my project. No one questioned that, and though many people no doubt inferred from my adopted English that I was not a local, no one objected to having a foreigner around. Perhaps my unusual background helped legitimize my interest in things that no doubt seemed self-explanatory to many of those involved.

It was through the various locals with a campaign pedigree and political connections that I later met the candidates and the senior staffers, introduced myself and my interest, and, often validated by people I had come to know early on, was given initial permission to visit the campaign offices (in April). Though lack of time quickly forced me to narrow down the number of districts I worked on, at this point I was still following developments in several potentially interesting areas in three states. Only after both candidates and campaign managers in Connecticut's 4th and

New Jersey's 7th district had approved my presence in April did I settle on these two, consider myself "in," and see my basic research design—a two-case minimal-variation comparative ethnography of campaign assemblages—as complete and ready to be executed.

I was quickly reminded, however, of a basic fact that should have been clear to me in advance: access is neither once and for all nor either/or. Several times my behavior (asking questions, carrying notebooks, snapping a picture) or even my mere presence caused problems. On two occasions in particular I feared I had irrevocably lost access to one of my cases.

The first incident occurred over the summer when the campaign manager in one of the campaigns saw me writing in my notebook on site and stopped to confront me with the charge that I was "interviewing" staffers, saying this was not what we had agreed on and warning me that I better "watch it" or I would no longer be welcome. Before I had much chance to reply, the campaign manager stormed off to pick up a phone that was ringing. I was worried about losing access and tried to understand what might have provoked the campaign manager. I concluded that my notebook and the notion of interviewing might have given the impression that some of my work would be put to journalistic use—something I had tried to make clear from the start that it would not. So I sent an email the same night reiterating that nothing would be published in any form before the election was over, that everything would be made anonymous, and that I would be returning to the office a few days later and hoped we could talk. When I did return, the campaign manager took time to briefly tell me "we're good." I attribute the incident to the stress of the work environment and the wariness of journalists and uncontrolled publicity that is part of the staffers' professional dispositions.[12]

The second incident was left more unresolved than the first. After one of the campaigns had had a staff shake-up and replaced the campaign manager, one of the surviving staffers whom I had known for some time asked me whether the new campaign manager knew who I was and what I was doing. I explained that I had introduced myself briefly but that our conversation had been cut short. The staffer advised me to "keep it quiet" and to "not bring it up unless you are asked," adding, "I think if [the campaign manager] thought about it for a second, you'd get chucked out." In this latter case I went with the rather self-serving interpretation that I had already secured approval from the candidate and the previous campaign manager, and that, after all, access was more important for me than trust or full transparency regarding what I was doing.

It seems that [senior staffer in CT] and [senior staffer in NJ] have a hard time figuring out how to think of me. Both are friendly, but also guarded, and seem somewhat puzzled by my presence. I have a feeling that they cannot imagine that I am doing what I am doing, that their world does not contain one like me, and that they regard me as a disruption. Especially [name] seems to have a controlling streak that I'll need to stay aware off. I am looking for a liminal experience that can help me get "in" with the campaigns, i.e. the police raid in Geertz' Balinese Cockfight experience.

—Research diary, June 14, 2008

Such a "liminal experience" never occurred.[13] I did not ever feel fully "in" or "understood," even if I was generally accepted or at least tolerated. Until the end my situation seemed somewhat precarious to me and not always particularly transparent to those around me. And yet my field-work was not covert, and I always told people about my research when they asked me what I was doing—often getting responses like "I've heard of you" as the word got around. I did not, however, always make sure to introduce myself as a fieldworker to everyone I met in the fast-paced and often-changing environment of the campaigns. To me this seemed methodologically unnecessary and a needless imposition. I almost always prefaced questions with an explanation of what I was doing, and often enough my behavior alone would alert people to the fact that I played an unusual role. I found it striking to be confronted again and again with how peculiar the practice of sustained fieldwork is to most people, even as I tried to explain it as analogous to what anthropologists do, to what usability researchers do, to what organizational consultants do, to what embedded reporters do (without the various ulterior motives that the lat-ter three have). I was struck in particular by one remark made by a staffer I often talked to, who said, "I've given up trying to figure out what it is you are doing, but it's nice to have you around."

I can't explain my project to people. Interesting. Partially a function, I think, of the fact that I use terms that are unfamiliar to many people (PhD student, research, etc.). From about this time, I notice I have started to explain it in much more low-key terms ("I'm a student, I do some work for the campaign, and will use it for some school work.") This seems to make sense to people.

—Research diary, October 5, 2008

Even as I had thus developed some rapport and, I liked to believe, trust with the staffers, the composition of the assemblages at hand meant that this was only a starting point for me and that a whole new challenge was to develop similar relations to the volunteers and part-timers and to position myself in a way that would be acceptable to the constantly changing populations of each of the three communities without identi-fying myself fully with either of them or becoming part of the conflicts between them. Whereas the volunteer community was generally open and accessible, whether people assumed I was "one of them," a staffer, or a part-timer, talking to part-timers on the occasions when they thought I was a staffer, or at least closely aligned with the staffers, was more problematic. In general, maintaining good standing with the staff community required more work than with any of the two other communities; it also had greater stakes—both for the staffers (who were the most invested in the campaign) and for me (because they control access to the campaign organization as a site).

STAYING IN

Staying in on-site meant making a decision about where on the continuum from participant to observer I wanted to operate.[14] I opted for a position as participant-observer and did a fair amount of campaign work myself. I adopted this position not as some sort of ideal middle road but because I believed it would afford both the freedom I needed to explore the wider assemblage and would be a way to ensure continued access. This position meant that I took part in the practices I observed, most importantly canvassing and phone banking, but always as a researcher. Relative to fully adopting the role of staffer, volunteer, or part-timer, this arguably gave me less access to each community but at least some access to all. Relative to the role of the outside observer, it gave me a chance to practically experience, and hence better analyze, the work people in the campaigns actually do.

It also provided me with a way to engage in the ongoing exchange that ethnographers like Sudhir Venkatesh argue is a premise for sustained fieldwork.[15] The fact that campaigns need all the help they can get for canvassing, phone banking, and a whole slew of additional menial tasks provides a suitable opening for a kind of exchange that is unlikely to compromise the validity of the research itself or the purpose of the assemblage. Staffers, volunteers, and part-timers all recognize people who are "workers" as legitimate, and becoming one of those people offered me a chance to become a more meaningful part of the site than as an observer, without becoming the kind of accomplice that Charles Tilly cautions against. So I stuck to this role, knocking on doors, calling voters, entering data, and otherwise doing more listening than talking, and I did my best to stay in.

Some level of trust is necessary to do fieldwork, and an element of rapport is certainly facilitating, but basically participant-observation is about *being there* for long periods of time. The defining quality of fieldwork as I practice it is not the elusive pursuit of communion between the self and the Other sometimes evoked by cultural anthropologists who are trying to "merge" with their subjects or become full "members" of a community (Erving Goffman, for one, sometimes seems to advocate this).[16] It is instead a more prosaic attempt to go from *here*, where I find myself situated, to *there*—to where the action is, to where the processes I want to analyze play out. And even if people trust you and like you, there are many situations in which they might not want you around if you do not do anything and do not play any recognizable role. Once you are in, however, what Duneier calls the "Becker principle" (named after ethnographer Howard Becker) kicks in. The idea is that the practical constraints, external demands, and individual dispositions that structure social processes virtually guarantee that life will eventually revert to normal, even with the fieldworker there. Ethnography *is* disturbing, especially in situations where some or all involved may think the outsider might hurt them in some way, but once that fear has been assuaged and the researcher has been naturalized to some degree, stronger forces than his or her presence will reassert themselves.[17]

Once in and involved in various exchanges, I still had to fashion and negotiate roles that were both useful in terms of research and socially acceptable on-site. I felt most comfortable on the one occasion when a staffer introduced me to a couple of volunteers and a visiting local elected official as the "office anthropologist," but this role was not one that was generally available in a setting where most had only the vaguest idea of what an anthropologist is or does. More common were situations where I was introduced or introduced myself as a student interested in politics or, depending on the circumstances, adopted a role as a member of one of the communities involved and tried to act it. Most often this would be a role as a volunteer, but I knocked on enough doors to be taken for a part-timer and was in the office often enough that some assumed I was on staff—in each case until I started introducing myself and asking questions.

Sometimes roles are offered rather than chosen, and decisions to accept or reject them become involved in the ongoing exchange on the site. If I was asked to stand in for a junior staffer or key volunteer, or to fill out a part-timer's slot on a canvassing team, I would oblige unless I had definite plans to do otherwise (interview someone, go to a specific event, observe something in particular). These offers were sometimes very concrete. On several occasions I was asked if I wanted to come on staff as a field organizer; a number of times I was offered part-time pay for my canvassing work; and close to Election Day, staffers in both campaigns wanted to be able to count on me as a volunteer phone bank coordinator. In all of these cases I refused as politely as I could to try to maintain my freedom of movement and retain acceptable on-site identities without becoming a fixed or dependable part of the situation—I did not want to be fixed or depended upon. The idea of the ethnographer as a marginal figure is widespread, but it is important to keep in mind that there are different degrees and kinds of marginality, and they are adopted or imposed for varying reasons. Each refusal to take up a role offered would remind people of my ulterior motives as a researcher. "You don't really care whether we win or not, do you?" one staffer asked me, and I was left again in the uncomfortable position of having to explain that while personally I would rather see a Democrat than a Republican represent the district, no, indeed, it did not matter to me professionally how things turned out, and my research was more important for me than the outcome of the election. This is not a popular stance in a campaign assemblage where everyone wants to win (even if to different degrees and for different reasons).

The importance of exchange and the roles available for facilitating research became particularly clear by comparison when it came to gaining access to various allies and getting interviews with them. Most local Democratic organizations and activist groups generally welcomed me, but more bureaucratic entities like unions, state parties, and D.C.-based organizations were less forthcoming. Here I would generally be referred to brief interviews, often with various PR people, and was in no position to offer them anything much in exchange for their time. The one thing everyone was most interested in—information about how others in the assemblage were doing—was what I least of all wanted to offer, fearful that I would lose access if I lost whatever confidence people had in me if I wittingly or unwittingly started trafficking sometimes sensitive information. Whether asked by people in one district about the other, or drilled by one actor in an assemblage about another, I tried to share only what I thought was in principle already available information—what had been announced openly at meetings, or what was already out on blogs or in newspapers. This was not always easy, however, as conversational dynamics and mutual confidentialities take on a life of their own.

OK, so the campaigns get work out of me, I get access. Fine. But often, the staffers are interested in the information I can traffic between different groups. There is some stuff I should try not to divulge. I don't want to end up ratting on someone, as I did at [event] where I told [name] about how [a staffer at an allied organization] viewed the campaign. Why do I do this?

—Research diary, June 4, 2008

Why can't I keep my f*cking trap shut? At least once a week, I blurt out with things I shouldn't share.

—Research diary, August 19, 2008

For some research subjects, simple attention and the additional idea of making it into print is gratifying enough for them to give access or grant an interview and talk frankly.[18] In these situations, what the researcher gives in "exchange" is simply reinforcement of a certain desirable sense of self. Under such conditions a position as a pure observer is entirely viable for the researcher. I think I could have adopted this, too, had I studied only volunteers and activist groups. But among the staffers and the party and campaign organizations, and with many allies, the countervailing interests in secrecy often seem to trump these inclinations to be open to the researcher. This limits access. A willingness to opt for participant-observation or even full participation seems more suitable under such circumstances, at least in situations where there is enough menial work to go around. (Remember how staffers ultimately find that they simply need people who "aren't crazy and don't look crazy"? Apparently I qualified.) Even after all the time I spent working on-site, cultivating ties, and ensuring referrals for further interviews, it still took me a year to track down and secure interviews with some of the off-site principals whom I had never met in person but wanted to speak with. Some never agreed to talk to me.

INTERVIEWS

I conducted a total of fifty-nine semistructured and open-ended interviews with various people to supplement my field research. A few were short, fifteen minutes granted unwillingly, with little of substance being said, but many of them were long, often much longer than I had anticipated, running for well over an hour, and in one case almost three. Most of the interviews were with people who were involved in the assemblages or in politics more widely in the districts in question. Some were with more senior figures around the country who have or have had an important role in the development of field campaigns in or around the Democratic Party but who had nothing in particular to do with my two cases. All interviews took place off-site, in many instances over the phone. Forty were conducted before Election Day, the rest after. In addition, I conducted two small focus groups, each with three volunteers who had worked on the campaigns (these turned out to produce little new data, so I have not quoted from them here and did not conduct more). Interviewees from the assemblages were chosen to flesh out my sense of the three communities and the various allies involved and to create a setting where I could talk to people outside the constraints of the campaigns themselves. The remaining were chosen because they figured in the secondary sources I perused or because they were recommended by people

I had already spoken to.[19] I did not have one main informant in any of the districts, but in both cases there were two or three from each of the communities of staffers, volunteers, and part-timers whom I talked with often. Out of the more than a thousand people involved in one way or another in each assemblage, I estimate that I talked at least once with about a hundred people on-site in each and spoke in more depth with about twenty-five.

Most interviews mainly confirmed what I had already seen, heard, or experienced in the field. Some helped me flesh out historical or technical details not always visible on-site. Reading the transcripts again, I was struck by how much my questions changed over time. My early interviews are consistently plagued by the problem Pierre Bourdieu calls the "scholastic fallacy," the confusion of the research subject's practical problems with the researcher's intellectual problems.[20] These initial conversations are replete with hypothetical questions, where I introduce alternative ways in which things could be done, or are done by others, in one case prompting a senior staffer to cut me off, saying, "Look, there are many ways in which we *could* do things, okay? But this is how we do it here." In later interviews, I talked less and leveraged my own accumulating practical experience and understanding to try to avoid these clashes, while retaining, I hope, a critical distance to the naturalized practices of the various political operatives.

CAMPAIGN ASSEMBLAGES AS RESEARCH OBJECTS

The time and trouble it took to track down the out-of-state actors illustrate a challenge that accompanies fieldwork focused on campaign assemblages. I could have narrowed my empirical focus to look exclusively at the campaign offices as sites, observing only the staffers and volunteers working there while ignoring the part-timers who mostly are on the streets, or I could have looked exclusively at the campaign organizations and the staffers who populate them. But realizing early on that practices of personalized political communication involve many more actors than those present in the office or employed full-time by the campaign organization, I retained my focus on the wider campaign assemblages. These are temporary and heterogeneous entities engaged in geographically distributed practices. As research objects (and sites) they are more akin to movie productions than to corporate headquarters. Unlike the formal organizations or relatively clearly delimited communities that are the objects of many ethnographies, campaign assemblages appear and disappear in quick succession, and any real-time study of them involves making choices about where to go and when, with the clock ticking in the background. Even in the case of congressional districts, just the core organizations in each of them quickly grew to include several offices, twenty staffers or more, and enrolled hundreds of volunteers and part-timers. Allied organizations ran or opened many more locations and involved many more people.

Operating alone, the ethnographer has to make choices, not only about where to be, but also about who to talk to and work with—staffers, volunteers, part-timers, campaigns, or allies, out-of-state operators or locals. The workdays of the staffers themselves are demanding enough, from the early fall and onward from 10 A.M. to 10 P.M. and sometimes more. I also faced a two-hour commute each way and the regular task of turning the jottings in my notebooks into field notes. Consider the practical challenges involved: I spent five to seven days split between the two districts from July onward (three to five days a week before), and a normal rule of thumb is that each hour of fieldwork requires at least another hour to write field notes. I had some of that time every morning and night on the trains, but not enough. Early on I decided that I wanted extensive field notes written shortly after each trip, so I took a day off most weeks until October to catch up on my notes. Even so, I spent two weeks in November writing up field notes from several notebooks I had filled in the final, busy weeks. The decision to write extensive field notes along the way gave me more than a thousand pages of data to work with later, but it also cost me time in the field while the elections were under way. Some ethnographers rely only on a few recorded memos to themselves, their jottings, and their memory, and while I realize that there are situations when this might be a defensible choice, in general I doubt much can reliably be inferred from such malleable and impermanent records.

Taking assemblages rather than offices or organizations as one's focus entails certain trade-offs. For example, although there is an unfilled need for a more classical "cultural" ethnography of campaigns—an attempt to capture and understand the life-world, meanings, and experiences of, for instance, the staffers who work so hard on them—I do not think this book is it.[21] The research design should have been different to really accumulate the data for such "thick description." I neither describe nor analyze here facets of campaigns that are irrelevant for my analytical interest in practical processes of personalized political communication (the pervasive machismo, the cult of the candidate, the magical thinking, etc.). Clifford Geertz has famously defined the task of the cultural anthropologist as being able to distinguish between a twitch and a wink,[22] but for a more analytically oriented ethnographer, it is worth keeping in mind that there are questions for which it matters very little whether something is a twitch or a wink. Thus, I have continuously kept the category and practices of personalized political communication at the center stage of my research, analysis, and writing, focusing on it not only in my data gathering but also in the very structure of this book (building it around contacting, organizing, and targeting rather than, for example, the communities or actors involved). I thus fall in line with an increasing number of attempts to break some of the limitations that traditional ethnographic research has sometimes been perceived to suffer from.[23] As opposed to single-site studies of supposedly self-contained communities, culturalist approaches, or sites understood as representing one side of some of the dichotomies that have haunted sociology in particular (micro/macro, lifeworld/system, practice/structure), more and more authors today argue for multisite studies that follow practices beyond the spatially and socially delimited setting that one starts with.[24]

THE PULL OF THE PROFESSIONALS

As I made these decisions about what in each assemblage to study and when, I noticed a phenomenon I think of as the "pull of the professionals." To ensure that I covered both districts roughly equally and equally systematically, I kept a log of my field notes and interviews that I consulted frequently as I plotted my next steps along the way. Even having decided in advance that I wanted to trace the wider assemblage and do research in all three involved communities, I could see from my log over the summer that I usually ended up spending most of my time with the staffers, both when in the offices and when on the streets or at events.

> When with people, especially in the field, I of course have to follow their sense of what is important, but also struggle against the tendency to focus everything on what the elected official/candidate is doing, or what is/is not on TV. It is cable television in August, for Christ sake! Who cares? It surprises a lot of people that I am interested in what *they* are doing. It in particular surprises a lot of staffers that I am interested in what the volunteers and especially the part-timers are doing. I shouldn't let the staffers lead me away from everyone else.
> —Research diary, August 2, 2008

I attribute this pull to three factors. First of all, once the researcher is accepted on the site, staffers are easier to study than volunteers or part-timers. Once one is in the office, staffers are at hand, often enjoy company during their breaks, and always need help with something. After just a few days in each district, I knew the majority of the staffers by name, whereas most of the volunteers and part-timers remained more anonymous multitudes, in and out in a steady flow. Secondly, there is no doubt an element of social homophily involved too. In almost every respect, the staffers were more like me than the members of any other community involved. Staffers are predominantly young, male, college-educated, white, and often of middle-class background (like me). Not so with the volunteers (who are often older) and the part-timers (many of whom are minorities and from less-privileged backgrounds). Thirdly, the staffers often have a lot to say and are convinced that what they do matters, whereas volunteers and in particular part-timers sometimes have little to say and occasionally doubt the value of what they do—even in cases where the three communities are involved in the *very same activity*, as with canvassing or phone banking.

The pull of the professionals can have a pernicious influence over the iterative process of ongoing research. As field notes and interview transcripts continuously underline the importance of staffers and what they do, and as they exert their pull, they may draw the researcher ever closer into their orbit at the expense of time with the other communities involved, a drift from studying an entire process to studying its management. As I became aware of this potential problem, I decided to invert the paths that had led me into the core organization and to trace the ties that tied volunteers, part-timers, and allies into the assemblage the other way, to interview volunteers and allies off-site, to attend public events and meetings and visit allied organizations in accordance with the everyday rhythms of the assemblage. I have come to think of this as a double movement, first from a full-time engagement in the district at large and inward to a full-time engagement in the core organization, and then from there outward again to a split engagement with heavy emphasis on the offices and the streets where the staffers, volunteers, and part-timers work, combined with systematic attempts to maintain focus on the wider assemblage. This approach is aligned with Bruno Latour's idea that one should "follow the actors," but I would underline that following is only one side; the other is the analytically informed decision of which actors to follow, when, where, and why. One cannot study everything, and to suggest otherwise, as some actor-network theorists sometimes seem to do, is an unhelpful throwback to naïve empiricism, no matter how sophisticated the analytical vocabulary used.[25]

THE CHALLENGE OF CONVERSATION

From August onward I started following the actual interactions between callers and canvassers and the voters they encountered in greater detail. The first step was to pay utmost attention to others' and my own actual conversations with voters, try to memorize them, and jot down extensive preliminary notes immediately afterward. Doing this is awkward and intensely demanding compared to less intrusive fieldwork oriented toward capturing only the most important snippets of conversation, general patterns of action, and the ambience of everyday work. A few people started making fun of how often I suddenly retreated to the men's room. I experimented with a second step: bringing a digital recorder with me both in the offices for phone banking sessions and on the street for canvassing. This came with a separate set of problems, however. On the one hand, volunteers and part-timers were visibly uncomfortable with the recorder, changed their behavior noticeably when it was on, and sometimes objected to its being used at all. On the other hand, I quickly realized that getting voters' consent to recording interactions that are already complicated and fragile would be hard. I did make some recordings, a few of them covert, but soon abandoned this practice as indefensible and unworkable in light of the strains it put on my relations with the volunteers and part-timers and the research-ethical problems it presented.

This means that in most cases where I use quotes, they are reconstructed from my on-site jottings, as fleshed out in field notes written soon afterward.[26] Mitchell Duneier has been an important critic of this somewhat misleading use of quotation marks, arguing that ethnographers should use recorders to get language right. Others suggest that a more lenient standard is acceptable.[27] I agree in principle with Duneier's position and recognize the problems inherent in presenting notes as quotes, especially jottings made under strenuous conditions by an often somewhat worse-for-wear non-native speaker from a different social background. But I still think it is useful to use quotation marks to distinguish words taken down as utterances. In using them, I have engaged in one of the multiple translations involved in ethnography, this one akin to the translation of talk into prose in quotes from interviews. There is writing craftsmanship involved in that, but it is craftsmanship oriented toward truths rather than aesthetic or dramatic effects. Again, I realize the limits and dangers inherent in this practice and therefore have not subjected my imperfect data to truly micro-oriented techniques like discourse or conversation analysis.

WRITING THIS BOOK

As many have observed, prose is the most important form of data visualization and the main kind of scientific rhetoric available to ethnographers, who rarely have equations, tables, or logs of lab experiments to show for their effort.[28] The campaigns I studied are gone, and the jottings I made, the artifacts I collected, the impressions I was left with, along with my field notes and my interview transcripts, will remain mine alone to ensure that the people involved can remain anonymous. This text is all I have to show what I saw, how I see it, and how I came to see it that way. There is no public data set I can refer to, no single, synoptic way in which situations and events happened or were played out that I can simply relate to the reader. This basic condition, integral to ethnography, spurred considerable interest in the poetics of anthropology in the 1980s, sparked both by the deceptively simple matter-of-fact writing style of some earlier ethnographers and a postmodernist and multiculturalist fear that the univocal accounts produced helped impose particular readings on peoples' multivocal experiences.[29]

In writing this book I have sought a balance between my sympathy for these critiques and my own more pragmatist and empiricist inclinations. I draw attention to my writing here not out of authorial narcissism or epistemological hypochondria, but because I recognize that it plays a role not only in conveying but also in constituting my arguments. I have tried to write what I saw, but I realize how deceptively simple the injunction to do that is. Three rhetorical decisions in particular bear mentioning here: first, the consistent anonymization of the people I spoke to; secondly, the use of episodes in each chapter; and finally, the way in which a few technical terms from the social sciences are used to bracket the meanings of natural language and guide the research design, execution, and the construction of the argument.

In his book *Sidewalk*, Mitchell Duneier offers a trenchant critique of the standard ethnographic practice of anonymizing people and sometimes even research sites, referring to them only by pseudonym. He argues that using real place and personal names holds the ethnographer to a higher standard and that the use of fictitious names often protects the researcher more than the research subjects, who rarely request them. Duneier suggests that they are therefore normally unnecessary and even undesirable. I cannot underline enough that anonymity and pseudonyms were neither in this study—to the contrary, they were often requested, necessary, and, I think, desirable. Many of the people involved in the two assemblages were extremely wary of being identified, especially concerned with being associated with quotes that could be construed as critical of others involved. Particularly staffers in the campaign, party, or allied organizations, and long-term local volunteers and party regulars with ongoing stakes in district-level politics would, on the one hand, be often eloquent and incisive critics of each other, and, on the other hand, insist that I did not quote them by name. Even though I had promised anonymity from the start, months after the fieldwork was completed I was still receiving emails from people asking me not to quote them by name. Many people I interviewed expressed similar sentiments. Some volunteers and part-timers were indifferent to being named or expressed no preferences, but early on, as I negotiated access to the sites, I decided to simply promise everyone anonymity, making clear I would use pseudonyms and quote people only with reference to their position. For those involved in the campaigns, some voices and many scenes throughout the book will be recognizable (though some sensitive ones have deliberately been written to make them less so), but outsiders would have to go to considerable lengths to identify any of the people involved with the quotes used and situations described. Even where it has pained me as a writer, I sometimes have kept references to people's position and personal characteristics deliberately vague (as in the discussion above of one campaign manager's fear of interviews, a passage that is virtually begging for the use of at least "him" or "her" instead of "the campaign manager"). For staffers in particular, suggesting I would do otherwise would have severely limited my access, and perhaps even made the project impossible. Loyalty is often considered a cardinal virtue in politics, and the ability to stay mum a close second, so it was possible that people's professional prospects and reputations could be damaged if they were associated personally with some of what they told me.

In all chapters I describe a number of episodes I have observed or taken part in. They serve three purposes. First, they are meant to take you there, to provide the vicarious experience that I think makes ethnographies so potentially compelling. They offer a more impressionistic illustration of my data than quotes and descriptions integrated into the main text, pieces of data that easily slip into the matter-of-fact tone that the postmodernists attacked during the debates in the 1980s. The episodes are as close as I get to sharing my primary data. Secondly, the episodes serve to underline the important point that personalized political communication, even when analyzed and conveyed in writing, must be understood first and foremost as a practice and thus cannot be rendered accurately solely through quotes. Thirdly, the episodes serve to remind both my readers and me of how loosely reality often fits our attempts to order it. The episodes are closer to the aperspectival and disjoint cacophony of social life than the more analytically ordered narrative in which I insert them; both are necessary in order to provide both a general understanding and reminders of its limitations.[30] They have been crafted with these three purposes in mind. Some episodes are close to being virtual quotes from my field notes. Others are composed from my jottings, recollections, and from interview data. I have not constructed synthetic scenes or composite characters anywhere in this book.

The use of technical terms from the social sciences—most notably my own notion of "personalized political communication" and those imported from sociology, "interaction," "socio-technical," and so forth—serves a similar purpose when coupled with the natural language in which I have tried to write most of the book. No one who has listened to Herbert J. Gans's incisive critique of the alienating and self-emasculating effects of the use of "sociologese" in place of proper English can use the word "assemblage" lightly.[31] But it still serves a purpose to "bracket" our taken-for-granted assumptions about what a political campaign is and analyze it from the third position that can be created around a technical vocabulary that is foreign to the situation at hand. Kenneth Burke to the contrary, language does not do our thinking for us, but we do our thinking with it, and hence we have to think carefully about it while we do so. I hope the reader will find the use I have made of these concepts analytically generative. They seem so to me; they have helped me structure my thinking beyond the logics of practice encountered and recounted, and should facilitate the translation of what I have seen into a form that is pertinent for scholarly debates. What I have pursued here is not an exercise in thick description, but what has been called "analytic ethnography," and a few choice terms have helped me structure my data, analyze it, and position my argument in relation to the various academic debates I aim to contribute to.[32] I hope further research will strengthen, qualify, or challenge the arguments made here and will investigate Republican campaigns, campaigns for other offices, under different circumstances, and during later cycles, will explore all of these sites that are positively clamoring for the kind of ethnographic work that has so much to offer to communications research, political science, and sociology. I hope I have demonstrated how it can be done and what can be achieved.

Notes

1. Entman 1989.
2. Twenty percent is a little less than the national average of 28 percent who reported being contacted in person by the Obama campaign in 2008, or the 26 percent who reported being contacted in person by the Kerry campaign and its allies in 2004 (see Barone 2006; CBS 2008). Both figures were presumably considerably higher in battleground states than elsewhere and, of course, represent only one side's efforts. (See Beck and Heidemann 2010 for an analysis of the changing strategic priorities of field campaigns.) In addition it should be noted that ground wars are waged somewhat differently in states that allow no-excuse early voting, where the final weekend of get-out-the-vote work is much more focused and the earlier field program more extensive.
3. Fiorina et al. 2009.
4. Putnam 2000; Verba, Schlozman, and Brady 1995.
5. Holbrook 1996; Johnston, Hagen, and Jamieson 2004; Rosenstone and Hansen 1993; Skocpol 2003.
6. Lichterman 1996; Munson 2008; Warren 2001.
7. Fisher 2006; Gosnell 1939; Marwell 2007.
8. Blake 1972.
9. Some have spoken of the "personalization" of political communication (Swanson and Mancini 1996) and mean by that something different from what I call "personalized political communication"—namely, an increased focus in both news coverage and campaign communications on individual politicians rather than interests and ideologies.
10. Jensen 2010.
11. Fenno 1978.
12. See, for example, Bennett and Entman 2001; Graber 2006; Iyengar and Kinder 1987; Negrine and Stanyer 2007; Norris 2000; Zaller 1999.
13. Beck et al. 2002; Eliasoph 1998; Gamson 1992; Huckfeldt and Sprague 1995; Mutz 2002; Walsh 2004.
14. Magleby and Patterson 2006.
15. Abramson, Aldrich, and Rohde 2010; Green and Coffey 2007; Herrnson 2004; G. Jacobson 2009; Johnson 2009; Shea and Burton 2006; Trent and Friedenberg 2008.
16. For a few exceptions, see Beck et al. 2002; Huckfeldt and Sprague 1995; and Ubertaccio 2009.
17. For an overview, see Green and Gerber 2008. See also Gillespie 2010; Masket 2009; Nickerson 2006.

18. Gosnell 1939; Lazarsfeld et al. 1948. See also Denver, Hands, and MacAllister 2004; Pattie, Johnston, and Fieldhouse 1995; and Whiteley and Seyd 2003 for examples of British studies documenting the impact of local "constituency campaigning" in the United Kingdom.

19. Altheide and Snow 1979; Mazzoleni and Schulz 1999.

20. See, for example, Norris 2000, 179.

21. Dalton and Wattenberg 2000; Skocpol 2003.

22. See, for instance, Bennett and Entman 2001; Cook 1998.

23. Mazzoleni and Schulz 1999, 249.

24. Castells 2007, 238, my emphasis.

25. See Arnold (2004) and Clarke and Evans (1983) on the limited coverage of much congressional politics.

26. Plouffe 2009, 378–79, my emphasis.

27. For communications equivalents of modernization theorists, see, for example, Blumler and Kavenagh (1999) and Norris (2000).

28. See Bennett and Iyengar 2008; Bennett and Manheim 2006; Gitlin 2001; Neuman 1996; Turow 1997.

29. Shenk 1997.

30. Prior 2007.

31. Green and Gerber 2008.

32. Herrnson 1995, 200.

33. Herrnson 2004, 236.

34. Weir and Ganz 1999.

35. Bergan et al. 2005.

36. See, for instance, Plouffe 2009.

37. DeLanda 2006; Girard and Stark 2007; Latour 2005; Sassen 2006.

38. Fantasia and Voss 2004; Fisher 2006; Ware 1985; Wattenberg 1996.

39. Levitz 2010; Fisher 2006.

40. Jamieson 2009, 45.

41. The fact that there is money involved does not mean their involvement does not have political and civic dimensions. First of all, of course, their work is meant to influence the election. Secondly, the experience of engaging in what Dana Fisher (2006) has called "paid activism" contributes to the part-timers' view and understanding of what politics is like.

42. Chadwick 2007; Hindman 2008; Howard 2006; Karpf 2009; Kreiss 2009; Nielsen 2009; Nielsen 2010; Vaccari 2008.

43. Malchow 2004.

44. This fact problematizes the major reason offered by some political scientists for not paying close attention to electioneering: in Larry Bartels's (1992, 264) succinct formulation, "In a world where most campaigners make reasonably effective use of reasonably similar resources and technologies most of the time, much of their effort will necessarily be without visible impact, simply because every campaigner's efforts are balanced against more or less equally effective efforts to produce the opposite effect." There is little evidence to suggest we live in such a world. Competing campaigns are not always equally effective. They often have access to different resources and technologies, and thus their efforts probably rarely balance each other.

45. Venkatesh 2002.
46. Merton 1987.

CHAPTER 2 THE GROUND WAR ENTERS THE TWENTY-FIRST CENTURY

1. Schudson 1998.
2. Dinkin 1989.
3. Blumenthal 1980; Ornstein and Mann 2000.
4. Aldrich 1995.
5. Herrnson 1988.
6. McGerr 1986.
7. Berry 1984; Maisel 2007; Wattenberg 1996.
8. Wilson 1962.
9. Ware 1985.
10. See Karpf 2009.
11. Rozell, Wilcox, and Madland 2006; Sabato 1981; Wattenberg 1991.
12. Dark 2001.
13. Clawson and Clawson 1999; Goldfield 1986.
14. Skocpol 2003.
15. Altschuler and Blumin 2000.
16. Green and Gerber 2008; Rosenstone and Hansen 1993.
17. Gerber and Green 2000, 662.
18. Norris 2000, 179.
19. Dulio 2004; Medvic 2001; Sabato 1981; Thurber and Nelson 2000.
20. See Aldrich (1995); Herrnson (1988); and Koldny (1998) on party organizations, and Blumberg et al. (2009); Green and Coffey (2007); Green and Farmer (2003); Green and Shea (1996); and Green and Shea (1999) on Ohio.
21. Rose 1992; Salmore and Salmore 2008.
22. Institute of Politics 2002, 229.
23. Ibid.
24. Jamieson 2001, 218.
25. Barone 2006.
26. See Masters 2004. All volunteer numbers should be treated with caution, since they are usually estimates based on self-reporting by political organizations eager to play up their popular support. In any case, raw numbers say nothing about how many hours people have actually worked. One dedicated activist working ten hours can do more for a campaign than ten people dropping by to chip in a halfhearted hour each.
27. Edsall 2000.
28. Broder 2000.
29. Jamieson 2001, 219.
30. Barone 2006.
31. Franke-Ruta and Meyerson 2004. Predictive dialing systems automatically call through a pre-determined list of phone numbers and connect callers to their targets, thus minimizing the time spent punching in numbers or waiting

for people to pick up the phone. They are widely used in telemarketing and the service industries, but only used occasionally by political campaigns.

32. Alexander 1976; Sorauf 1992.

33. Malbin 2006.

34. Green and Farmer 2003, 203.

35. Green and Shea 1997.

36. Gerber and Green 2000.

37. Malchow 2004.

38. Broder 2001.

39. Semiatin 2008, 90.

40. Magleby and Monson 2004.

41. Kiely 2002.

42. Carney 2006.

43. Balz 2003.

44. Edsall 2006.

45. Magleby and Monson 2004.

46. As Galvin (2010) has shown, most postwar Republican presidents have been more avid party builders than their Democratic counterparts.

47. Balz and Broder 2002.

48. Malbin 2006.

49. Typically, 501(c)s operate for religious, charitable, scientific, or educational purposes and can engage in very limited political activities, typically voter registration. On the other hand, 527s are committees formed primarily to influence elections through issue advocacy or mobilization efforts. They are free to do so as long as they do not coordinate with individual candidates or parties or engage in candidate advocacy.

50. Bergan et al. 2005.

51. Jamieson 2006, 35–36.

52. Campaign Finance Institute 2006.

53. Barone 2006.

54. Bai 2004; Institute of Politics 2006; Jamieson 2006.

55. Edsall quoted in Institute of Politics 2006, 213. See Fisher 2006 for a similar point.

56. Federal Election Commission 2007.

57. Skinner 2005.

58. Institute of Politics 2006, 230.

59. Edsall 2005.

60. Green and Coffey 2007.

61. Balz 2004a.

62. Edsall 2006; Hamburger and Wallsten 2006.

63. Kerbel 2009.

64. Kreiss 2009.

65. Balz 2004b.

66. Democratic National Committee 2005.

67. Kamarck 2006; Bowers 2008.

68. Quoted in Bai 2006.

69. Blumberg et al. 2009.
70. Suddes 2006.
71. Jacobson 2006.
72. Jamieson 2009, 40.
73. See Jamieson 2009, 31.
74. Thomas 2010.
75. Plouffe 2009.
76. Institute of Politics 2009, 98.
77. Plouffe 2009.
78. Perlstein 2001.
79. Dickinson 2008.
80. See Jamieson 2009, 42.
81. Quoted on TechPresident 2009.
82. Plouffe 2009.
83. Quoted in Institute of Politics 2007.
84. Blumberg et al. 2009.
85. Ibid., 16.
86. Hamburger and Wallsten 2006.
87. Thomas 2009.
88. Bowers 2008.
89. Part of the process was pure political calculation, part of it an extensive consultation involving five hundred thousand people from the email list in an online survey and thousands at meetings (Cillizza 2009). See Galvin (2010) for examples of previous postwar Democratic presidents who built their own parallel organizations rather than engage in party building.
90. Saslow 2009; Eggen 2009.
91. Zeleny 2010.
92. Bacon 2010.
93. Figure for total spending taken from the Center for Responsive Politics' website, www.opensecrets.org.
94. Parks 2010.
95. Melber 2010.

Chapter 3 Contacting Voters at Home

1. Thompson 1995, 84.
2. Goffman 1959.
3. See, for instance, Webster 1968.
4. Goffman 1982.
5. Duneier 1999, 198.
6. There are clear differences in how much respect is afforded to people's presentation of self by voters, partially dependent on age, class, gender, and race, but I do not have the data to analyze these systematically. See Gillespie (2010) for an analysis of some parallel issues based on focus group research.
7. Schwartz 1968.

8. Eliasoph 1998.

9. Hochschild 1979, 1982; Leidner 1993, 1999.

10. Bennett and Manheim 2006.

11. Cameron 2000.

12. One says "the scripts matter more for the lawyers than for us," referring to the campaign finance regulations that cover expenses shared between different candidates.

13. See Gillespie 2010; Nickerson 2007.

14. See, for example, Mazeland 2004.

15. There are more dramatic examples of interactions going well beyond what staffers are comfortable with, such as volunteers getting into sometimes quite heated arguments with voters.

16. See Panagopoulos 2009; Nickerson 2007; and Green and Gerber 2008 for an overview.

17. Gillespie 2010.

18. Green and Gerber 2008; Nickerson 2006. A growing body of research based on a combination of experimental methods and contemporary psychological theory (and in some cases behavioral economics) is working through a whole range of different approaches in terms of content, form, and media for mobilizational messages. See, for instance, Arceneaux and Nickerson 2009; Gerber, Green, and Larimer 2010; Nickerson 2005; and Nickerson and Rogers 2010, plus Issenberg 2010 for a journalistic account.

19. Leidner 1993.

20. Boorom et al. 1998; Ligas 2004; Mittal and Lassar 1996.

21. Ganz 2009b.

Chapter 4 Organizing Campaign Assemblages

1. Weber 1968; Michels 1915.

2. Beunza and Stark 2004; Clemens 1993; March and Olsen 1989.

3. Castells 2000.

4. Piore and Sabel 1984.

5. Leidner 1993.

6. Hernnson 2008; Sabato 1981.

7. Medvic 2001; Dulio 2004; Patterson 2002.

8. Sabel 1991; Bibby 1999; McCarthy and Zald 1977.

9. As pointed out by Magleby, Monson, and Patterson 2007.

10. Powell 1990.

11. One might add "convention" and "charisma" to the mix, to return to the Weberian roots and include a more explicit historical dimension to the analysis (Weber 1968), and of course the term "network" has many other meanings in addition to the sense in which it is used here.

12. See Herrnson 1988 and Kolodny 1998.

13. There are campaigns, both successful and unsuccessful, that have experimented with other forms of organizing, some of them less hierarchical, many of

them definitely not "by the book." In addition to the campaigns of Barack Obama and Howard Dean, those of Gary Hart, Jesse Jackson, and Paul Wellstone are recent prominent examples from the Democratic Party.

14. Wilson 1995.

15. Campaign organizations are predominantly staffed by men, especially in field, and the women who worked there often complained about the "frat boy" atmosphere and a sometimes sexist work environment.

16. Hernnson 2008; Miller, Wlezien, and Hildreth 1991; Walker 1991.

17. Powell 1990.

18. Over time, long-term incumbents often build a coterie of professionals around them, some working in their office, some for allied organizations, some in corporate jobs, but many of whom will find ways to staff campaign organizations when necessary. These candidates need not rely on de-territorialized professionals (though some bring a few on board if desired).

19. In his book *The Amateur Democrats*, James Q. Wilson (1962) suggests a distinction between "professionals" and "amateurs" in politics not on the basis of their skills or sophistication but on the basis of whether they are preoccupied with electoral outcome or find politics intrinsically interesting. While his description of the "amateurs" he studied, 1950s reform Democrats, is reminiscent of the civically and communally motivated volunteers I met during my fieldwork, the outcome—winning—is a concern shared by all communities involved, and both staffers and volunteers are highly partisan. What differs are the additional motivations and whether winning is of primary importance. Whereas staffers have a vocational view of politics and are overwhelmingly concerned with winning, volunteers have more of a civic view while remaining very concerned with winning, and part-timers would like to win but see the whole thing primarily as a casual job (and are generally not particularly partisan).

20. MoveOn and more recently the Obama campaign have experimented with "distributed phone banks," an arrangement where individual volunteers can make calls from home by logging on to a secure website that will provide them with a script, contact details for target voters, and a template for recording response data. The staffers in Connecticut and New Jersey were generally skeptical of such innovations, worrying that people would "stray from the script" and "not get that much work done." "I'd rather have them here and try to keep the energy in the room," says one.

21. Nickerson 2006, 2007; Green and Gerber 2008.

CHAPTER 5 TARGETING VOTERS FOR PERSONAL CONTACTS

1. Bennett and Manheim 2006.

2. Assume that previously 65 percent of those reminded to vote and activated because of the GOTV contact voted for the "right" candidate, and the rest voted for the opponent, and that the new political targeting changes this to 80 percent. From a partisan point of view, the net gain of each additional voter who is turned out is then $0.80 - 0.20 = 0.60$ as opposed to $0.65 - 0.35 = 0.30$.

3. See Gandy (1993) and Howard and Kreiss (2009) on privacy, Gandy (2001) and Elmer (2004) on control, and Turow (1997, 2006) on segmentation. Sosnik, Dowd, and Fournier (2006) provides an industry perspective.

4. Ganz 1993; Hillygus and Shields 2008.

5. Malchow 2003; Wielhouwer 2003.

6. Castells 2000; Hindman 2009.

7. There is no clear line that separates predictive modeling from a whole slew of related statistical techniques used in marketing and elsewhere and branded as "data mining," "behavioral targeting," etc. For my purposes it suffices to define predictive modeling as any kind of quantitative analysis trying to predict individual-level behavior on the basis of individual-level data.

8. Godwin 1988; Hillygus and Shield 2008.

9. Bai 2004.

10. Edsall and Grimaldi 2004.

11. Some consultants confidently claim they can predict voting tendencies with 90 percent accuracy (Cillizza 2007). However, the 80 percent figure was repeated to me in several interviews and has been mentioned in the trade press, too, so I will stick to this more conservative approximation.

12. Latour 1987, 131.

13. Precincts vary in size, containing on average about eleven hundred registered voters but ranging from as little as four hundred to as many as four thousand.

14. Blaemire 2002.

15. Malchow 2003.

16. Gosnell 1939; Key 1949.

17. Green and Shea 1996.

18. Malchow 2003, 4.

19. Catalist 2009.

20. See Hillygus and Shield 2008; Howard 2006.

21. As information scientists have often noted, quantitative data is constituted through standardized classifications that require a degree of shared understanding and agreement on how terms are used—understanding and agreement that is not always to be found (Bowker and Star 1999).

22. Using enough manpower and tried-and-trusted routines, the Hillsville Democratic Town Committee accomplished successfully at a local level and in an off-line way what the so-called Project Houdini unsuccessfully tried to do at the national level in an online way for the Barack Obama campaign—a near-real-time narrowing down of the GOTV universe to include only those voters who had yet to vote.

23. See, for instance, Marwell 2007.

24. See Wielhouver (2003) on Lincoln's "perfect list." The Clarkson quote is from McGerr (1986, 94).

25. Varon 2004.

26. Malchow 2003.

27. Blaemire 2002.

28. Meyerson 2003.

29. In contrast, when lists are balkanized along geographic lines, one party organization in a particular state or county may have a twenty-year record on Ms. Smith, but when she moves across the line that information does not follow, and her profile will be built from scratch in her new location.

30. Quoted in Farhi 2004.

31. Journalistic coverage of the use of new technologies and tools in politics is full of such inflated hype from supposedly authoritative sources who often know better.

32. Cillizza 2003.

33. See, for instance, Gertner 2004.

34. Jaquith 2006.

35. Ibid.

36. Cillizza 2003.

37. See Tynan 2004.

38. Compare Wielhouver 2003 and Ganz 1993.

CHAPTER 6 ALWAYS FIGHTING THE SAME GROUND WAR?

1. Wallsten 2008.

2. Dickinson 2008.

3. Eliasoph 1998; Hibbing and Theiss-Morse 2002.

4. Goffman 1959, 1982; Hochschild 1979, 1983; Leidner 1993, 1999.

5. Gosnell 1939; Lazarsfeld et al. 1948; Gerber and Green 2008.

6. Ansolabehere and Iyengar 1995; Ansolabehere et al. 1994; Patterson 1993; Cappella and Jamieson 1996; Godwin 1988.

7. Bennett and Iyengar 2009; Neuman, Park, and Panek 2009; Prior 2007.

8. Steffens 1904.

9. See Clemens (1997) and Wilson (1962) for a historical discussion, and Dark (2001); Karpf (2009); and Kerbel (2009) for contemporary examples. Business interests and various right-wing activist groups, most recently the so-called Tea Parties, push the Republican Party in similar ways (see Williamson, Skocpol, and Coggins 2011).

10. Wallsten 2010.

11. Simon 1957.

12. Stark 2009.

13. See, for instance, Medvic 2001; Patterson 2002; Sabato 1981.

14. Johnson 2007.

15. Wilson 1962; Ware 1985.

16. Erie 1988; Grimshaw 1992.

17. See Abbott (1988) for a sociological analysis.

18. Weir and Ganz 1997.

19. McAdam, Tarrow, and Tilly 2001; Munson 2008; Rosenstone and Hansen 1993; Verba, Schlozman, and Brady 1995.

20. Skocpol 2003; Skocpol, Ganz, and Munson 2000.

21. Skocpol 2003; Ware 1985.

22. Barber 2003; Gutmann and Thompson 2004; and Held 2006.

23. Patterson 2002; and Schier 2000.

24. Clemens 1997; Skocpol 2003.

25. Morris P. Fiorina (1999) has rightly warned against the tendency to assume that civic engagement is always a good in itself and pointed out that ideologically motivated activists have contributed to the partisan polarization American electoral politics have seen in recent years. The absence of direct means of influence afforded by campaign assemblages indicates that low-turnout primaries are more likely drivers of this effect than electoral activism. The fact that campaign volunteers have not only ideological but also instrumental and intrinsic motivations suggests they may not even want to impress their exact beliefs on the candidates they support.

26. Green and Gerber 2008.

RESEARCH APPENDIX

1. Gans 1962; Latour and Woolgar 1986; Bourdieu 1992.

2. Duneier 2002; Emerson et al. 1995; Gans 1982.

3. I use "fieldwork" and "participant-observation" interchangeably in the narrow sense recommended by Gans (1999), i.e., to signify actual firsthand research on-site. I use the more general term "ethnography" in the broader sense it has acquired, as a combination of a wide range of predominantly qualitative methods, including fieldwork, but also interviews, historical research, and the collection of artifacts on site.

4. Duneier 2002, 1568.

5. See, for example, Auyero 2000; Becker 1998; Katz 2001; Katz 2002; Latour 2005; Tilly 2008.

6. In a sense this position offers an important qualification to the idea that participant-observation is a "time-consuming" method. While it is certainly true that fieldwork takes time, what is more important is that it generates data that is not available in any other way, and questions of time consumption are thus secondary to the more fundamental issue of whether and to what degree one wants or needs to do fieldwork in order to develop and answer ones' questions.

7. Emerson et al. 1995.

8. Ragin 1992, 217.

9. In many uncontested districts, large-scale field operations are unnecessary, as unpromising electoral conditions and incumbents' brimming war chests deter challengers, and the ritual of regular elections plus some direct mail and paid media suffice to remind a portion of the electorate to renew the representatives' mandate every term.

10. Marcus 1995. See Newman (1999) and Marwell (2007) for examples of comparative designs.

11. See, for instance, Gans (1962) on the occasional methodological need to "take sides."

12. In most campaigns one can be fired for speaking to journalists or bloggers without authorization. Staffers in allied organizations and even regulars in local

party organizations and activists groups are equally ambivalent about publicity, always willing to talk about others, happy to showcase things that go well, but reluctant to speak openly about problems and conflicts.

13. In his seminal work *The Interpretation of Culture* (1973), Clifford Geertz argues that an unexpected police raid, in which he, just like everyone around him, fled the scene of the illegal cockfight he was observing, was an experience that helped overcome the barriers between him—the ethnographer—and the local Balinese he was out to study.

14. Gans 1962, 338–39.

15. See Venkatesh 2002.

16. See Goffman 1989.

17. Duneier 1999, 338. See also Becker 1998 and Gans 1962, 345.

18. Gans 1982.

19. I think the combination of controlled comparison between two cases and the triangulation between fieldwork, interviews, and secondary sources allows me to substantiate the arguments developed here. I have to say, though, that I regret that I did not survey the staffers, volunteers, and part-timers involved. Even with predictably low response rates, such additional data would have allowed me to flesh out my sense of people's various backgrounds and also use terms like "most," "many," and "the majority of" with greater certainty and precision than I do.

20. Bourdieu 2003.

21. See Mahler (forthcoming) for steps toward a more classical "cultural" ethnography of campaigns.

22. Geertz 1973.

23. For a sustained contemporary critique, see Katz 2001; Katz 2002.

24. See Marcus (1995) for an overview, or Burawoy (1998) on the "extended case method," Duneier (1999) on the "extended place method," or Latour (2005) on "following the actors."

25. The double move was a trade-off too. While it gave me a broader data set, I continue to believe that I might have gotten access to more campaign meetings, documents, and data on contacts and numbers had I subjected myself more fully to the pull of the professionals on a single site. My strategy means I at least interviewed, and very often visited, most major actors at least once along the way, so it is only in a few instances that I have had to rely solely on postelection interviews, with all of their inherent dangers of retrospective rationalizations.

26. Quotes from interviews are marked as such in the text and are mostly from detailed transcripts. A few are from handwritten notes when people objected to recordings.

27. Contrast Duneier (1999) with, for example, Gans (1982) and Van Maanen (1988).

28. Born 2004; Emerson et al. 1995.

29. See, for example, Clifford and Marcus 1986 and Geertz 1988.

30. Some have suggested that ethnographic writing should break with the representational logics that often lead us (whoever "we" are—thinkers, writers, readers?) to reify and categorize what is written and instead "evoke" the experience of the field (see Clifford and Marcus 1986). I personally think the distinction

between "representing" and "evoking" is a sleight of hand that cannot avoid the basic fact that language is a form of violence we do to the world, and the question is how and why we do it, not what we call it. (I take my cue from James [1995] and Wittgenstein [1991] on this.)

31. Gans 1989.

32. Lofland 1995; Snow et al. 2003.

References

Abbott, Andrew D. 1988. *The System of Professions: An Essay on the Division of Expert Labor.* Chicago: University of Chicago Press.

Abramson, Paul R., John Herbert Aldrich, and David W. Rohde. 2010. *Change and Continuity in the 2008 Elections.* Washington, D.C.: CQ Press.

Aldrich, John H. 1995. *Why Parties? The Origin and Transformation of Political Parties in America.* Chicago: University of Chicago Press.

Alexander, Herbert E. 1976. *Financing Politics: Money, Elections, and Political Reform.* Washington, D.C.: Congressional Quarterly Press.

Altheide, David L., and Robert P. Snow. 1979. *Media Logic.* Beverly Hills, Calif: Sage Publications.

Altschuler, Glenn C., and Stuart M. Blumin. 2000. *Rude Republic: Americans and Their Politics in the Nineteenth Century.* Princeton, N.J.: Princeton University Press.

Ansolabehere, Stephen, and Shanto Iyengar. 1995. *Going Negative: How Attack Ads Shrink and Polarize the Electorate.* New York: Free Press.

Ansolabehere, Stephen, Shanto Iyengar, Adam Simon, and Nicholas Valentino. 1994. "Does Attack Advertising Demobilize the Electorate?" *American Political Science Review* 88 (4): 829–38.

Arnold, R. Douglas. 2004. *Congress, the Press, and Political Accountability.* New York: Russell Sage Foundation.

Arceneaux, Kevin, and David W. Nickerson. 2009. "Comparing Negative and Positive Campaign Messages." *American Politics Research* 38 (1): 54–83.

Auyero, Javier. 2000. *Poor People's Politics: Peronist Survival Networks and the Legacy of Evita.* Durham, N.C.: Duke University Press.

———. 2009. The Political Ethnographer's Compagnon. http://essays.ssrc.org/tilly/auyero.

Bacon, Perry. 2010. "As Elections Near, Voter Outreach Intensifies." *Washington Post,* November 1.

Bai, Matt. 2004. "The Multilevel Marketing of the President." *New York Times Magazine,* April 25.

———. 2006. "The Inside Agitator." *New York Times Magazine,* October 1.

Balz, Dan. 2003. "Getting the Votes—And the Kudos." *Washington Post,* January 1, sec. A.

———. 2004a. "DNC Chief Advises Learning from GOP." *Washington Post,* December 11, sec. A.

———. 2004b. "Campaign for DNC Chief Begins; Candidates Say Party Must Rebuild State Chapters, Offer Resounding Message." *Washington Post,* December 12, sec. A.

Balz, Dan, and David S. Broder. 2002. "Close Election Turns on Voter Turnout." *Washington Post,* November 1, sec. A.

Barber, Benjamin R. 2003. *Strong Democracy: Participatory Politics for a New Age*. Berkeley: University of California Press.

Barone, Michael. 2006. *Almanac of American Politics*. Washington, D.C: National Journal.

Bartels, Larry. 1992. "The Impact of Electioneering in the United States." In *Electioneering: A Comparative Study in Continuity and Change*, edited by David Butler and Austin Ranney. New York: Oxford University Press.

Beck, Paul Allen, Russell J. Dalton, Steven Green, and Robert Huckfeldt. 2002. "The Social Calculus of Voting: Interpersonal, Media, and Organizational Influences on Presidential Choices." *American Political Science Review* 96 (1): 57–73.

Beck, Paul Allen, and Erik Heidemann. 2010. Changing Strategies in Grassroots Canvassing: 1956–2008. Social Science Research Network. SSRN eLibrary (August 26). http://papers.ssrn.com/sol3/papers.cfm?abstract_id=1666576.

Becker, Howard S. 1998. *Tricks of the Trade: How to Think about Your Research While You're Doing It*. Chicago: University of Chicago Press.

Bennett, W. Lance, and Robert M. Entman, eds. 2001. *Mediated Politics: Communication in the Future of Democracy*. New York: Cambridge University Press.

Bennett, W. Lance, and Shanto Iyengar. 2008. "A New Era of Minimal Effects? The Changing Foundations of Political Communication." *Journal of Communication* 58 (4): 707–31.

———. 2009. "The Shifting Foundations of Political Communication: Responding to a Defense of the Media Effects Paradigm." *Journal of Communication* 60 (1): 35–39.

Bennett, W. Lance, and Jarol B. Manheim. 2006. "The One-Step Flow of Communication." *Annals of the American Academy of Political and Social Science* 608 (1): 213–32.

Bergan, Daniel E., Alan S. Gerber, Donald P. Green, and Costas Panagopoulos. 2005. "Grassroots Mobilization and Voter Turnout in 2004." *Public Opinion Quarterly* 69 (5): 760–77.

Berry, Jeffrey M. 1984. *The Interest Group Society*. Boston: Little, Brown.

Beunza, Daniel, and David Stark. 2004. "Tools of the Trade: The Socio-Technology of Arbitrage in a Wall Street Trading Room." *Industrial and Corporate Change* 13 (2): 369–400.

Bibby, John F. 1999. "Party Networks: National-State Integration, Allied Groups, and Issue Activists." In *The State of the Parties*, edited by John Clifford Green and Daniel M. Shea. Lanham, Md.: Rowman and Littlefield.

Blaemire, Bob. 2002. "Voter Files: Yesterday, Today, Tomorrow." *Campaigns and Elections*, June.

Blake, Reed H. 1972. "Medio Communication: A Conceptualization." Presented at the International Communication Association conference in San Francisco, April 19. http://www.eric.ed.gov/ERICWebPortal/contentdelivery/servlet/ERICServlet?accno=ED062785.

Blumberg, Melaine J., William C. Binning, Sarah K. Lewis, and John C. Green. 2009. "Party-on-the-Periphery." Presented at the State of the Parties: 2008 and Beyond conference in Akron, Ohio, October 15. http://www.uakron.edu/bliss/docs/Blumberg2009_State_of_the_Parties_Draft__Edited_.pdf.

Blumenthal, Sidney. 1980. *The Permanent Campaign: Inside the World of Elite Political Operatives*. Boston: Beacon Press.

Blumler, Jay G., and Dennis Kavanagh. 1999. "The Third Age of Political Communication: Influences and Features." *Political Communication* 16 (3): 209.

Boorom, Michael L., Jerry R. Goolsby, and Rosemary P. Ramsey. 1998. "Relational Communication Traits and Their Effect on Adaptiveness and Sales Performance." *Journal of the Academy of Marketing Science* 26 (1): 16–30.

Born, Georgina. 2004. *Uncertain Vision: Birt, Dyke, and the Reinvention of the BBC*. London: Secker and Warburg.

Bourdieu, Pierre. 1992. *An Invitation to Reflexive Sociology*. Chicago: University of Chicago Press.

———. 2003. "Participant Objectivation." *Journal of the Royal Anthropological Institute* 9 (2): 281–94.

Bowers, Chris. 2008. "Dean Out, Fifty-State Strategy Likely Done." OpenLeft, November 10. http://www.openleft.com/showDiary.do?diaryId=9854.

Bowker, Geoffrey C., and Susan Leigh Star. 1999. *Sorting Things Out: Classification and Its Consequences*. Cambridge: MIT Press.

Broder, David S. 2000. "Democrats Tuning Up for Turnout; Nationwide Effort Set; Special Challenges Seen." *Washington Post*, August 21, sec. A.

———. 2001. "Shoe Leather Politicking." *Washington Post*, June 13, sec. A.

Burawoy, Michael. 1998. "The Extended Case Method." *Sociological Theory* 16 (1): 4–33.

Cameron, Deborah. 2000. *Good to Talk? Living and Working in a Communication Culture*. London: Sage.

Campaign Finance Institute. 2006. Federal 527 Organizations in the 2004 Election Cycle. http://www.cfinst.org/pdf/federal/interestgroup/Federal527s_2004Cycle_Raising200K.pdf.

Cappella, Joseph N., and Kathleen Hall Jamieson. 1996. "News Frames, Political Cynicism, and Media Cynicism." *Annals of the American Academy of Political and Social Science* 546 (1): 71–84.

Carney, James. 2006. "The Republicans' Secret Weapon." *Time*, October 1.

Castells, Manuel. 2000. *The Rise of the Network Society*. 2nd ed. Oxford: Blackwell.

———. 2007. "Communication, Power, and Counter-power in the Network Society." *International Journal of Communication* 1: 238–66.

CBS. 2008. Americans Look Ahead with Optimism (poll). Press release. November 11. http://www.cbsnews.com/htdocs/pdf/NOV08B-postelection.pdf.

Chadwick, Andrew. 2007. "Digital Network Repertoires and Organizational Hybridity." *Political Communication* 24 (3): 283.

Cillizza, Chris. 2003. "Critics Slam 'Demzilla.'" *Roll Call*, June 5.

———. 2007. "Romney's Data Cruncher." *Washington Post*, July 5.

———. 2009. "Obama Announces Grass-Roots Lobby." *Washington Post*, January 19.

Clarke, Peter, and Susan H. Evans. 1983. *Covering Campaigns: Journalism in Congressional Elections*. Stanford, Calif.: Stanford University Press.

Clawson, Dan, and Mary Ann Clawson. 1999. "What Has Happened to the U.S. Labor Movement? Union Decline and Renewal." *Annual Review of Sociology* 25: 95–119.

Clemens, Elisabeth S. 1993. "Organizational Repertoires and Institutional Change: Women's Groups and the Transformation of U.S. Politics, 1890–1920." *American Journal of Sociology* 98 (4): 755–98.

————. 1997. *The People's Lobby: Organizational Innovation and the Rise of Interest Group Politics in the United States, 1890–1925*. Chicago: University of Chicago Press.

Clifford, James, and George E. Marcus, eds. 1986. *Writing Culture: The Poetics and Politics of Ethnography*. Berkeley: University of California Press.

Cook, Timothy E. 1998. *Governing with the News: The News Media as a Political Institution*. Chicago: University of Chicago Press.

Dalton, Russell J., and Martin P. Wattenberg, eds. 2000. *Parties without Partisans: Political Change in Advanced Industrial Democracies*. Oxford: Oxford University Press.

Dark, Taylor E. 2001. *The Unions and the Democrats: An Enduring Alliance*. Ithaca: ILR Press.

DeLanda, Manuel. 2006. *A New Philosophy of Society: Assemblage Theory and Social Complexity*. London: Continuum.

Democratic National Committee. 2005. 50-state strategy. http://www.democrats .org/a/party/a_50_state_strategy.

Denver, David, Gordon Hands, and Iain MacAllister. 2004. "The Electoral Impact of Constituency Campaigning in Britain, 1992–2001." *Political Studies* 52 (2): 289–306.

Dickinson, Tim. 2008. "The Machinery of Hope." *Rolling Stone*, March 20.

Dinkin, Robert J. 1989. *Campaigning in America: A History of Election Practices*. New York: Greenwood Press.

Dulio, David A. 2004. *For Better or Worse? How Political Consultants Are Changing Elections in the United States*. Albany: State University of New York Press.

Duneier, Mitchell. 1999. *Sidewalk*. New York: Farrar, Straus and Giroux.

————. 2002. "What Kind of Combat Sport Is Sociology?" *American Journal of Sociology* 107 (6): 1551–76.

Edsall, Thomas B. 2000. "Unions Mobilize to Beat Bush, Regain House." *Washington Post*, March 27, sec. A.

————. 2005. "Soros-Backed Activist Group Disbands as Interest Fades." *Washington Post*, August 3, sec. A.

————. 2006. *Building Red America: The New Conservative Coalition and the Drive for Permanent Power*. New York: Basic Books.

Edsall, Thomas B., and James V. Grimaldi. 2004. "On Nov. 2, GOP Got More Bang for Its Billion, Analysis Shows." *Washington Post*, December 30, sec. A.

Eggen, Dan. 2009. "Obama's Machine Sputters in Effort to Push Budget." *Washington Post*, April 6.

Eliasoph, Nina. 1998. *Avoiding Politics: How Americans Produce Apathy in Everyday Life*. Cambridge, U.K: Cambridge University Press.

Elmer, Greg. 2004. *Profiling Machines: Mapping the Personal Information Economy*. Cambridge: MIT Press.

Emerson, Robert M., Rachel I. Fretz, and Linda L. Shaw. 1995. *Writing Ethnographic Fieldnotes*. Chicago: University of Chicago Press.

Entman, Robert M. 1989. *Democracy without Citizens: Media and the Decay of American Politics*. New York: Oxford University Press.

Erie, Steven P. 1988. *Rainbow's End: Irish-Americans and the Dilemmas of Urban Machine Politics, 1840–1985*. Berkeley: University of California Press.

Fantasia, Rick, and Kim Voss. 2004. *Hard Work: Remaking the American Labor Movement*. Berkeley: University of California Press.

Farhi, Paul. 2004. "Parties Square Off in a Database Duel." *Washington Post*, July 20, sec. A.

Federal Election Commission. 2007. "FEC to Collect $775,000 Civil Penalty from America Coming Together." August 29. Press release. http://www.fec.gov/press/press2007/20070829act.shtml.

Fenno, Richard F. 1978. *Home Style: House Members in Their Districts*. New York: HarperCollins.

Fiorina, Morris P. 1999. "Extreme Voices: A Dark Side of Civic Engagement." In *Civic Engagement and American Democracy*, edited by Theda Skocpol and Morris P. Fiorina, 395–425. New York: Brookings Institution Press.

Fiorina, Morris P., Paul E. Peterson, Bertram Johnson, and William G. Mayer. 2009. *The New American Democracy*. 6th ed. New York: Longman.

Fisher, Dana. 2006. *Activism, Inc.: How the Outsourcing of Grassroots Campaigns Is Strangling Progressive Politics in America*. Stanford, Calif.: Stanford University Press.

Franke-Ruta, Garance, and Harold Meyerson. 2004. "The GOP Deploys." *American Prospect*, February 1.

Galvin, Daniel. 2010. *Presidential Party Building: Dwight D. Eisenhower to George W. Bush*. Princeton, N.J.: Princeton University Press.

Gamson, William A. 1992. *Talking Politics*. Cambridge, U.K.: Cambridge University Press.

Gandy, Oscar H. 1993. *The Panoptic Sort: A Political Economy of Personal Information*. Critical Studies in Communication and in the Cultural Industries. Boulder, Colo: Westview.

———. 2001. "Dividing Practices: Segmentation and Targeting in the Emerging Public Sphere." In *Mediated Politics*, edited by W. Lance Bennett and Robert M Entman, 141–59. New York: Cambridge University Press.

Gans, Herbert J. 1962. *The Urban Villagers: Group and Class in the Life of Italian-Americans*. New York: Free Press of Glencoe.

———. 1982. *The Levittowners: Ways of Life and Politics in a New Suburban Community*. New York: Columbia University Press.

———. 1989. "Sociology in America: The Discipline and the Public." American Sociological Association, 1988 Presidential Address. *American Sociological Review* 54 (1): 1–16.

———. 1999. "Participant Observation in the Era of 'Ethnography.'" *Journal of Contemporary Ethnography* 28 (5): 540–48.

Ganz, Marshall. 1993. "Voters in the Crosshairs." *America Prospect*, December 1.

———. 2009a. *Why David Sometimes Wins: Leadership, Organization, and Strategy in the California Farm Worker Movement*. Oxford: Oxford University Press.

————. 2009b. "Why Stories Matter." *Sojourners*, March.

Geertz, Clifford. 1973. *The Interpretation of Cultures; Selected Essays*. New York: Basic Books.

————. 1988. *Works and Lives: The Anthropologist as Author*. Stanford, Calif.: Stanford University Press.

Gerber, Alan S., and Donald P. Green. 2000. "The Effects of Canvassing, Telephone Calls, and Direct Mail on Voter Turnout: A Field Experiment." *American Political Science Review* 94 (3): 653–63.

Gerber, Alan S., Donald P. Green, and Christopher W. Larimer. 2010. "An Experiment Testing the Relative Effectiveness of Encouraging Voter Participation by Inducing Feelings of Pride or Shame." *Political Behavior* 32 (3): 409–22.

Gertner, Jon. 2004. "The Very, Very Personal Is the Political." *New York Times Magazine*, February 15.

Gillespie, A. 2010. "Canvasser Affect and Voter Response: Results from National Focus Groups." *American Politics Research* 38 (4): 718–58.

Girard, Monique, and David Stark. 2007. "Socio-Technologies of Assembly: Sense Making and Demonstration in Rebuilding Lower Manhattan." In *Governance and Information Technology*, edited by David Lazer and Viktor Mayer-Schoenberger, 145–76. New York: Oxford University Press.

Gitlin, Todd. 2001. *Media Unlimited: How the Torrent of Images and Sounds Overwhelms Our Lives*. New York: Metropolitan Books.

Godwin, R. Kenneth. 1988. *One Billion Dollars of Influence: The Direct Marketing of Politics*. Chatham, N.J: Chatham House.

Goffman, Erving. 1959. *The Presentation of Self in Everyday Life*. Garden City, N.Y: Doubleday.

————. 1982. *Interaction Ritual: Essays on Face-to-Face Behavior*. New York: Pantheon Books.

————. 1989. On Fieldwork. *Journal of Contemporary Ethnography* 18 (2): 123–32.

Goldfield, Michael. 1986. "Labor in American Politics: Its Current Weakness." *Journal of Politics* 48 (1): 2–29.

Gosnell, Harold Foote. 1939. *Machine Politics: Chicago Model*. Chicago: University of Chicago Press.

Graber, Doris A. 2006. *Mass Media and American Politics*. 7th ed. Washington, D.C: CQ Press.

Green, Donald P., and Alan S. Gerber. 2008. *Get Out the Vote: How to Increase Voter Turnout*. 2nd ed. Washington, D.C: Brookings Institution Press.

Green, John C., and Daniel J. Coffey, eds. 2007. *The State of the Parties: The Changing Role of Contemporary American Politics*. 5th ed. People, Passions, and Power. Lanham, Md.: Rowman and Littlefield.

Green, John C., and Rick Farmer, eds. 2003. *The State of the Parties: The Changing Role of Contemporary American Parties*. 4th ed. People, Passions, and Power. Lanham, Md.: Rowman and Littlefield.

Green, John C., and Daniel M. Shea, eds. 1996. *The State of the Parties: The Changing Role of Contemporary American Parties*. 2nd ed. People, Passions, and Power. Lanham, Md.: Rowman and Littlefield.

———. 1999. *The State of the Parties: The Changing Role of Contemporary American Parties*. 3rd ed. People, Passions, and Power. Lanham, Md.: Rowman and Littlefield.

Grimshaw, William J. 1992. *Bitter Fruit: Black Politics and the Chicago Machine, 1931–1991*. Chicago: University of Chicago Press.

Gutmann, Amy, and Dennis Thompson. 2004. *Why Deliberative Democracy?* Princeton, N.J.: Princeton University Press.

Hamburger, Tom, and Peter Wallsten. 2006. *One Party Country: The Republican Plan for Dominance in the 21st Century*. Hoboken, N.J.: John Wiley and Sons.

Held, David. 2006. *Models of Democracy*. Cambridge, U.K.: Polity.

Herrnson, Paul S. 1988. *Party Campaigning in the 1980s*. Cambridge, Mass.: Harvard University Press.

———. 1995. *Congressional Elections: Campaigning at Home and in Washington*. Washington, D.C: CQ Press.

———. 2004. *Congressional Elections: Campaigning at Home and in Washington*. Washington, D.C: CQ Press.

Hibbing, John R., and Elizabeth Theiss-Morse. 2002. *Stealth Democracy: Americans' Beliefs about How Government Should Work*. Cambridge, U.K.: Cambridge University Press.

Hillygus, D. Sunshine, and Todd G. Shields. 2008. *The Persuadable Voter: Wedge Issues in Presidential Campaigns*. Princeton, N.J.: Princeton University Press.

Hindman, Matthew. 2008. *The Myth of Digital Democracy*. Princeton, N.J.: Princeton University Press.

Hochschild, Arlie R. 1979. "Emotion Work, Feeling Rules, and Social Structure." *American Journal of Sociology* 85 (3): 551–75.

———. 1983. *The Managed Heart: Commercialization of Human Feeling*. Berkeley: University of California Press.

Holbrook, Thomas M. 1996. *Do Campaigns Matter?* Thousand Oaks: Sage Publications.

Howard, Philip N. 2006. *New Media Campaigns and the Managed Citizen*. New York: Cambridge University Press.

Howard, Philip N., and Daniel Kreiss. 2009. "Political Parties and Voter Privacy: Australia, Canada, the United Kingdom, and United States in Comparative Perspective." World Information Access Project Paper. Seattle: University of Washington. http://www.wiareport.org/index.php/publications/working-papers.

Huckfeldt, R. Robert, and John D. Sprague. 1995. *Citizens, Politics, and Social Communication: Information and Influence in an Election Campaign*. Cambridge, U.K.: Cambridge University Press.

Institute of Politics. 2002. *Campaign for President: The Managers Look at 2000*. New Hampshire: Hollis Publishing Company.

———. 2006. *Campaign for President: The Managers Look at 2004*. Lanham, Md.: Rowman and Littlefield.

———. 2007. Looking Ahead Discussion Sessions, Democrats. http://www.iop.harvard.edu/Programs/Campaign-2008-Looking-Ahead/Looking-Ahead-Discussion-Sessions-DEMS.

———. 2009. *Campaign for President: The Managers Look at 2008.* Lanham, Md.: Rowman and Littlefield.

Issenberg, Sasha. 2010. "How Behavioral Science Is Remaking Politics." *New York Times Magazine*, October 29.

Iyengar, Shanto, and Donald R. Kinder. 1987. *News That Matters: Television and American Opinion.* Chicago: University of Chicago Press.

Jacobson, Gary C. 2009. *The Politics of Congressional Elections.* 7th ed. New York: Pearson/Longman.

Jacobson, Louise. 2006. "Ohio: Time for the Once-in-a-Generation Political Shake-up?" *Roll Call*, March 29.

James, William. 1995. *Pragmatism.* New York: Dover Publications.

Jamieson, Kathleen Hall, ed. 2001. *Electing the President, 2000: The Insiders' View.* Philadelphia: University of Pennsylvania Press.

———. 2006. *Electing the President, 2004: The Insider's View.* Philadelphia: University of Pennsylvania Press.

———. 2009. *Electing the President, 2008: The Insiders' View.* Philadelphia: University of Pennsylvania Press.

Jaquith, Waldo. 2006. "The Demzilla Downfall." *Campaigns and Elections*, May.

Jensen, Klaus Bruhn. 2010. *Media Convergence: The Three Degrees of Network, Mass, and Interpersonal Communication.* London: Routledge.

Johnson, Dennis W. 2007. *No Place for Amateurs: How Political Consultants Are Reshaping American Democracy.* New York: Routledge.

Johnson, Dennis W., ed. 2009. *Routledge Handbook of Political Management.* New York: Routledge.

Johnston, R., Michael Gray Hagen, and Kathleen Hall Jamieson. 2004. *The 2000 Presidential Election and the Foundations of Party Politics.* Houndmills, Basingstoke: Cambridge University Press.

Kamarck, Elaine. 2006. "Assessing Howard Dean's Fifty State Strategy and the 2006 Midterm Elections." *Forum* 4 (3): article 5.

Karpf, David A. 2009. "Unexpected Transformations: The Internet's Effects on Political Associations in American Politics." Unpublished doctoral dissertation. University of Pennsylvania.

Katz, Jack. 2001. "From How to Why: On Luminous Description and Causal Inference in Ethnography (Part 1)." *Ethnography* 2 (4): 443–73.

———. 2002. "From How to Why: On Luminous Description and Causal Inference in Ethnography (Part 2)." *Ethnography* 3 (1): 63–90.

Kerbel, Matthew. 2009. *Netroots: Online Progressives and the Transformation of American Politics.* Boulder, Colo.: Paradigm.

Key, V. O. 1949. *Southern Politics in State and Nation.* New York: A. A. Knopf.

Kiely, Kathy. 2002. "In the End, 'Ground Game' May Decide Closest Races." *USA Today*, November 4, sec. A.

Kolodny, Robin. 1998. *Pursuing Majorities: Congressional Campaign Committees in American Politics.* Norman: University of Oklahoma Press.

Kreiss, Daniel. 2009. "Developing the 'Good Citizen': Digital Artifacts, Peer Networks, and Formal Organization during the 2003–2004 Howard Dean Campaign." *Journal of Information Technology and Politics* 6 (3): 281–97.

Latour, Bruno. 1987. *Science in Action: How to Follow Scientists and Engineers through Society*. Cambridge, Mass: Harvard University Press.

———. 2005. *Reassembling the Social: An Introduction to Actor-Network-Theory*. Oxford, U.K.: Oxford University Press.

Latour, Bruno, and Steve Woolgar. 1986. *Laboratory Life: The Construction of Scientific Facts*. Princeton, N.J.: Princeton University Press.

Lazarsfeld, Paul Felix, Bernard Berelson, and Hazel Gaudet. 1948. *The People's Choice: How the Voter Makes up His Mind in a Presidential Campaign*. 2nd ed. New York: Columbia Univ. Press.

Leidner, Robin. 1993. *Fast Food, Fast Talk: Service Work and the Routinization of Everyday Life*. Berkeley: University of California Press.

———. 1999. "Emotional Labor in Service Work." *Annals of the American Academy of Political and Social Science* 561 (1): 81–95.

Levitz, Jennifer. 2010. "To Protest Hiring of Nonunion Help, Union Hires Nonunion Pickets." wsj.com, July 16, sec. A-hed. http://online.wsj.com/article/SB10001424052748704288204575362763101099660.html.

Lichterman, Paul. 1996. *The Search for Political Community: American Activists Reinventing Commitment*. Cambridge, U.K.: Cambridge University Press.

Ligas, Mark. 2004. "Personalizing Services Encounters: The Role of Service Provider Actions in Developing Customer Trust." *Services Marketing Quarterly* 25 (4): 33–51.

Lofland, John. 1995. "Analytic Ethnography: Features, Failings, and Futures." *Journal of Contemporary Ethnography* 24 (1): 30–67.

Magleby, David B., and J. Quin Monson, eds. 2004. *The Last Hurrah? Soft Money and Issue Advocacy in the 2002 Congressional Elections*. Washington, D.C.: Brookings Institution Press.

Magleby, David B., J. Quin Monson, and Kelly D. Patterson, eds. 2007. *Dancing without Partners: How Candidates, Parties, and Interest Groups Interact in the Presidential Campaign*. Lanham, Md.: Rowman and Littlefield.

Magleby, David B., and Kelly D. Patterson. 2006. "Stepping Out of the Shadows? Ground-War Activity in 2004." In *The Election after Reform*, edited by Michael J. Malbin, 161–84. Rowman and Littlefield.

Mahler, Matthew. Forthcoming. "The Day before Election Day." *Ethnography*.

Maisel, Louis Sandy. 2007. *American Political Parties and Elections: A Very Short Introduction*. Very Short Introductions. New York: Oxford University Press.

Malbin, Michael J, ed. 2006. *The Election after Reform: Money, Politics, and the Bipartisan Campaign Reform Act*. Lanham, Md.: Rowman and Littlefield.

Malchow, Hal. 2003. *The New Political Targeting*. Washington, D.C.: Campaigns and Elections Press.

———. 2004. "Shattering Myths about Getting out the Vote." *Campaigns and Elections*.

March, James G., and Johan P. Olsen. 1989. *Rediscovering Institutions: The Organizational Basis of Politics*. New York: Free Press.

Marcus, George E. 1995. "Ethnography in/of the World System: The Emergence of Multi-sited Ethnography." *Annual Review of Anthropology* 24 (1): 95–117.

Marwell, Nicole P. 2007. *Bargaining for Brooklyn: Community Organizations in the Entrepreneurial City*. Chicago: University of Chicago Press.

Masket, Seth E. 2009. "Did Obama's Ground Game Matter? The Influence of Local Field Offices during the 2008 Presidential Election." *Public Opinion Quarterly* 73 (5): 1023–39.

Mazeland, Harrie. 2004. "Responding to the Double Implication of Telemarketers' Opinion Queries." *Discourse Studies* 6 (1): 95–115.

Mazzoleni, Gianpietro, and Winfried Schulz. 1999. "'Mediatization' of Politics: A Challenge for Democracy?" *Political Communication* 16 (3): 247.

McAdam, Doug, Sidney G. Tarrow, and Charles Tilly. 2001. *Dynamics of Contention*. New York: Cambridge University Press.

McCarthy, John D., and Mayer N. Zald. 1977. "Resource Mobilization and Social Movements: A Partial Theory." *American Journal of Sociology* 82 (6): 1212–41.

McGerr, Michael E. 1986. *The Decline of Popular Politics: The American North, 1865–1928*. New York: Oxford University Press.

Medvic, Stephen K. 2001. *Political Consultants in U.S. Congressional Elections*. Columbus: Ohio State University Press.

Melber, Ari. 2010. "Year One of Organizing for America: The Permanent Field Campaign in a Digital Age." A TechPresident Special Report, http://techpresident.com/files/report_Year_One_of_Organizing_for_America_Melber.pdf.

Merton, Robert K. 1987. "Three Fragments from a Sociologist's Notebooks: Establishing the Phenomenon, Specified Ignorance, and Strategic Research Materials." *Annual Review of Sociology* 13: 1–29.

Meyerson, Harold. 2003. "Judging Terry." *American Prospect*, December 1.

Michels, Robert. 1915. *Political Parties: A Sociological Study of the Oligarchical Tendencies of Modern Democracy*. New York: Hearst's International Library Co.

Miller, Arthur H., Christopher Wlezien, and Anne Hildreth. 1991. "A Reference Group Theory of Partisan Coalitions." *Journal of Politics* 53 (4): 1134–49.

Mittal, Banwari, and Walfried M. Lassar. 1996. "The Role of Personalization in Service Encounters." *Journal of Retailing* 72 (1): 95–109.

Munson, Ziad W. 2008. *The Making of Pro-Life Activists: How Social Movement Mobilization Works*. Chicago: University of Chicago Press.

Mutz, Diana C. 2002. "The Consequences of Cross-Cutting Networks for Political Participation." *American Journal of Political Science* 46 (4): 838–55.

Negrine, Ralph M., and James Stanyer, eds. 2007. *The Political Communication Reader*. London: Routledge.

Neuman, W. Russell. 1996. "Political Communications Infrastructure." *Annals of the American Academy of Political and Social Science* 546 (July): 9–21.

Neuman, W. Russell, Yong Jin Park, and Elliot Panek. 2009. "Tracking the Flow of Information into the Home: An Empirical Assessment of the Digital Revolution in the U.S. from 1960–2005." Presented at the International Communication Association conference in Chicago.

Newman, Katherine S. 1999. *No Shame in My Game: The Working Poor in the Inner City*. New York: Knopf and the Russell Sage Foundation.

Nickerson, David W. 2005. "Partisan Mobilization Using Volunteer Phone Banks and Door Hangers." The *ANNALS of the American Academy of Political and Social Science* 601 (1): 10–27.

———. 2006. "Volunteer Phone Calls Can Increase Turnout: Evidence from Eight Field Experiments." *American Politics Research* 34 (3): 271–92.

———. 2007. "Quality Is Job One: Professional and Volunteer Voter Mobilization Calls." *American Journal of Political Science* 51 (2): 269–82.

Nickerson, David W., and Todd Rogers. 2010. "Do You Have a Voting Plan?" *Psychological Science* 21 (2): 194 –99.

Nielsen, Rasmus Kleis. 2009. "The Labors of Internet-Assisted Activism: Overcommunication, Miscommunication, and Communicative Overload." *Journal of Information Technology and Politics* 6 (3): 267–80.

———. 2010. "Mundane Internet Tools, Mobilizing Practices, and the Coproduction of Citizenship in Political Campaigns." *New Media and Society* 13 (5): 755–71.

Norris, Pippa. 2000. *A Virtuous Circle: Political Communications in Postindustrial Societies*. Cambridge, U.K.: Cambridge University Press.

Ornstein, Norman J., and Thomas E. Mann, eds. 2000. *The Permanent Campaign and Its Future*. Washington, D.C: American Enterprise Institute.

Panagopoulos, Costas. 2009. "Partisan and Nonpartisan Message Content and Voter Mobilization." *Political Research Quarterly* 62 (1): 70 –76.

Parks, James. 2010. "Trumka: Be Proud of Union GOTV Effort, Get Ready Again to Fight for Jobs." AFL-CIO Now Blog. http://blog.aflcio.org/2010/11/03/trumka-be-proud-of-union-gotv-effort-get-ready-again-to-fight-for-jobs.

Patterson, Thomas E. 1993. *Out of Order*. New York: A. Knopf.

———. 2002. *The Vanishing Voter: Public Involvement in an Age of Uncertainty*. New York: Alfred A. Knopf.

Pattie, Charles J., R. J. Johnston, and Edward A. Fieldhouse. 1995. "Winning the Local Vote: The Effectiveness of Constituency Campaign Spending in Great Britain, 1983–1992." *American Political Science Review* 89 (4): 969–83.

Perlstein, Rick. 2001. *Before the Storm: Barry Goldwater and the Unmaking of the American Consensus*. New York: Hill and Wang.

Piore, Michael J., and Charles F. Sabel. 1984. *The Second Industrial Divide: Possibilities for Prosperity*. New York: Basic Books.

Plouffe, David. 2009. *The Audacity to Win: The Inside Story and Lessons of Barack Obama's Historic Victory*. New York: Viking.

Powell, Walter W. 1990. "Neither Market Nor Hierarchy: Network Forms of Organization." *Research in Organizational Behavior* 12: 295–336.

Prior, Markus. 2007. *Post-Broadcast Democracy: How Media Choice Increases Inequality in Political Involvement and Polarizes Elections*. New York: Cambridge University Press.

Putnam, Robert D. 2000. *Bowling Alone: The Collapse and Revival of American Community*. New York: Simon and Schuster.

Ragin, Charles C. 1992. "Casing" and the Process of Social Inquiry. In *What Is a Case? Exploring the Foundations of Social Inquiry*, edited by Charles C. Ragin and Howard S. Becker, 217–26. New York: Cambridge University Press.

Rose, Gary L. 1992. *Connecticut Politics at the Crossroads*. Lanham, Md.: University Press of America.

Rosenstone, Steven J., and John Mark Hansen. 1993. *Mobilization, Participation, and Democracy in America*. New York: Macmillan.

Rozell, Mark J., Clyde Wilcox, and David Madland. 2006. *Interest Groups in American Campaigns*. Washington, D.C.: CQ Press.

Sabato, Larry. 1981. *The Rise of Political Consultants: New Ways of Winning Elections*. New York: Basic Books.

Sabel, Charles F. 1991. "Moebius-Strip Organizations and Open Labor Markets: Some consequences of the Reintegration of Conception and Execution in a Volatile Economy." In *Social Theory for a Changing Society*, edited by Pierre Bourdieu and James S Coleman, 23–61. New York: Russell Sage Foundation.

Salmore, Barbara G., and Stephen A. Salmore. 2008. *New Jersey Politics and Government: The Suburbs Come of Age*. New Brunswick, N.J.: Rivergate Books.

Saslow, Eli. 2009. "Grass-Roots Battle Tests the Obama Movement." *Washington Post*, August 23.

Sassen, Saskia. 2006. *Territory, Authority, Rights: From Medieval to Global Assemblages*. Princeton, N.J.: Princeton University Press.

Schier, Steven E. 2000. *By Invitation Only: The Rise of Exclusive Politics in the United States*. Pittsburgh: University of Pittsburgh Press.

Schudson, Michael. 1998. *The Good Citizen: A History of American Civic Life*. New York: Free Press.

———. 2003. *The Sociology of News*. New York: Norton.

Schwartz, Barry. 1968. "The Social Psychology of Privacy." *American Journal of Sociology* 73 (6): 741–52.

Semiatin, Richard J., ed. 2008. *Campaigns on the Cutting Edge*. Washington, D.C: CQ Press.

Shea, Daniel M., and Michael J. Burton. 2006. *Campaign Craft: The Strategies, Tactics, and Art of Political Campaign Management*. Westport, Conn.: Praeger.

Shenk, David. 1997. *Data Smog: Surviving the Information Glut*. San Francisco: HarperEdge.

Skinner, Richard M. 2005. "Do 527's Add Up to a Party? Thinking about the 'Shadows' of Politics." *Forum* 3 (3): article 5. http://www.bepress.com/forum/vol3/iss3/art5.

Skocpol, Theda. 2003. *Diminished Democracy: From Membership to Management in American Civic Life*. Norman: University of Oklahoma Press.

Skocpol, Theda, Marshall Ganz, and Ziad Munson. 2000. "A Nation of Organizers: The Institutional Origins of Civic Voluntarism in the United States." *American Political Science Review* 94 (3): 527–46.

Snow, David A., Calvin Morrill, and Leon Anderson. 2003. "Elaborating Analytic Ethnography: Linking Fieldwork and Theory." *Ethnography* 4 (2): 181–200.

Sorauf, Frank J. 1992. *Inside Campaign Finance: Myths and Realities*. New York: Yale University Press.

Sosnik, Doug, Matthew J. Dowd, and Ron Fournier. 2006. *Applebee's America: How Successful Political, Business, and Religious Leaders Connect with the New American Community*. New York: Simon and Schuster.

Stark, David. 2009. *The Sense of Dissonance: Accounts of Worth in Economic Life*. Princeton, N.J.: Princeton University Press.

Steffens, Lincoln. 1904. *The Shame of the Cities*. New York: McClure, Phillips and Co.

Suddes, Thomas. 2006. "NE Ohio Is Key to Senate Contest." *Cleveland Plain Dealer*, July 5, Metro.

Swanson, David L., and Paolo Mancini, eds. 1996. *Politics, Media, and Modern Democracy: An International Study of Innovations in Electoral Campaigning and Their Consequences*. Westport, Conn.: Praeger.

Techpresident. 2009. Quote of the Day. December 14. http://techpresident.com/blog-entry/quote-day.

Thomas, Evan. 2009. *A Long Time Coming: The Inspiring, Combative 2008 Campaign and the Historic Election of Barack Obama*. New York: PublicAffairs.

Thompson, John B. 1995. *The Media and Modernity: A Social Theory of the Media*. Stanford, Calif.: Stanford University Press.

Thurber, James A., and Candice J. Nelson, eds. 2000. *Campaign Warriors: The Role of Political Consultants in Elections*. Washington, D.C: Brookings Institution Press.

Tilly, Charles. 2008. *Explaining Social Processes*. Boulder: Paradigm.

Trent, Judith S., and Robert V. Friedenberg. 2008. *Political Campaign Communication: Principles and Practices*. Lanham, Md.: Rowman and Littlefield.

Turow, Joseph. 1997. *Breaking Up America: Advertisers and the New Media World*. Chicago: University of Chicago Press.

———. 2006. *Niche Envy: Marketing Discrimination in the Digital Age*. Cambridge: MIT Press.

Tynan, Daniel. 2004. "GOP Voter Vault Shipped Overseas." PC World, September 24. http://www.pcworld.com/article/117930/gop_voter_vault_shipped_overseas.html.

Ubertaccio, Peter N. 2009. "Network Marketing and American Political Parties." In *Routledge Handbook of Political Management*, edited by Dennis W Johnson, 509–23. New York: Routledge.

Van Maanen, John. 1988. *Tales of the Field: On Writing Ethnography*. Chicago: University of Chicago Press.

Varon, Elana. 2004. "Election 2004: IT on the Campaign Trail." *CIO* Magazine, June 1. http://www.cio.com/article/32314.

Venkatesh, Sudhir. 2002. "'Doin' the Hustle': Constructing the Ethnographer in the American Ghetto." *Ethnography* 3 (1): 91–111.

Verba, Sidney, Kay Lehman Schlozman, and Henry E Brady. 1995. *Voice and Equality: Civic Voluntarism in American Politics*. Cambridge, Mass: Harvard University Press.

Walker, Jack L. 1991. *Mobilizing Interest Groups in America: Patrons, Professions, and Social Movements*. Ann Arbor: University of Michigan Press.

Wallsten, Peter. 2008. "A GOP Machine Sits Silent." *LA Times*, June 9. http://articles.latimes.com/2008/jun/09/nation/na-ohio9.

———. 2010. "Chief of Staff Draws Fire From Left as Obama Falters." wsj.com, January 26, sec. Politics and Policy. http://online.wsj.com/article/SB10001424052748703808904575025030384695158.html?mod=WSJ_latestheadlines#printMode.

Walsh, Katherine C. 2004. *Talking about Politics: Informal Groups and Social Identity in American Life*. Chicago: University of Chicago Press.

Ware, Alan. 1985. *The Breakdown of Democratic Party Organization, 1940–1980*. Oxford, U.K: Clarendon Press.

Warren, Mark R. 2001. *Dry Bones Rattling: Community Building to Revitalize American Democracy*. Princeton, N.J: Princeton University Press.

Wattenberg, Martin P. 1991. *The Rise of Candidate-Centered Politics: Presidential Elections of the 1980s*. Cambridge, Mass: Harvard University Press.

———. 1996. *The Decline of American Political Parties, 1952–1994*. Cambridge, Mass: Harvard University Press.

Weber, Max. 1968. *Economy and Society; an Outline of Interpretive Sociology*. New York: Bedminster Press.

Weir, Margaret, and Marshall Ganz. 1997. "Reconnecting People and Politics." In *The New Majority*, edited by Stanley B. Greenberg and Theda Skocpol. New Haven, Conn.: Yale University Press.

Whiteley, P., and P. Seyd. 2003. "How to Win a Landslide by Really Trying: The Effects of Local Campaigning on Voting in the 1997 British General Election." *Electoral Studies* 22 (2): 301–24.

Wielhouwer, Peter W. 2003. "In Search of Lincoln's Perfect List: Targeting in Grassroots Campaigns." *American Politics Research* 31 (6): 632–69.

Williamson, Vanessa, Theda Skocpol, and John Coggin. 2011. "The Tea Party and the Remaking of Republican Conservatism." *Perspectives on Politics* 9 (1): 25–43.

Wilson, James Q. 1962. *The Amateur Democrat: Club Politics in Three Cities*. Chicago: University of Chicago Press.

———. 1995. *Political Organizations*. Princeton, N.J.: Princeton University Press.

Wittgenstein, Ludwig. 1991. *Philosophical Investigations*. Oxford, U.K.: Blackwell.

Zaller, John. 1999. A Theory of Media Politics. Unpublished manuscript, dated October 24, 1999. http://www.sscnet.ucla.edu/polisci/faculty/zaller/media%20politics%20book%20.pdf.

Zeleny, Jeff. 2010. "Democrats Counting on Strength of Obama's Network." *New York Times*, October 26, A17.

Index

DATE DUE

APR 07 2013	
DEC 2 4 2013	